Examining Science Teaching in Elementary School from the Perspective of a Teacher and Learner

CRITICAL EDUCATION PRACTICE
VOLUME 18
GARLAND REFERENCE LIBRARY OF SOCIAL SCIENCE
VOLUME 1140

CRITICAL EDUCATION PRACTICE

SHIRLEY R. STEINBERG AND JOE L. KINCHELOE, *SERIES EDITORS*

BECOMING A STUDENT OF TEACHING
*Methodologies for Exploring
Self and School Context*
by Robert V. Bullough, Jr.
and Andrew Gitlin

OCCUPIED READING
*Critical Foundations for
an Ecological Theory*
by Alan A. Block

DEMOCRACY, MULTICULTURALISM,
AND THE COMMUNITY COLLEGE
A Critical Perspective
by Robert A. Rhoads
and James R. Valadez

ANATOMY OF A COLLABORATION
*Study of a College of Education/
Public School Partnership*
by Judith J. Slater

TEACHING MATHEMATICS
Toward a Sound Alternative
by Brent Davis

INNER-CITY SCHOOLS,
MULTICULTURALISM,
AND TEACHER EDUCATION
A Professional Journey
by Frederick L. Yeo

RETHINKING LANGUAGE ARTS
Passion and Practice
by Nina Zaragoza

EDUCATIONAL REFORM
A Deweyan Perspective
by Douglas J. Simpson
and Michael J. B. Jackson

LIBERATION THEOLOGY
AND CRITICAL PEDAGOGY
IN TODAY'S CATHOLIC SCHOOLS
Social Justice in Action
by Thomas Oldenski

CURRICULUM
Toward New Identities
edited by William F. Pinar

WRITING EDUCATIONAL BIOGRAPHY
*Explorations in
Qualitative Research*
edited by Craig Kridel

EVERYBODY BELONGS
*Changing Negative Attitudes
Toward Classmates with Disabilities*
by Arthur Shapiro

TEACHING FROM UNDERSTANDING
Teacher As Interpretive Inquirer
edited by Julia L. Ellis

PEDAGOGY AND THE POLITICS
OF THE BODY
A Critical Praxis
by Sherry B. Shapiro

CRITICAL ART PEDAGOGY
*Foundations for
Postmodern Art Education*
by Richard Cary

THE POST-FORMAL READER
Cognition and Education
edited by Shirley R. Steinberg,
Joe L. Kincheloe,
and Patricia H. Hinchey

BECOMING MULTICULTURAL
*Personal and Social Construction
through Critical Teaching*
edited by Terry Ford

EXAMINING SCIENCE TEACHING IN
ELEMENTARY SCHOOL FROM THE
PERSPECTIVE OF A TEACHER AND
LEARNER
by Margery D. Osborne

Examining Science Teaching in Elementary School from the Perspective of a Teacher and Learner

BY

Margery D. Osborne

Routledge
Taylor & Francis Group
New York   London

First published by Garland Publishing, Inc.

This edition published 2013 by Routledge

Routledge	Routledge
Taylor & Francis Group	Taylor & Francis Group
711 Third Avenue	2 Park Square, Milton Park
New York, NY 10017	Abingdon, Oxon OX14 4RN

Routledge is an imprint of the Taylor & Francis Group, an informa business

Library of Congress Cataloging-in-Publication Data

Osborne, Margery D.
    Examining science teaching in elementary school from the perspective of
a teacher and learner / by Margery D. Osborne.
        p. cm. — (Garland reference library of social science ; v. 1136
Critical education practice ; v. 18)
    Includes bibliographical references (p.) and index.
    ISBN 0–8153–2569–X (alk. paper)
    1. Science —Study and teaching. 2. Instructional systems—Design.
I. Title. II. Series: Garland reference library of social science ; v. 1136. III.
Series: Garland reference library of social science. Critical practice
education ; vol. 18.
LB1585.077   1999
372.3'5—dc21   99-25535
                                                                        CIP

Contents

Acknowledgments   vii

**Chapter 1 Introduction and a Review of Some Aspects
of Hermaneutics**   3

Chapter 2 The Role of Design in Science and Teaching   15

The First Class: Figuring Out What To Do   16

The Second Class: Science Talk And Explorations   26

Discussing Problems Of Design   37

Discussion Of Science Increases   39

Discussion Of Science And The Role Of Metaphor   42

*How Discussing The Act Of Design Facilitates
A Recognition Of Human Agency In Science*   46

*The Last Class: A Consideration Of Background
As Well As Foreground: What This
Can Mean In Science*   49

Conclusion   52

Chapter 3 Patterns and Understanding   57

An Outline Of The Unit On Music And Patterns   58

*Beginning Our Explorations Of Patterns:
What Is A Pattern, How Is It Constructed,
How Is It Used?*   62

*Starting To Explore Music Through Patterns:
Constructing Relationships*   67

*Asking Scientific Questions Intertwined
With Experimentation: Working Within
The Emerging Patterns*   78

*Encouraging Experimentation By Questioning
Relationships*   83

*The Development Of Method: Communication And
Community*   87

Method, Experimentation, Making Sense Of Phenomena   95

What Is Music? What Is Science? The Discussion Begins   103

The Meanings Of Variables, Defining Words   113

Defining Words Continued: Comparing/Constructing
     Similarities And Differences   116

Defining Words Continued: What Is A Pattern
     In And Out Of A Context? Playing With Context
     To Think About Meaning   122

What Is Music? Using Patterns To Examine
     A Fundamental Question   128

Conclusion   134

Chapter 4 Knowing   141

A Description Of The Unit On The Solar System   142

What Do You Measure When You Weigh Something?
     Finding The Fundamental Questions   144

What Is Gravity?
     Our Goals And Objectives Evolve   158

Constructing And Testing Scientific Theories
     And The Development Of A Community:
     Out Into The Solar System   167

Gravity And The Solar System Continued.
     I Realize We Have Changed Direction   176

Connecting Gravity To Motion. Connecting
     To Each Other's Ideas   179

Defining Words, Making Statements Of Knowing:
     The Development Of Uncertainty   192

Conclusion: The Role Of The Community   200

Chapter 5 Teaching: Knowing and Learning   205

First Story: Dinosaur Stories--Substance Or Process,
     Choosing Instructional Goals   208

Second Story: Martin Luther King Jr.--
     The Personal And The Political
     In The Social Constructivist Classroom   217

Discussion: Places Of Conflict As Places Of Change   220

Chapter 6 Conclusion   227

Appendix A: School and Classroom Descriptions   237

Appendix B: Children's Country of Origin and Pseudonyms   241

References   245

Index   251

Acknowledgments

This book owes immensely to many people. I want to thank, in particular, G.W. McDiarmid and Deborah Ball who, with great patience, helped me write this as a thesis when I was a doctoral student at Michigan State University. The two classroom teachers I worked with, Kathy Valentine and Sylvia Rundquist, were immeasurably important in creating the wonderful classrooms where I taught. The atmosphere which enabled the children to do such provocative experimentation and thinking is due to them.

In turning my thesis into a book I wish to acknowledge the sensitive and penetrating suggestions of Ian Westbury. Thank you so much for your time and help, Ian. Throughout the whole of this writing effort I have to recognize the great intellectual, emotional, and spiritual encouragement I received from my closest friends Jeremy Price and Angie Calabrese-Barton.

Finally I want to thank my two children, Larkin and Cornelia. Both engaged the text in ways no one else could, attending classes, making their own penetrating comments about the ideas, falling asleep at night as I read drafts to them as bedtime stories, laughing at the dialogue, and trying out the science.

Examining Science Teaching in Elementary School from the Perspective of a Teacher and Learner

CHAPTER 1

Introduction and a Review of Some Aspects of Hermeneutics

This book is about how relationships—between subject matter and teacher, subject matter and children, children and the teacher—are constructed in the context of teaching science in the lower elementary grades. Relationships are dynamic and shifting. Rather than try to characterize them, it is easier to try to characterize their dynamism—how they change. Therefore this book is a study of how relationships evolve, how they are initiated, and how they change over time as the components interact and effect one another.

I have been teaching science in a school with a highly diverse population. In this book I have used stories of those classes to reflect upon the nature of teaching and upon the relationships involved in teaching. I ask the questions: How is a practice, based upon certain ideals about science, children and learning constructed? How do these ideals shape the relationships between people and between people and things in classrooms?

This work draws on my readings of Hannah Arendt, *The Life of the Mind* and *Eichmann in Jerusalem*; Jean-Paul Sartre, *Search for a Method*; Jacque Derrida, *The Truth about Painting*; Luce Irigaray, *The Speculum of the Other Woman*; Julia Kristeva, *Woman's Time*; and Martin Heidegger, *Being and Time*. These readings and other readings in hermeneutics, semiotics, poststructuralism, and feminism have shaped my thinking about how subject and object are defined through relationships.

Many would argue, in a number of different ways, that the subject-object relationship is not created and maintained by the subject standing apart from the object—looking at the object from a distance. Rather, the basis of the relationship is in recognizing what the object shares with the subject. The relationship becomes one that isn't purely one of recognizing similarities, but is also one of comparing differences. "The semiotic continuum must be split if signification is to be produced."[1] The "object" of inquiry must be differentiated, extracted from a background. This relationship is the "signifying process" in which meaning is constructed through a continuous comparative movement between identities shared and identities defined oppositionally. This is intimately tied to the process of naming. The act of naming is fundamental in doing science. Naming a variable in science separates it from the continuum, gives it identity when before it was part of another. For example, energy: the concept of energy is a humanmade idea that can only be quantified and qualified after it has been named. Before that, it was part of the totality of the phenomenon. Once named, it acquires substance and reality. The children in my class also play with the act of naming, of reducing a phenomenon into parts. For example, in talking about music (Chapter 3), they separate the "whole" into pattern, rhythm, and beat. How the children then work to make sense of music and sound is fundamentally shaped by these variables. But how do they partition the whole into the three? What is included and excluded in each of the terms? Doing this determines meaning and use and occurs through use (application) and reflection on meaning (listening to the sounds identified as one or the other and talking about this with each other).

The sharing of components of identity—overlapping parts of the definitions of things—and recognizing these shared identities, is important because otherwise there could be no understanding (Rommetveit, 1980). For example, the children find that the words pattern, rhythm and beat overlap and are different in definition and the children use their understandings of each one to construct their understandings of the others. According to Derrida (1976, 1987), defining what is shared and what is not so that "objects" can be recognized occurs through framing—creating a frame around the "other." This frame is the context of the object and is also a context in which the subjects can place themselves. For example, a teacher could be teaching science or literacy skills not recognized as such until the time period is demarcated (named) "language arts time" or "science period." This context composes the basis or background of the relationship between subject and object, something not normally articulated or examined "for itself." The context or frame is continuously remade by the recognition and examination of similarities and differences as the object's definition is refined—there is a developing meaning of "science" from what is done in "science period" that is different from what is done at other times. How that is understood, though, is through an interplay between and examination of differences and similarities of those actions during science period and other actions. Finally, thinking about similarities and differences can also cause us to become aware of qualities of the surrounding context.

In science the naming of an idea or object often obscures both its background (frame) and its history. Through the scientific process an idea is often refined and even redefined, further obscuring history and the "oneness-that-once-was." There are two aspects of science. The first is progressive. Science is done for what it can do to transform an object or the environment or even ourselves. This hides both the past and the nature of the science. The other aspect allows a new, critical reflection upon both the scientific concepts themselves and upon the continuum. Science is a balance of these two aspects as is teaching. Teaching involves reaching toward a goal which in turn can cause reflection upon both the goal itself and the process. When and why are each of these two aspects of science and teaching in play?

> The real question is whether one sees the function of reflection as bringing something to awareness in order to confront what is in fact accepted with other possibilities—so that one can either throw it out or reject the other possibilities and accept what the tradition de facto is presenting—or whether bringing something to awareness *always dissolves what one has previously accepted.*[2]

Does thinking about the object make us increasingly blind to qualities of the frame or can we turn our understandings of the object back to a critical examination of the frame? In the children's explorations of the nature of musical sounds, the usefulness of the concepts they are developing is balanced between what they can do with them and what new thoughts are enabled as they examine both music and language. In defining pattern, rhythm, and beat they work to construct music of their own. They apply these concepts to bird song and ask whether or not it is really music or is, rather, language—they think new thoughts about the phenomenon and in turn question the usefulness of the labels. This process of becoming both cognizant of assumptions and questioning those assumptions is the essence of arguments of critical theorists such as Habermas (1991) as well as Arendt in *Eichmann in Jerusalem*. I think that in the course of teaching, reflection on assumptions and classifications also can occur. In the process of transforming both the children, the subject matter, and myself during teaching there are opportunities to reflect on this transformation as well as the assumptions that underlie them. I write about this in Chapters 4 and 5.

The subject-object relationship is defined by what the object and the subject share as much as by how they are different. Now the instruments that the subject uses to "look" at the object must also be able to access similarities as well as differences. In order to do this, these instruments mimic in some way the qualities of the object under study and also the qualities of the subject. There would be little point in teaching children if they were clones of myself. They are intrinsically different. I also could not teach them if we did not share certain things—for example, a language. A similarity, which is fundamental to the relationship such as language, shapes what can be learned about differences—both between the children and myself and between children—as they debate the meanings of scientific words by discussing their different ideas, they learn about each other as well as the science. Language is a tool, an instrument in the relationship reflecting and shaping it. It embodies the culture which contains the relationship and is instrumental in altering it. Its ability to be a tool is grounded in similarities between subject and object. Its purpose can be to "see" differences or similarities. The lenses, tools, and instruments used by the subject to look at the object selectively focus or image the similarities and differences. If these lenses mimic the subject only rather than the object, the image seen is of the object rather than the subject. The lens is a mirror and the study is a false one (Irigaray, 1985).

Both the context and the instruments that shape and enable us to look at an object are designed by us (the subjects) purposefully—to be able to do particular things. We choose (consciously or unconsciously) how things appear to us as well as objects choose their appearance: presentation is a purposeful act (Arendt, 1978). This also means it is a conscious act, at least on some level—we choose what we want others to see about us. This makes the subject-object relationship a reversible one. If a child in my class is the object to me, then I am also an object to him. If every act is one of self-display, then it is that fact that makes acts meaningful—they are so because of their purpose to the actor.

> [When I choose what to show, how to show it] I am not merely reacting to whatever qualities may be given me; I am making an act of deliberate choice among the various potentialities of conduct with which the world has presented me. Out of such acts arise finally what we call character or personality, the conglomeration of a number of identifiable qualities gathered together into a comprehensible and reliably identifiable whole.[3]

Now I think, as suggested by Foucault (1979), that this presentation or self-display can be a form of play—trying on different self-images, trying on different effects on the observer enabled by this back and forth, shifting subject-object identity. The idea of purposeful self-display also links the creation of subject-object identity directly to method, to the things done by either subject or object. Defining subject or object is through method. Neither the subject nor the object exists as a concept without the actions or thoughts in between the two that construct and shape the relationship. Again, this is also what I feel Derrida (1987) is saying with his idea of framing—the things, actions, context that set the object apart from a continuum.

If the subject-object relationship is based upon both self-presentation and perception that is purposeful—where both the object and the subject want to do something—it is motivated by a *need*. Sartre differentiates between *desire* and *need*. In *Being and Nothingness* (1965), he claims that acts of free will are motivated by desire. In *Search for a Method* (1963), he modifies this to need. The difference between desire and need, it seems to me, is one of an intellectual desire versus more emotional, felt need. To desire is in your head, to need is in your gut. Most importantly, need addresses a vanishing point—needs can never be satiated. Desires can, however, and then one can move beyond them. I think of Sartre's need as similar to bell hooks' (1990) "yearning"—a longing which emanates from the heart as well as the mind, which shapes thought, actions, and emotions and which is not satiated even when directly addressed. The subject-object identity shifts in response to how this need is acted on and perceived.

The tension between what is known and unknown which I write about as central to both the act of teaching and of doing science reflect needs. For a scientist, the need to discover can't be fulfilled—each new discovery uncovers new questions. Likewise for a teacher—goals in teaching and learning are always moving away, constantly redefined as progress or even just change occurs. Presentation of self, of science, of relationships becomes a vehicle for expressing and acting upon this need, but on the other hand, so does perception—both sides of the subject-object relationship are shaped by need.

Presentation is also a symbolic act, I think. It is a way of expressing something hidden. This as similar to Levi-Strauss's description of ritual as symbolic:

> [I]t is a matter of provoking an experience; as this experience becomes structured, regulatory mechanisms beyond the subject's control are spontaneously set in motion and lead to an orderly functioning.[4]

These regulatory mechanisms occur in a classroom because the act of self-presentation is a social act to which others react. This is really another explanation of how expressions of thoughts, needs, and actions become method. The symbolic quality of actions, where actions mean something other than what they appear, is at the heart of Julia Kristeva's (1986) concept of cyclical time. Actions, when perceived in a generalized sense, repeat over and over, form a cycle, are in cyclical time. They also define a method (methodical). Because they repeat, they acquire a transcendence in meaning; each time they occur the setting is different, their meaning is different (yet the same), and they become generalizable in consequence and form beyond the immediate actions of a particular moment. For example, when I ask for the class' attention by turning off the lights, I am not turning off the lights to make the room dark, but for a different purpose. The act has acquired a meaning other than the obvious one. It is symbolic of something other than what it does. The action has a generalized meaning—that the children should give me their attention—and a meaning specific to the instance. For example, at one time I may be stopping misbehavior, at another I may be calling the class to large group discussion. Actions reflect something about the actor, about the actor's beliefs about the perceiver, and about the actor's beliefs concerning what they are acting on. My use of the lights as a signal implies that I believe the children need me to signal that certain actions are appropriate, and that I know what the appropriate behavior is. The act of perceiving is also an interpretive one, and is active, not passive. The subject brings a lens to seeing also shaped by purposes and beliefs. The children are interpreting my actions in both a general and specific manner.

Heidegger argues that it is artificial to separate subject and object, as is implied in metaphors about the subject "seeing" the object. The subject and object occupy the same worldspace, lifespace: "By drawing a distinction that I (the subject) am perceiving something else (the object), I have stepped back from the primacy of experience and understanding that operates without reflection." Heidegger does not deny that we exist purposefully in this world, that we are trying to do certain things. He claims that this purposefulness involves decisions— what to do and what not to do, and how to go about doing these things. These decisions are founded upon uncertainty; they reflect needs for things that we don't have yet and hence don't know about. We make decisions on the basis of things felt, not articulated. The actions necessitated by decisions are symbolic interpretations of their unarticulated foundation.

This further defines Derrida's framing context. The frame is also a symbolic miasma of assumptions. We act using "skills and practices" from which we can articulate "beliefs, rules, . . . principles" by examining the background in light of our actions. I think that this idea of how we come to do the things that we do is central to thinking about the everyday decisions and choices that we make in teaching (Buchmann, 1986; Connelly & Clandinin, 1990). The background to the things that I do when I am teaching is unarticulated knowledge of science, children, teaching, context, as well as how I feel about those things founded in my history and also in the goals that I have set for my teaching. Acts of teaching are manifestations of a web constructed of these things, which add up to an "understanding" of the moment. This moment itself is not extractable from the situation itself. It's only when I can remove myself from the moment that I can think *about* my actions, knowledge, and choices. The same is true in the process of doing the science. This is why the question of design in science is so interesting. To design an experiment or a course of action represents this thinking that can go on outside the moment, but participating in science, utilizing the design, means immersion in the moment. The children in my second grade classroom are asked to participate in both of these ways of thinking as we explore soap bubbles. They design experiments and then they enact them, and finally we discuss their activities—thus, we move in and out of immersion in the moment.

The blending of subject and object, the dynamic between them constructed in a relationship composed of methods, purposes, and needs, is related for me to a concept that Julia Kristeva calls female subjectivity:

> According to Kristeva, female subjectivity would seem to be linked both to *cyclical* time (repetition) and to *monumental* time (eternity), at least in so far as both are ways of conceptualizing time from the perspective of motherhood and reproduction. The time of history, however, can be characterized as *linear* time: time as project, teleology, departure, progression and arrival. This linear time is also that of language considered as the enunciation of a *sequence* of words.[5]

The relationship between subject and object conceptualized as metaphorical, symbol-ridden method is patterned. Qualities of it repeat and it becomes a design. This is how a method can be defined and also how meaning can be found in method—method can be abstracted from a background of random action and it attains its own symbolic, transcendental meaning. The subject and object evolve, though, through the relationship—they become something different from what they were before. Then how does method respond to this?

> [F]emale subjectivity as it gives itself up to intuition becomes a problem with respect to a certain conception of time: time as project, teleology, linear and prospective unfolding: time as departure, progression and arrival—in other words, the time of history.[6]

Method is at the intersection between these two world concepts. It is the place where the battle between cyclical time and historical time occurs. As an example, teaching: There is an internal conflict for me when I am teaching—I need to understand, stay in one place and contemplate what I know about children, science, myself, and how I am able to know it, but I also need to change—to teach, to do things, to learn. Method serves both concepts of time; it is progressive (historical), in the service of change, and it is symbolic (cyclical), repeating. Thinking of method as purposeful is not the same as the false causality of history in which events are looked back on from the perspective of an outcome, nor is it transcendental in the sense of pointing to an inner truth which transcends individual instantiations. Method is in historical time because it is not willy-nilly, the relationship between the subject and the object is purposeful, each is trying to do something to the object or with the object as audience. This purpose isn't necessarily realized, but change is. Method is in symbolic time because of its own repetitive qualities and also because it allows the subject to look at the object in ways that are "framed," that have meaning. This is why talking about method as a form of design is important. In thinking about method and design as metaphorically linked, I wish to think of the word *design* as a verb and also as a noun. As a noun, the word *design* captures the abstract qualities of a pattern signifying something transcendent. As a verb it should be understood as a plan, an activity oriented toward a goal. Teaching, learning, science as methods have both of these qualities.

As people develop relationships they learn, and they develop a purpose, methods, and methodical ways of interacting. These methodical ways of interacting define patterns that enable our relationships. In particular, they allow us to understand each other and the purposes behind what we are doing. Methodical actions and method are at the heart of relationships: they are at the heart of science and also of teaching. They enable the construction of a community in the class— a relationship among diverse people enabled by a common pursuit. Method allows people to understand each other and live together even when doing, thinking, desiring very different things. It allows people to appreciate their differences as well as their similarities.

But method is seductive—it stops our thinking as well as enables our thinking. To act methodically means we are acting in expected ways. We aren't thinking about our actions. When doing this we forget the assumptions, the value choices hidden within the things we are doing. Action becomes oriented toward a goal, toward the future, toward realizing a purpose. Method allows one to live within a relationship without thinking about it, but at the core of science and teaching is a questioning of relationships—a need to see and develop new qualities. To be able to do this necessitates a recognition of assumptions and a questioning and reevaluation of them. It requires that those living within relationships periodically deconstruct them and rebuild them differently.

In the second chapter of this book, I wish to explore an example of design in teaching and in science through a description of a unit I taught in a first and second grade combination class. This unit is ostensibly about soap bubbles. The underlying concept it is about is experimental design. There are two forms of design occurring in these classes: the design that the children and I participate in as we explore the soap bubbles; and that between myself, the children, and the materials we are using to design the teaching. I talk about how the children use their previous understandings of many things to construct both new knowledge and also scientific process as we explore the bubbles. I also talk about how I use my knowledge to frame this pursuit and how this knowledge is altered as the children and I interact around the science and with each other.

In Chapter 3, I explore another design problem, that of designing, or maybe redesigning (redefining) the science so that I can maintain some particular goals in my teaching. Making a claim that both teaching and science are methods is, by my definition, making a claim that they are both purposeful activities with particular goals. That makes no claim that the goals for both are the same or that they are articulated ahead of time. My point in the argument that I have just presented about what method is, is that goals, as part of the "need" that motivates action, are in part unarticulated. Some instructional goals are acknowledged at the outset of teaching, yet the experience of designing, interacting, et cetera, make evident other goals not previously articulated. Through my work in the classroom I come to recognize the goals (values) that I am using to shape my teaching. I learn to recognize what my teaching symbolizes. When, through interactions with others, I come to realize these meanings and that they are not consistent with each other, I choose to work to redesign the science so that I can maintain the goals of my teaching. I don't do this in the abstract or all at once. Rather, I do this incrementally, as I teach and as I need.

The story portrayed in the third chapter concerns teaching sound by asking the question, What is music? I embedded the teaching of the science of sound in the exploration of music because this allows me to examine an intertwinement of questions science and aesthetics, a connection often not recognized by nonscientists. The story is an illustration about how the definitions of words, both naming and defining meaning, which along with method are the fundamental components of a science, is a process in itself. A more radical example of redesigning science is found in the fourth chapter, which narrates the tale of teaching a third grade class about gravity.

The stories told in each of these chapters continue to engage the larger conversations about children's science learning and teacher knowledge and learning. They also address ideas about the role of the children's home cultures in these classes. In the story of music teaching I make the argument that through discussion of the science, a unique classroom culture is generated. This culture adds onto and respects the children's home cultures. This development of a classroom culture around scientific explorations and discussions is central to my thinking about how the children come to learn in science and also about how I use my pedagogical knowledge to learn about teaching, the science, and the children. This is also true in the story of gravity, but here qualities of the "things"—knowledge as well as ways of thinking and expressing themselves—the children bring to class and use to construct this classroom culture are often problematic and cause me to think about how I am portraying the science and also how the science is evolving in my own head.

The fifth chapter of this book is specifically about how teaching is based upon knowing, but is also a process of coming to know. The process of design and therefore method isn't only a process of demonstrating what a person already knows; it's also a process of coming to know, of learning. This story quite explicitly addresses the questions of teacher learning and the role that thinking about the child's home culture has in teaching. The science itself is no longer the focus.

Much has been written about what teachers need to know about children, diverse learners, subject matter, and teaching skills. Little has been written about how a teacher changes as she tries to act upon that knowledge—how as she translates her knowledge into actions and interactions, it changes as the teacher is confronted with the demands of a complex situation. As the children interacting with the science are confronted by things that they don't know or things that they need to know differently, a teacher as she interacts with the children or with the subject matter discovers things that she doesn't know, and she must act to change her practice and the knowledge that practice is based upon. This means fundamentally rethinking the value choices—emotional and moral as well as intellectual—upon which the knowledge is constructed. This book is an attempt to trace the course of this cycle of thinking, knowing, and learning for one teacher—myself.

I explore this through my interactions with children and with a variety of phenomena—sound, music, gravity, soap bubbles, and dinosaurs. Each story of this book recounts a story of these interactions and developing relationships. Each addresses the question of how teaching practice is constructed and also altered and evolved as these relationships develop.

NOTES

1. Kristeva (1986), Women's time, 13.
2. Gadamer (1976), *Philosophical hermeneutics*, 34.
3. Arendt (1978), *The life of the mind*, 37.
4. Levi-Strauss (1963/76), *Structural anthropology*, 198.
5. Moi, T. (1986), Marginality and subversion: Julia Kristeva, 187.
6. Kristeva (1986), Woman's time, 192.

CHAPTER 2

The Role of Design
in Science and Teaching

The school in which I teach the science units described in this book is a public elementary school which primarily serves the children of married students at Michigan State University. The population of this school is diverse; it is not characterized by a particular class or ethnic background. The children represent approximately fifty cultures from around the world. I have given all the children pseudonyms which preserve as much as possible an indication of their culture. There is a list of children with their country of origin in Appendix 2 of this book. The classes in which I worked were a first grade, a first and second grade combination, and a third grade. These classes each had approximately twenty children (in this school district, English as Second Language children counted as two in enrollment statistics). I say approximately because the number of children changed over the course of the year as children left and new children replaced them when their parents enrolled in or graduated from the university. The children listed in Appendix 2 are children who stayed for a length of time but did not necessarily complete the year. Children who only came at the very end of the year or who only stayed for a short amount of time are not included.

The story I tell in this chapter involves a very long science unit on soap bubbles which was taught in the first and second grade combination class. The unit lasted from early November through winter and spring, and concluded in late May. It was intertwined with two other science units; a short one on growing plants (December), and another long one on patterns which was begun in October, continued through our exploration of music and sound, and ended in June on the last day of school. This last unit is discussed in detail in Chapter 3 of this book.

THE FIRST CLASS: FIGURING OUT WHAT TO DO

November 7
The children come in from recess and we discuss what we will be doing now in science class. While they were outside, I made up tubs of bubble solution using dishwashing soap and water. I have decided that each table of three or four children will have one plastic washtub of bubble solution. First we set up the room by putting down pads of newspapers on the desks. When we are ready, I give them the bubble solution and ten minutes to experiment with it. I give no other instructions than that. They are restricted to stay in their own pods and to using only their hands to make the bubbles. I have given them no implements. This is purposeful: I wish to maximize the children's sensual contact with the material and I want this contact to be just between them and the soap solution (and of course with other children in the class—there was much discussion in all this) without anything else added in.

I stop the whole thing and ask the children to form a learning circle for our first conversation. I have certain possible directions that we might go from this first activity laid out in my head and I want to see which of these things the children have located for themselves and if I push a little bit, very gently on those things, how the children respond to this. I am trying to locate *what* about soap bubbles the children are actually going to be able to pursue and discover given that in the teaching that I do with this age group I am disinclined actually to *tell* them information to explain the things that we observe. My mental list of things we might explore includes bubble shape, bubble size, colors in bubbles, why bubbles form in the first place, and why they pop.

I start the discussion by asking what people were able to see when they were making bubbles. Thomas said, "Well, something I made, I put my two hands . . . first I blew a bubble, then I caught it in one hand then I put my other hand on top then I got this long string." He mimes this with his hands. I name what he has made a "cylinder." Other children have tried similar things and start discussing this. I get up and draw what I think he has made on the board (Fig. 2.1).

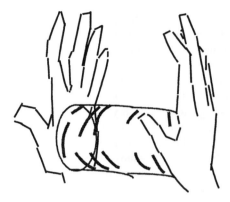

Figure 2.1

I quiet the room and ask Thomas if this is what he means. He agrees.

> *Thomas*: And it was not two [bubbles], sometimes people catch bubbles like that but what I do is sometimes I catch one and put it in the other hand, sometimes I catch two and put it [*together, he shows us with his hands*] and then you see the silver coin in the middle . . .

I start to ask Thomas about this silver coin but he wants to talk more about how he made the cylinder. He says that it requires two hands. A bubble in just one hand is "fat out of my hand but when my hand goes on it, it goes straight up." When he puts another hand on the bubble it elongates into a cylinder. This is the essence of an explanation of why bubbles are the shapes that they are—they are fluids that take a shape imposed upon them. I repeat his description of how he made the cylinder and ask him to confirm that.

> *Thomas*: Yes but what I think is funny is, see, it was sort of fat when I just had it . . . here I'll [*He does this with the bubble solution—I have brought a tub up to the front of the room*] But it's fat then it starts going up. It turns into a straight person, like kids playing, they get in line so fast, like when they are playing, they're all fat and then when they say line up, it's just *whup*!

I ask if anyone else has done anything like what Thomas is talking about. Ricky says that he did something like this without making the silver coin and he found when you pull the bubble cylinder too far, it stretches and then pops.

In this first short conversation we have started talking about the shape of bubbles and why they break, but in a more complex way than could have been suggested from my abstracted mental list. The discussion about shapes is also about the intersection of shapes, and the discussion of popping bubbles is combined with consideration of size. Now Andy adds in that he saw Kwanhyo blow a bubble that fell to the floor and, rather than breaking, bounced. Thus, the conditions which make a bubble break aren't purely those of size.

Emily adds her observations about bubbles breaking—that you can only stretch them so far—and then Suni says,"I had one, I had one, see I catched the balloon and then I put the other hand on it and stretched it and kept stretching it, then I had one balloon and then when I stretched it, I had two." I asked him if this was like Thomas's. Thomas interjects,"Yeah 'cause it broke." I say, "Oh, so, but it didn't break and there was nothing, it broke and you had two bubbles." This particular phenomenon, that bubbles can divide into two or more *or* break, is a new connection for me which is allowed, I think, by the messy, social qualities of how we are discovering things—in class with others and then all together again as we talk about things and put ideas together. For me this means as we talk about the things we have done and what we think about them, we hear new ideas, different ways of thinking than those we have constructed alone. This has an implicitly critical quality—as someone says something different from my own ideas, I compare and assess. That, though, is dependent upon my ability to listen and truly hear (understand) what the other is saying. This combined with a desire to do new things or think new thoughts rather than justify my own or replicate others is the essence of the creativity integral to the concept of design I am attempting to foster in this class and describe as a component of teaching. I think this can only be achieved through conversation around topics in which the children are genuinely interested. This, though, has a cyclical quality—the children also become genuinely interested because of the conversation.

An'gele tells us about her technique of bubble blowing, "Um, when I was doing it, I just, would just, dip my hands in the water, I had two hands, I went like this, and I got like a little crystal ball, a little circle in my hand like this . . . " She shows us (Fig. 2.2):

Figure 2.2.

Then she tells us that she was able to make a cylinder like Thomas described using her other hand. Cory adds, "When I put, um, one in my hands and then I took it out, I blew and little tiny bubbles came out of my fingers." Each time a child says what he has done I draw him out a bit in his description. I do this to develop the language that the children are using and to continue my search for something that can be developed into a theme. To do the latter, I want to increase the "dwell" time on any particular observation or statement to see if it is developed further and if it resonates with others. I talked in the introduction to this chapter of how a design stands out from a background. I am looking for this design to begin to emerge. I listen to the things the children say about what they have done and in response to each other for repetitions in ideas, for echoes that pull one idea into prominence over others. I am looking for the emergence of a foreground over a background.

The language that I am using to describe this process is deceptive; it implies a passivity but in truth it is the combined interactions in conversation between us all, the desire to communicate, that causes the emergence of a theme. Part of my role is to recognize the common-alities in the statements the children make and work to construct the conversation to contain that theme more prominently—so that over time separate ideas and observations become part of a whole and the children begin to work together on common ideas and questions. For example, after An'gele and Cory describe to us the mechanics of making bubbles for them and describe what they were able to make, Sakti says this, "I blowed a bubble like this and I held my hand like this and I blowed it and it kind of went like this and then it was this big and it popped." I repeat, "It popped? Did it ever become separate from your hands? Did you ever get it so it was like separate from your hands or was it always attached to your hands?" She says that it remained attached to her hands. Her comments are connected to and add to all the other children's observations. It's this that gives me a feeling of a common topic for us to pursue. Both the children and I are taking a role in developing and creating this, but it's a complicated pattern of playing off each other.

Shumshad claims that when he pulled his hand out of the water a bubble was made between his fingers and even an enclosed spherical bubble, held in his hand, followed the edges of his fingers. He continues describing to us how the bubble film travels up the sides of his wet fingers, clings to his fingers. A bubble not held this way was shaped like a "crystal ball." This is an addition to Thomas's early description of how to form a cylinder: a free bubble is round but it will cling "sometimes" to a surface and be reshaped by that surface.

We continue talking about technique, and I try to suggest an exploration of bubble size, one of my original ideas about what this might be about that hasn't been mentioned yet. I don't want things closing down on one topic yet. This is in part because all the various things I have listed in my mind that we might be exploring—size, source, color, shape, et cetera—are connected, as the children demonstrate in their talk. I know that in order to develop understanding of any one it won't be done in isolation of the others. The variables are connected and we are going to want to recognize and develop these connections to be able to theorize explanations.

At this point in our conversation, however, I think we should focus a bit on size. I want this discussion to be connected to a discussion of how the children actually made the bubbles. The size of a bubble depends upon how much air you blow into it, and also on how large the initial film the bubble comes from is. I say to the class that I saw Ho Sook making bubbles a different way from the description others have given. I demonstrate this (Fig. 2.3).

Then I ask how those bubbles differed from bubbles made the other way, like An'gele had shown us. Ho Sook says that they are

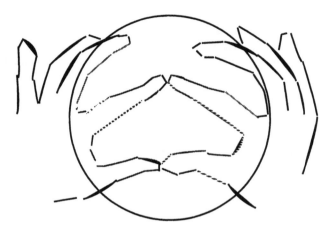

Figure 2.3

smaller. This is not so; they are larger, and Paula disagrees—she was also blowing bubbles this way and hers were much larger. Many children debate this until Teton introduces something new: he saw rainbows when he made a cylinder. I ask what he thinks might make the rainbows. Paula responds, "The bubble soap, when all the bubble soap . . . and the lights . . . when the lights come down, it seems like all these rainbow things are swirling around."

> *Teacher:* You saw them swirling around?
> *Danping:* You know what? When I was looking at the rainbow . . . first you know when I'd put my hands together and then I'd go like that [*blow the bubble through her hands like Ho Sook and Paula did*] and then I'd see the rainbows first . . . they'd be thick and then they'd be skinny and then they'd curl everywhere.

I ask her why she thinks they did that and she replies that she saw it occur as the bubble stretched. I repeat the whole thing, putting the two sets of observations together to emphasize the implied causality. "Danping is saying that at first her rainbows were real big and then they got skinnier and skinnier and started to swirl around and that was as the bubble got bigger."

Now I blow a bubble and ask what they see. Shumshad says, "Um it was kind of like a bag that you made." Suni says, "Like blowing a real balloon but you were blowing that." Andy adds that as I blew, it got bigger and longer, and Teton says that at the top of the bubble he saw a large rainbow that changed like Danping told us about. Cory adds, "Yeah it went skinny skinny and then it went longer longer and then when it got to the, um, end it showed the colors, it was purple, green and black." Thomas tells us that he saw the rainbow go up and move especially when the bubble was about to break. Then Emily and Benjamin try describing how the bubble changed shape as I was blowing it.

I blow another bubble and the children continue talking amongst themselves about the shape changes until Kwanhyo says, "It was going on your hand like this and then it went like this, it curved and then it was going on your hand like this, . . . " I say that then it broke. Sueh-yen says that it was like a ghost and that it "turned it bigger and bigger and then it was moving and then it popped." Cory says that before it popped, it looked like "fire and smoke on the back." I blow another and then another. The second pops and generates the first question that I choose to pursue by experimentation and observation. I want to model a form of dialectic between the two for the children.

I ask what the children saw when the second bubble broke. Paula says that she saw it stick to my arms before it popped. I ask if anyone saw it exactly when it popped, and Cory says, "Yeah it went all over you, first it went down and then it touched the bowl and then it went phoof!" I ask if it popped all over or just in one place and that break spread. I want them to look harder and harder; when no one can answer this I blow another bubble. Cory says that it popped in one place and others say all over. I blow another. Now Danping describes what she was able to see. "Um it went sort of like a circle and then it went a little bit down and it went off one this [*she gestures with her hands*]." Cory adds, "First it went down, then it popped then . . . and it went in one place, 'cause it only went down, all of them went down, it went . . . " He gestures with his hands and I catch on, "Oh 'cause it's like everything fell?" Shumshad describes it perfectly, "Yeah like raindrops."

Next Cory asks me to try to make Thomas's silver coin construction. I do this while Thomas tells me how (Fig. 2.4).

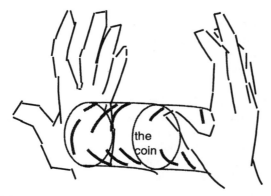

Figure 2.4

I ask if the children can see the coin. Thomas adds, "Well it's really not a coin it's really just a line that's circled." I stretch the bubbles until they break, then have to do it again. Cory exclaims, "The rainbows are going very fast!" I notice, "They are as soon as I made it stretch, the rainbows went really fast." Cory says, "It's from the lights!" I make another.

> *Thomas*: Now hook it! There's going to be a coin now see all around that, . . .
> *Paula*: Now turn it the other side it looks like one of those lamps that you put fire in, . . .
> *Emily*: The coin was invisible!
> *Thomas*: See!!
> *Dan*: Oh I see it, . . .

"I see it!" everybody is shouting. The bubble pops and I do it again; Thomas tells me step-by-step how to do it this time. Finally we get the cylinder made and a "coin" in the center. Thomas says, "There see that round thing, it's clear but it looks like a coin." I agree and point out that it is flat. It pops and we make another. Lots of children start talking about this, describing what they think it looks like. For instance, Cory says that he thinks it looks like a snowman.

I have Thomas come up and sit in the center and make the coins himself. He has problems getting the two bubbles to reattach. (This is an interesting problem, by the way: two bubbles don't always want to "stick" to each other.) I get Thomas to talk as he is working, to say the thing that he is making or trying to make as he does this. This has two effects—to get him to slow down and to focus the audience. Once he's made one, I ask the kids to direct comments and questions to Thomas. Cory asks him how he makes it—when he puts it together. Thomas does another play-by-play as he makes a second. Then he does a third. I ask Cory why he thinks that it makes that flat surface in between the two bubbles. He replies, "I think if it touches something else it can turn flat. Or it got squished in the middle and it didn't pop." Thomas says, "This is what I think, the way the bubbles attach is I think the way it happens. You see my hand makes the bubbles go out and these bubbles go together." Andy says, "Well I think when it goes together the other bubble sort of pushes it and makes it flat when they come together and it makes the coin." Then Thomas says that he doesn't know if it should really be called a coin because it's not that "but that's just what he named it." I say that's okay because it is flat so it looks like a coin, it tells us that it's flat, it's a good description. Andy says that he agrees "it looks like a coin." The children in this sequence have appropriated the observation, question, experimentation dialectic I demonstrated, extending it by starting to theorize around the dynamics of bubble surfaces.

I start to end class by asking the children what they think they learned from doing this. Thomas says that he learned that bubbles stretch and he's learned how to do that. Cory has learned that he can make it very big. I ask what they are going to do next time. Thomas says that he is going to make one that goes over his head like a spaceman. Cory says that he is going to try to make one that goes up and will fly around the room. I ask them to think about that for next time.

I use the word *design* as either a noun or verb, or sometimes I can mean both. I think in the first class of this unit what is portrayed is designing not so much a design—although I think as the teacher a shadow of a design already existed in my head that gains solidity as the class progressed. I did find things in this class through the discussions about the shapes of bubbles that I could locate as things that we would at least partially focus on in the next few classes. There are, though, designs (the noun) to be found in this also. There is the way that I am teaching—the questions that I ask to focus the conversation on descriptions of things made and of how the children went about making those things, qualities of the conversation itself that I model and develop (e.g., the subject of the silver coin—the science grows out of what people have discovered on their own). This is a design because it follows a pattern. I conduct conversations in certain ways in which there are rules of behavior. I develop the science over and over again through this conversation which always starts with observation, and moves to explanation and further experimentation, driven by questions rather than answers. There are also the "things," types of bubbles and observations expressed metaphorically, that the children produce in the conversation. These are the results of their interactions with the bubble solution and other children contextualized in the task I have given them. These things are designed because they are made purposely, either to fulfill my task, because a child sees someone else make one, or possibly because of a developing interest in something previously known or discovered accidentally. It's the way I teach that these done things become works in progress, designs become incomplete, become symbolic of partial acts of designing.

This story (and the stories in the other chapters of this book) are written from transcripts of the class. In transforming those transcripts into a story, I have reduced and edited what was said by the children and by me and also descriptions of what we did. In doing this and in choosing to focus on science content (e.g., rather than on control issues) I have, strangely enough, deleted much of the patterned activity of the class. I find this strange because if this is a story of design, and design as a noun is a pattern, then I have deleted a large portion of that design.

The repetitive acts I am talking about are things such as turning out the lights to get the children's attention, the mental processes I go through to decide who to call on and when in class discussions, descriptions of speech patterns or activity patterns of individual children. These small patterns enable and compose the larger design. They are microcosms of my dialectic between the atemporality and temporality of patterns. We recognize patterns because they repeat in time, they become a quality of the passage of time but they also punctuate and differentiate particular moments in time; they exist for themselves.

The act of design, however, does appear to be an interaction among materials, the person and metaphorical images of purpose, as Schon (1984) would claim, when we examine the bubbles the children have made—Thomas's coin, for example, which he was able to make because of the qualities of the soap solution and of his own acts. These were shaped by his person and his past history, which were in turn developed by his growing personal aesthetic. Thomas spends a lot of time designing Lego constructions and competing with them in local children's clubs. I believe you can see this background in his work with the bubbles—he made bubbles and the first thing he did with them was try to attach them together. People who play with Legos don't just gaze at them, they try to build things with them. The idea of building something is certainly purposeful, and transporting this idea to working with bubbles is equally metaphorical. What do bubbles and Legos have in common? Not very much from my perspective, but quite a lot from Thomas's. As the teacher engaged in the act of design, I have ideas about what we should be doing in these classes and these ideas start to take on concrete shapes as I interact with the children and the soap bubbles through the children. It's purposeful because I have a purpose: I want the children to engage in experimental design where they find out things and develop ideas. That purpose is metaphorical to me because it's shaped comparatively with other things that I have done in science, things that are like and unlike this.

In the next class we continue to discuss bubble shapes, but now the children start to postulate theories to explain those shapes. I act to keep the children cognizant of their role in shaping the bubbles. Unlike other observation-based science we have done (e.g., the unit on music described in the next chapter), in a fundamental way, the bubbles take the shapes they do because of what the children do in forming them (as well as because of their own intrinsic properties). Recognizing the role of the experimenter is paramount. Discovering the intrinsic properties of bubbles comes through either the success or the failure of the design of the experiment (both can tell you information and augment your understanding). There can be no illusion of the experimenter's passivity. I try to keep the children cognizant of their role. This goal shapes many of my decisions in the whole of this unit.

THE SECOND CLASS: SCIENCE TALK AND EXPLORATIONS

November 12

I start by asking all the children to try to make the cylinder and coin that Thomas and Ricky had shown us. By telling them to do something in particular, I set a problem in which their actions as well as the qualities of the outcome play a role. After ten minutes, the children come to a learning circle to talk about their experiences. I bring a basin of bubble solution in case we need it.

I ask, "How many people made their cylinder and the silver coin? Were any people not able to make them? Kwanhyo, you weren't able to make them?" A number of children have had some problem making the silver coin. My intention in asking this question, which I do many times in the subsequent classes, is to find out about these difficulties that the children have in making their creations and to uncover what things the children do about those problems. This isn't particularly to help the children to achieve their original visions, but rather to hear how they alter their mental designs because of difficulties or the strategies they develop to try to circumvent these problems. I also wish to hear the things the children have found out about the soap solution in the process of running up against difficulties. In this instance, the children talk about their problems and exchange hints and techniques. This again progresses to theorizing about the science.

Cory describes the way he was able to make the bubbles: "When I was blowing a cylinder, when I got very far it, um, they were both big bubbles and when I made the cylinder it was a big cylinder and inside of it, I looked, and inside of it it looked like there was a circle inside of it." Thomas exclaims, "That was the coin." Cory, however, says no it wasn't, it was a "flat part." Thomas says again "that was the coin." I ask Cory to describe his bubble again and agree that was the silver coin. Then I ask, "Why do you think, you guys, why do you think the silver coin is flat. I mean, the bubble is round [*I indicate curved with my hands*] but the silver coin is flat." Cory says, "Because when you stick it together it makes something flat," and Danping adds, "It squashes each other." I ask her what squashes each other means.

This is more than just a description of something she has seen. It is an idea about why what she has seen is the way that it is—why the silver coin is flat. She has to be clear about what she is talking about for others to understand and for us in the class to be able to go any further with her ideas. Because this topic of the silver coin and the shape of the silver coin seems to keep resurfacing and because things can be said about it that are both derived from what the children can observe with the bubbles and connect with other more fundamental scientific principles about pressure and directional pressure, I have pretty much decided what I want the class to pursue when she makes her statement about the two bubbles squashing each other to make the coin. This has become a really interesting cut on the question I had originally thought we might be pursuing concerning the shapes of bubbles. A free bubble is round because of the pressure of the air inside it pushing out equally in all directions. This isn't at all obvious—why is the air pushing, for example? The concept has suddenly become more accessible because in Thomas's construction there are two bubbles pushing against one another, so in some parts they are round, but where they connect they are flat. The flatness and roundness become understandable as connected concepts. It's obvious that the flat part is caused by the bubbles pushing together, so the pushing that goes on elsewhere is pushing the bubble film out and round.

Danping says, "Because the bubbles is squashing each other and it makes . . . like this goes like this [*she gestures with her hands*] and it just squashes this, it's almost like two bubbles both put in one but it just squashes it and lays down flat in the middle." Cory adds, "Like a flat nose." Next Thomas tells us:

> I can explain it better because it's sort of like . . . see this? This is what it's like. It's flat but it's round because it's skinny, you can see in both sides but, but what we mean by it's flat is it's very skinny like this . . . but it's also round.

I ask, "Why is it round?" and Thomas replies that the coin is round because the bubble is round and it is inside the bubble. This is where I get the next refinement to my plans for the subsequent classes. In the future we will begin talking about the shapes of bubble films and the shapes created by their intersections. The aspects of design we will participate in involve controlling the placement of those planes and predicting their intersections.

Thomas and, in a minute, Danping, are saying that the shape of the bubble controls the shape of the intersections between the bubbles. This observation will become key during the ensuing weeks. For my next question, I return to asking why the coin is flat. Thomas says, "Because it's inside the bubble and if it wasn't, I wouldn't have called it a coin, for one thing, I would have called it an I don't know." I respond by summarizing the discussion, ignoring Thomas's last bit of logic. "So Thomas says first of all that the silver coin is round because the bubble's round and when they come together it's still going to be round and Danping says that it's flat, . . . " Thomas breaks in to state, "It *is* flat!" I continue, "Danping says it's flat because the two bubbles are pushing on each other.

> *Thomas*: Right.
> *Danping*: I know why it's round because the bubble is round, right? And the edges are round so when you squash them it's going to make a round coin, it's not a square coin. That would be if it was a square one.
> *Teacher*: Hum, Cory what were you saying?

Danping has just made a very nice elaboration on Thomas's explanation for why the coin is round. I want us to stay on the question of why the coin is flat because we are very close to making sense of that.

> *Cory*: Um, that there's no air inside the flat thing so it makes it flat. I think that there's no air in it.
> *Teacher*: Oh, I thought when you first started to say that . . . I thought you said that there is no air inside the bubbles.
> *Cory*: There is. But inside the flat thing there isn't. There's nothing.

This is a pretty important concept. Children this age have very interesting ideas about what air is and one of the places that they form their ideas is in blowing up things like bubbles and balloons. Having some idea about what is in the bubbles and where it comes from is important if we are going to think about shape and size and that they have any control over those things. I ask what other people think is inside the bubbles. Emily changes the subject, though, and says that she saw an "invisible line" that squiggled around the bubble. We will get back to what is in bubbles later. "It wasn't really invisible, it was hard to see but it, it was on the side and it would be like a rainbow and right here there would be like lines that would go [*she traces a wiggly line with her finger*] a whole bunch of lines and it was going like this very slowly or something." I say that I have seen something like this also.

I spent quite a lot of time with Danping and Ho Sook looking at these lines on their bubbles. There are two kinds of "lines" on the surface of the bubbles. One is formed by excess fluid flowing down the sides of the bubble to the bottom where it drips off. The second are interference color bands. The actual colors of these bands is dependent on the thickness of the bubble—the thicker they are, the brighter the color. When the bubble is very thin, they appear as black or gray lines. The speed the lines move is variable and is controlled by the flow of fluid over the bubble so the two types of lines are connected. This flow is more or less downward to the base of the bubble, but swirls around. Anyway, Ho Sook and Danping and I talked about how it seems to do with the "water" fluid on the bubbles. This is what Danping means when she now asks Emily if she is talking about the water. Emily doesn't understand this, however.

Emily tries to explain what she has seen to Danping, Ho Sook, and the class. "Here's the bubble [*she indicates a circle with her hands*] and then inside would be a little line about that big, you can barely see them and they're so white that they're like invisible and then like on the side there would be like a rainbow." Danping announces that she knows what Emily means and I ask her if what Emily has just described is the same as the water that Danping and I had observed running down the outside of her bubbles and dripping off the bottoms (Fig. 2.5).

Figure 2.5

Danping says, "No I think that she is talking about the lines that are in the bubble." From what I have observed myself, I ask, "Are they the same lines that sometimes look like they are colors and sometimes look like they are black and white?" Danping says that she isn't sure. I blow a bubble that we can look at while we talk more about this. I want them to associate the act with the bubble.

Emily: Did you see the lines in there?

Teacher: There's a bubble, why is that round?

Cory: 'Cause of the air that's in it.

Andy: The air is pushing. When it's going around, it's pushing.

Teacher: Okay hold it, Cory says because there's air in it makes it round and Andy says because the air that's inside is going around and around and pushing.

Danping: I think because your finger was round and you blow it so: (Fig. 2.6)

Figure 2.6

I ask if my fingers were square, would it make the bubble square? Some say yes and some no. I make a bubble An'gele's way (Fig. 2.7):

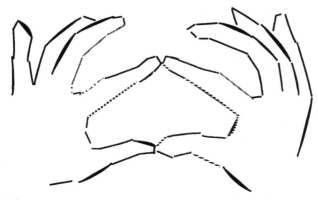

Figure 2.7

Then I point out that the hole between our hands from which the bubble forms isn't round. Andy says that it *changes* to round and Danping adds, "It first went like that [*elongated*] but then it went to round." Then Danping says that even though the hole between my hands is more or less triangular, the bubbles become round because "the bubbles down there are round so when you blow it, um, the littler bubbles get big so they're round." In other words, the bubbles already exist in the soap solution and in making them large we are just enlarging them.

Ricky asks if he can say something about how the air gets in.

> *Ricky*: 'Cause I think when people breathe, how they breathe out and
> then the air's in the room and then I think after you put it in your
> fingers like this and it's in there, I think the air comes here and it
> stops here and then when you blow, it goes out with the bubble.
> *Teacher*: 'Cause you're blowing it out?
> *Ricky*: No, because there's air in the room I think and then when you
> have it like this, the air comes in towards it and then when you
> blow, blow the bubble the air goes inside it when you blow.

Ricky is saying that when you blow you aren't blowing air into the bubble; rather you are making the opportunity for air from the room to go into the bubble. This comes up again later.

Then we return to why bubbles are round. Cory says that it's because you blow into it like with a balloon—you blow into it and it gets round. The air that gets into it makes it get round. If you blow too fast, the air will just go right through it and pop on the other side. I ask him if this is the same as what Andy said about the air going round and round, and he agrees that it is. If the air goes straight the bubble pops. Emily agrees with Ricky that it's the air in the classroom that goes into and makes it round. I ask again if it's the air that you blow in and am corrected that it's the air from the classroom. I ask her if it's something about the air itself that makes the bubble round or rather, like Andy and Cory have said, the motion of the air. She says it's the air—the air from the classroom combining with the air from the person blowing combines and makes a "weird" sort of air that goes into the bubble and is round. So I ask what would happen if I were to blow something else, not classroom air or my air into it—would it still be round? Danping says that all bubbles are round. I ask her why, and again she says because the little bubbles in the bubble soap are round.

Now all this is interesting, but I put it aside for the moment. I choose rather to ask the children to clarify their statements so that we can all be sure of them. Not to have the idea that the "placement" of the bubble film is at an equilibrium point between competing forces is a problem, but one we will work on. Their idea that the bubbles already exist in the bubble solution is interesting, and their idea that air can have shape is wrong. Neither of these ideas can really be addressed in the directions we seem to be heading in our interactions with the bubbles. Neither effect what we are doing, so there is no reason for me to want to work to confront them.

I ask if they all think that even when they can't see bubbles that there are still bubbles in the bubble soap. They all say yes, and Danping adds that these are what we blow up when we make the bigger bubbles. Andy says that he thinks the air inside is going around because of the movement of the color bands. He and Emily start talking about this. Andy says that these bands form right from when you start to blow.

An'gele says that she knows why you can put your finger into the bubble. She says that it is because the wet air in the water hooks onto your fingers so that you are able to go through. This is quite right—the bubble needs to be able to "wet" a thing that it clings to, otherwise it can't and will break. This is why two bubbles sometimes will and sometimes won't connect together to make the coin. We work on this a bit more, and the concepts behind it come up again and again. We go into this further starting with the next class when I ask the children both to use and to make implements to make bubbles with. The way that this works and the shapes of the resultant bubbles is determined by how the bubble solution is able to wet the materials we are using for construction. Now, though, Emily asks what would happen if you have one dry hand and you try to put that hand through the bubble. I tell the children that wet things can go through and dry things will break the bubble. We demonstrate this.

Then I say that I thought Danping's idea about why the coin was flat was a good one—I thought so, although I wasn't sure. I send them back to their seats and I ask them to blow a bubble and look for and at the lines Emily talked about and then to make a column and see what happens to the lines. They all start talking about how the lines start moving faster and faster as I stretch it. Emily points out that when I touch the bubble all the lines speed up and start to move toward my finger "like a magnet." The children do this until recess.

In this class, although we have continued to discuss bubble shape, we've added in more sophisticated observations about size and color. The children have also started postulating scientific theories to explain what they are seeing. I want to make sure that they connect the things that they see to the things that they are able to do. I want their view of experimental design to include themselves as the lens former: I want them to see themselves as active in the process of making observations and explanations about the science, and not start to fall into the fallacy that they aren't part of the process of seeing.

In the next class I decide that they should experiment with bubble size. To do this I give each child a lunchroom tray with a quarter inch of bubble solution on the bottom and a straw to blow the bubbles on the surface with. This allows the entire surface of the tray to form a bubble. The bubble can be very large because this surface is much larger than anything they can form with their hands. I also want them to use the straw because that distances them from the bubble. They are further away, and therefore they can look at the bubble differently. Using a straw also makes the act of blowing more focal, I think.

I want slowly to introduce tools. In the original task, the only tools were the children's hands and the solution. In the process of coming to use tools as tools, a person has to stop focusing their consciousness on the tool itself and place it on the outcome instead (Polanyi, 1966). At the beginning of using a tool, the tool itself is at focus. By having the children just use their hands in the bubble solution at the start, I wished to focus them on the properties of the bubble solution and their role in forming the bubbles. Now I can let them play with a new tool and let them develop new ways of seeing the bubble solution through this tool after, of course, they've explored the tool. The point of using tools is that they allow a person to see particular aspects of the things being worked on. This can be passive looking, like through a lens of a microscope, or it can be an active shaping, like a saw and wood. Mostly we do want to think about what the tool shows us about the object (subject) but (at least in science) we should also be mindful that the tool is selective and we can look backwards from what we see in the object to the tool and say things about the qualities of the tool.

This is also true of teaching. In the introduction to this chapter, I talk about the aspects of this class I have deleted in constructing this narrative. Many of these "things," such as turning out the lights to gain control of the class or thought processes I go through to decide who will talk and when, are tools of teaching that enable our explorations of bubbles and design. They also shape what happens in the class—things could happen differently if the tools were used differently or if those tools weren't used and others were. These are my choices because I want the class to look a particular way.

As a class we had to learn to recognize these actions as tools, as symbolic of something else. The children had to learn the meaning of lights-out and to respond to that meaning rather than to the mere fact of the lights being off. They had to learn the conversational patterns of the class. These had to become background, but in such a way that they could still delineate, articulate the things we should be paying attention to—my next instruction or a child's statement of an idea. We can look backward from the outcome and ask about the background patterns that enable the processes of the class, the designing of the class. That's not to say that I do that while I'm using those tools or that there aren't many and multiple levels of this background and the questions necessary to uncover them. For example, deciding who will talk when can get at particular thoughts about particular children in a context or can go further back and ask why I feel I need to be in control of conversation (to shape the science, to control behavior, to hear different children). We can also ask how these tools shape the science in a small sense (determine what we are doing) and in a large sense (determine the concept of science itself we are developing).

For the next three classes I continue to keep the exploration of bubbles open—exploring other, different variables in turn, rather than closing in on one particular direction. We talk more about bubble color, discussing and experimenting with this to some depth. We spend time thinking about the conditions that make bubbles pop. We continued discussing the shapes of bubbles and intersecting bubble films. Finally I start to narrow our explorations down to this last by having the children write about this question of shape and try to construct particular shapes with the bubbles. The arguments to explain phenomena become increasingly complex and concern the shapes formed by intersecting planes.

After November, I ended the first part of this unit in which the children made freeform bubbles. In the classes during December and January I gave the children three-dimensional geometric constructions that I had made out of straws and paper clips to dip in the bubble solution. I did this because I felt that at this point we should focus in on one aspect of the bubbles: their shape and the shapes made by the intersection of bubble films. The children used my geometric shapes for a week and then I set them the task of designing in their notebooks things that they would like to make for themselves out of the straws, predicting what they thought these constructions would look like after being dipped in the bubble solution, then attempting to make these things so that they could try them out. This turned out to be quite an interesting process to watch and participate in. It led to many discussions about the process of design as well as about the products themselves. As far as what the children discussed and thought about for the actual bubble shapes they were able to make, I think they explored what effect the shape of the external frame had on the resulting bubble film. There was a general feeling that the external shape controlled the shape of the bubble. This is true, but not as simplistic as it initially sounds. The shape of a bubble depends upon if you are looking at a two-dimensional or three-dimensional shape (if it is two-dimensional, the bubble film will follow the outline; if three-dimensional, the bubble will be a complex result of intersecting two-dimensional films), a shape with no irregularities (irregularities will warp the two-dimensionality), or a perfectly stationary shape. Discussions of the process of design centered on purpose—why design?—and the frustrations of translating designs, from paper or from one's head, into reality. This is very much what Schon (1984; 1990) is talking about, I think, when he calls design a metaphorically shaped process of dialectic between person and materials.

In the next phase of this unit we focus much more on this process of design, both in what we are doing and in our discussions. The science we talk about follows from the things we are able to make much more than the things that we design follow from the science. This is not the usual way we are taught to think about the processes of science (e.g. Popper). The point is that the designs (noun) and the process of design (verb) control the science and the class (teaching).

I return to my narrative about the class in February. By now the children have been working for two months with the straws, paper clips, and bubble solution. The children have become deeply involved with the problems of design and many of our discussions start with this: What have the children been able to do? What were they trying to do and what were the problems? From this we moved to discussions of the science of bubble making.

DISCUSSING PROBLEMS OF DESIGN

February 3

By the month of February, we have moved to a new phase of our explorations. I have asked the children first to make a drawing of a construction they would like to make and try out in the bubble solution. In addition, they are to write a sentence predicting what they think the resulting bubble film will look like. Then they are to attempt to make these constructions and finally try them out.

This process becomes an extremely fertile terrain: spurring children's creativity as well as our developing conversations about the nature of design in science. In think in part this is because the procedure of first making an idealized drawing and then trying to construct this image was filled with frustrations and problems. As children dealt with these they learned a great deal about the nature of the materials they were working with.

By the beginning of February everyone in the class has been able to make at least one thing with straws and paper clips and put it in the bubble solution. In our conversations about this process I ask the children to talk about whether or not it was easy for them to realize their idealized design and what they did to address the problems they confronted. The children talk about how they discover properties of the materials (straws, paper clips, bubble solution) in the context of this exercise—the materials don't act as the children wish them to almost forcing the children to discover other qualities and what can be done with these. This to me was what this whole thing was about, an interplay between design, material, and outcome. Schon talks about the design his students were engaged in as an interplay between aesthetics, the intellect, and emotive qualities of the individual with the qualities of the material available for construction.[1] Those students are engaged in the actions of design as they play with the materials. In my assignments, the children's initial design is on paper, a drawing and in the absence of interaction with the materials. I feel that by doing this I have generated a problem for the children.[2] They are trying to make something in particular. When they go to the straws and paper clips and finally the soap solution, they are trying to use those things to make their design. This could be very frustrating and usually involved either altering the design, discovering new properties of the materials, or discovering new, absorbing phenomena in what is actually made that makes the unexpected so valuable that the original plan is laid aside. This process is one of compromise, radical alteration or, for some children, complete abandonment of one design for another or for just empirically playing with the materials to try to make something. There was also a lot of discussion going on between children—between those who were able to turn their designs into real objects and those who were experiencing greater degrees of frustration. The reason that I did it this way was because I wanted the children to be thinking at the initial stages of design about what it was they were trying to make with the soap bubbles, and not so much with the straws. My idea in doing this was that I knew there would be big surprises in what they actually did make if their constructions were three dimensional.

The final step, trying out their constructions in the bubble solution, was always filled with discovery and surprise. They never got what they had anticipated except those children who made simple two-dimensional shapes. Now, I figured, this could have gone three ways: children could have then altered their constructions to *try* to make something in particular with the bubble films; they could have just been interested in what they did make or; they could have again worked empirically with their constructions and the bubble solution to try new things out. With the straws they mostly did the second thing. In the next part of this description, I give them wire to make their constructions (which is malleable enough to be easily shaped by the children), and virtually everyone that I could see moved to the third process of working empirically to shape their construction as they tried it out in the bubble solution. Wire lends itself to accidental forms and also to three dimensions much more easily.

The conversations this month progressed from talking about specific strategies the children developed for dealing with their design problems to talking philosophically about the meaning of the term design. In each instance, the children weigh their designs and the problems they found in implementing them against the effects they achieved. The decision to keep something that has not come out as desired or to continue to work to achieve a predetermined end is made by weighing the original "vision" against what is actually achieved. The final value is placed when the construction is *used*. When this happens, no matter what the qualities of the construction, something new is seen. The question is how much is this unexpected result valued by both the children and by me.

Making bubble constructions using wire in particular is both easier and harder to control. I invite the unexpected in our results. The children respond to this with a reduction in their struggles over trying to construct a particular design. Rather, children now seem to spend much more time reworking their constructions as they try them out in the bubble solution. The acts of design, construction, and empirical work with the construction are compressed.

The new constructions, as I have noted are much less controlled. When a child makes an apparently two-dimensional heart shape out of wire, it is rarely two-dimensional. It is always warped in multiple directions and asymmetric in outline. The wire itself once bent never becomes smooth and straight again—it retains little kinks and crenullations. All of these irregularities have repercussions when the constructions are used in the soap solution. The most obvious manifestation of this is in a change in the children's attempts to describe their creations in our subsequent talk. Rather than using geometric terms that assume a symmetry, the children in the next day's conversation resort to metaphor. This is fertile scientifically. Metaphor is a form of language use that is fundamentally comparative. It invites discussions of similarities and differences both descriptively and functionally. How does the new object *look* like a waterslide and how not? How does it *act* like a waterslide and how not? This talk is embedded in the conversations in the rest of the unit and it is instrumental in the increased intensity of our talk about the science rather than the design facets of the unit.

DISCUSSION OF SCIENCE INCREASES

February 27

I ask if anyone has finished their design and tried it in the bubble solution. A few have, like Cory and Danping. I find Danping's creation (a helix like the one I had once made and shown them) and ask her what it looked like when she dipped it. She says it looked like a piece of glass. I ask what other people think it might look like. Ricky says a slide. Emily says a waterslide. Cory says a bubble slide. Sueh-yen says a bubble can. I ask Danping to dip it in. When she does, the children notice a rainbow at the top of the helix.

Suni remarks that when he heard Danping say that it looked like a glass, he thought she meant that the bubble would be all over the shape

(I think he means like Sueh-yen's "bubble can"). He says, "I think that is what it will turn out to be if you don't have this middle part. I think it will be like a big piece of glass if it doesn't have this thing in the middle." I ask him what he means and he says that it will just have a bubble around the outside and not in the inside. I say that we should try that (we do later).

I pick up Emily's—she has made a heart out of the wire—and ask what the kids think that would look like with bubbles. Kwanhyo says that she thinks it will look like a "piece of heart." Thomas says, "It will look just like that (the heart) but with glass over it." I ask Emily to try it. When she does, Thomas says that is what he meant. Cory says that there are rainbows inside of it. Many kids exclaim over this. The prominence of colors in all of these constructions with the wire is because of the irregularities in the constructions that the children make. It is really hard to bend the wires without introducing kinks and curvature changes that are not regular. Also, planar constructions like this heart are not planar but are usually warped in irregular ways. These two factors cause the bubble surfaces to be bent in a number of different directions. This is not an effect that we were able to get with the straws and paper clips. When the bubble films are bent in these ways, the children see through the films easier. The films are under anisotropic tensions so that the light is refracting differently and the children are better able to see the effects of this. Cory and then others start naming the colors that they see. Then Cory notices that the rainbow disappears and "once the rainbow is gone the bubble pops." The bubble gets thinner and the colors are dependent on thickness and disappear as the bubble gets thinner and thinner.

Then I pick up Thomas's construction, which is made from aquarium pipe material rather than from the wire. He has made a series of curves which he has put together into a sort of dome. His construction is huge, bigger than the plastic basins that we have the bubble solution in. Thomas says that he doesn't know if it will work because maybe it is too big to fit. I ask him if this is what he had originally designed and he says yes. Now this is not what he had originally drawn, but as he altered his construction while he was making it he also went to his drawing and altered that. He was very careful to do this with each step of his changes. I think this is interesting because often the children didn't build what they had designed but usually they waited until they had completed a structure that they liked before they redrew their design. After Thomas tells me that he made what he designed, I ask if other people were able to make exactly what they had designed. Some say yes and some say no. I ask Teton and he says "not really." He says that he drew his picture and continued to think about it as he worked. Again, note how the acts of design are a dialectic between construction and realization, materials and their properties, vision of the final product and results.

I ask if people can predict what they think Thomas's construction will look like with bubbles. This marks the beginning of the children's talk, in which increased and fertile use of metaphor can be seen. Cory says, "Nothing or lots of circles and a rainbow inside." Alyosha says, "Like a circle on the bottom and whatever those are [*Thomas suggests circles*] and from those on the both sides, they go all the way up there." Cory says, "It would look like a butterfly." Shumshad adds, "It already looks like a rainbow." Dan thinks it is, "Like a wood basket where you put wood." Thomas argues, "Nothing, I don't think it will fit in." Then he tries it and gets a lot of bubbles in. It makes a very complex set of intersecting curves. Kwanhyo observes, "It looks like a glass basket, the top of it." Cory says, "Whenever he moves it, rainbows come, but it only works for the sides." Teacher, "Do you have to move it to get the rainbows?" Thomas says no, Cory says yes. An'gele asks if he could dip in the other part that he missed before and I ask what difference she thinks that would make. She says that she thinks it would look like a rainbow. "And maybe it would go up and down and also across." I try it by dipping in one side and then the other. I ask if it did what she thought it would and she says sort of. Cory asks me to do it again because he says that he saw the bubbles shifting inside the construction. "There was a crystal ball right here and then at the back of the wall, it was weird." Tity says that it looked like a sunset "because these [*the curved tubes*] look like a half of the sun." Suni says that he saw the back wall and crystal ball also and that he thought they looked like "a sun and the sun's baby."

Much of the children's description of these new constructions makes use of metaphor. The increased complexity of the new design has stimulated metaphor use—the shapes aren't given to easy description. Working on the science means developing language, agreeing on meanings: developing a community in the discourse community sense. At the start, the use of metaphor enables difference and similarity comparisons, which are fertile scientifically—it invites conversations about exactly what a child does mean. Also, the use of metaphor has implied explanation embedded within it, so these words are not purely descriptive. I think this is because the metaphors are functional words as well as descriptive. The words the children use— saws, rainbows, baskets, glass, slides—imply something about the way the object looks and also how the object is made and how it can function. Again, this echoes Schon's ideas about the use of metaphor in engineering and urban design.[3] This is where and how they become fertile ground for scientific discussion.

In the next class, the children continue to talk about their strategies for the construction of their designs. Note that they are actively reworking their constructions as they try them out in the bubble solution. Their use of metaphor goes from being descriptive to becoming generative scientifically—although I have a role in this change. I think because there is an increased discussion of the science, rather than of the acts of design (which was primarily individualistic), there is a coming together of ideas and people working together on one phenomenon. There would suddenly seem to be a community talking together about shared questions, profiting from differences and similarities.

DISCUSSION OF SCIENCE AND THE ROLE OF METAPHOR.

March 3

We start class looking at some of the constructions the children have made. In this discussion, the children start to have inspired ideas about the science. Please note how this is tied up with the use of metaphor and experimentation. The science is dependent both on how observations are described and how they can be acted on: metaphor becomes generative in design problems. The metaphors embedded in design capture aspects of the problem the design is constructed to address. In implementing the design, other aspects of the metaphor and of the problem become highlighted. Such implicit comparisons enable critical thinking about outcomes as well as process.

We look at a construction that no one claims. It is a spiral with no central axis (Fig. 2.8).

Suni says that he thinks it won't work as it is made, you have to close off the ends somehow. Emily says that she thinks it will make

Figure 2.8

another waterslide. Thomas says, "Well this is just a prediction but I think it will be covered here and it will be like a cone but this won't be filled because it's not connected but this would sort of be like a can, I think." I ask if that is what Suni meant when he said it should be connected. Sueh-yen thinks it will look like the helix. I ask if at the top where whoever made it had put a sort of circle but not quite closed it off there would be a bubble. Some say yes and some say no. Sakti says yes, because it's a loop. I ask if she thinks the loops in the spiral will make a bubble. She says that she doesn't think so; it will make a bubble at the top but not further down. I try it as it is. No bubble forms, and I ask why. Thomas says because air is getting into it. I ask what he means by that. He replies, "I think bubbles trap the air inside, but if there is a hole in the bubble it will just pop. Like if you, if there's a little hole, it blows up like a lightbulb, if you make a little hole in a lightbulb it will blow up, on or off." This is a very interesting metaphor to examine in this context. The science that we have been working on all these months is coming together here, as are the children on this one question and set of ideas. For the next few paragraphs of this discussion there is apparently a coalescence of children thinking and working together—a community.

I squeeze the rings together (Fig. 2.9) and dip it in. Suni says he knew this would work. I ask if they think that the pieces of wire actually have to touch each other to get a bubble. They all yell "yes" at me, and Suni says that is what he was trying to say before. I try just getting them real close without touching and try it. It doesn't work. I ask why doesn't it work. Thomas says because too much air is getting in,"like a lightbulb." Alyosha says that is the same thing with balloons. "If there is a hole in a balloon all the air will come out." I remind Suni what he had said about the spiral making a tube and ask why he thinks

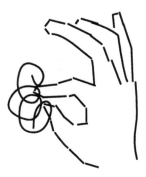

Figure 2.9

that didn't happen. Suni says, "See if you connect both of these then it will make a tube." He wants me to make circles at either end. He does this and Cory points out that it is "littler." We try this and it makes bubbles on the two ends but not in the middle. Suni remarks, "I think I know the reason, 'cause see this is smaller and these are different sizes than these two, they have to be in the same order." Shumshad wants to make a loop in the middle and he tries it and gets bubbles in the loops. I point out that there are still no bubbles between loops.

Suni wants me to try a piece of the original wire, which forms a slinky sort of shape. I get one. He thinks it is important that the loops are all the same size. The kids think that would work. Thomas says it won't work because "there's no support, it can go up but it can not go sideways. If it went sideways it would be hard for it. It's not too easy to go sideways, I don't know why but I don't think it will work." I ask Suni what he thinks of what Thomas said and he says he disagrees, he still thinks there will be bubbles along the side. He then says that he isn't sure if the bubbles will be from the inside (like the helix) or on the outside. Shumshad adds that he thinks they can't come from the inside, it won't work from the middle unless I squeeze it. Danping comments, "It will turn out nothing because it doesn't have a thing in the middle so I don't think . . . the bubble will just follow the inside part. So it has nothing to follow."

I try it and nothing happens. Thomas and Suni say that there weren't enough things to hold it and there has to be another part. I ask about Shumshad's suggestion. Danping says she thinks it will work because then it will have a circle. I try it and it does work. Cory says to let it go (maybe he thinks the bubbles will extend). I do and the bubbles break. Cory says that he thinks he knows why it won't make a bubble without the inner axis.: "Because maybe the water is slipping out and it has nothing to hold it in." Cory suggests connecting the wire loops with another wire. An'gele says it didn't make a bubble because just like everyone keeps calling the helix bubble a slide, "maybe the bubble keeps sliding down into the water and if you blink your eyes you can't see it."

There is some talk about the children's strategies for the construction of their designs. They still remark on the frustrations of trying to realize an ideal design, but much more they are actively reworking their constructions as they try them out in the bubble solution. The children seem much more ready to abandon initial ideas about their construction as they find new and interesting things in what they have made. As the children talk about their designs now they are actually talking about the results they obtained when they tried them in the bubble solution, and they talk in metaphors. Their use of metaphor goes from being descriptive to becoming scientifically generative. This is enabled by me in a manner analogous to the way I described searching for a theme during the first conversation the class had about bubbles: I am listening for commonalities in the things the children say; but now not just commonalities within the class, but also things that resonate with my scientific understandings. If I hear a number of children saying things that are fertile scientifically, I work to make the science come out. I do this by posing questions rather than by giving explanations. I want the children to continue to offer their own ideas and explanations and share them with each other. I think because there is an increased discussion of the science, there is a coming together of ideas and people working together on one phenomenon: the core of a community in an idealistic sense, meaning people talking together about shared questions and profiting from the different ideas each can bring.

In the next class there is even more explanatory scientific theory-making by the children. Note that their theories about how bubbles work are intimately tied to statements about the design of the experiment. There is an implicit recognition of the interrelationship of the design (which they have made) and the resulting bubbles. The things that they have seen and are trying to describe and explain they know that they have made—the result must be explained by a combination of attribution to their own actions and the qualities of the

bubble solution itself. There is an implicit appreciation of the interdependence of the phenomenon and themselves as active shapers of the
results. The results are dependent upon what *they* do. Again, note the
evidence of a community with the children working on the same idea
and talking in a manner about their construction and ideas that has been
developed and validated through the organic process of the community
itself.

HOW DISCUSSING THE ACT OF DESIGN FACILITATES
A RECOGNITION OF HUMAN AGENCY IN SCIENCE.

March 5
We look at Andy's creation. Children say it looks like a hat (Fig. 2.10).

Figure 2.10

I dip it in and say that in one place the bubbles seem to go straight
across but in other places the bubbles come together, such as in a
tetrahedral shape we had tried in the fall (Fig. 2.11).

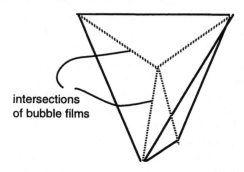

intersections
of bubble films

Figure 2.11

I ask why they do that in one place but not in other places. Thomas says that it's because there is a triangle. I ask him what difference that makes and then if he is seeing a triangle in the wire (because I didn't see that). He says yes and shows me where, and I ask if he means a part that is curvy. He says yes, but that doesn't matter. Suni says that the wires are like a triangle and it's because the wires come together into three that the tetrahedron effect is achieved. Abeni says that she thinks the straight part of the bubbles are like that because there the wires are straight but in the other part the wires come together. Suni says that if the wires went differently and made a different shape so would the bubbles. Shumshad has noticed something and poses a question about it. He asks why in one place do the bubbles curve up. Suni replies that because there is "no gravity over here, I think there's . . . it doesn't feel a lot of gravity that holds it down so they just try to stick up and stick together so they make a kind of a hole." Cory says that they stick up because of the wire, and that's the way Andy made it. He also tells us to look very closely and we will see that the wires aren't really straight, but are curved. He points out that we need to look from different angles. It can look straight from one angle and curved from another. Then he says that "maybe the bubbles have to hook on to something so they have to go to there [*creating the curve*]."

I break one of the bubble films by mistake and ask if anyone noticed what happened when I did that. Cory says that the intersections between the bubbles which defined the shape we were talking about moved. We do some more of this, popping different ones. At first we get a triangle and then as we progressively pop bubbles we get the circle. Shumshad says that when he pops it, it causes the intersection between bubble films to move down. We do it again. Shumshad says that the triangle bubbles hold the bubble creation up and when they break it goes down. Suni says that he thinks it wouldn't do that if the wire shape was a square. He seems to be saying that the shape created by the intersection is created by the wires being too close together and with a square the wires would be further apart. Cory says that he thinks popping one effects the others, because "if you look very close, I think the bubbles go over the wiring, they hook onto the wiring."

Suni suggests that if there were a wire across the bottom of them it would hold the circle even with the other bubbles. Then the bubble would be able to "hook on." Shumshad suggests that we pop the bubbles from the bottom first rather then from the top like we had been doing. This changes the whole thing. The intersection moves up, different bubbles get differentially bigger, and in the end we have windows in the upper spaces between the wires. Shumshad says that he thought when he did this that by popping one of the bottom films he would have popped them all. He says he thought this because the film he chose to pop was touching all of the others.

An'gele says that she knows why one part pops before another part. She says that one part "has better gravity and plus this part was sort of harder to make and this part is bendy and it's harder for the bubble to go bendy then straight." Alyosha says that the bubble intersection is in the position it is because the bubbles hold it up and the air is pushing it up. Suni thinks that something funny happens, a funny shape is formed when just one bubble is popped.

We start again making and testing the wire creations.

In this class the geometric and metaphorical descriptions of the bubble construction are closely tied with the children's explanatory scientific theorymaking. Their theories are about how bubbles work (that there is a play between gravity and the frame of the structure which determines the placement of bubble intersections, that the existence of the bubble films themselves are dependent upon the ability of the bubble solution to "hook" on to the wires). Explanation of phenomena is intimately tied with statements about the design of the experiment. As they work on these ideas, the children are talking together—there is an increasing sense of ideas shared and growing because they are being shared. Again, I feel that this is a manifestation of the community developed around a purpose and shared activity in the class.

In the next, our final class about bubbles, we refocus on why there are colors in rainbows, holograms, and bubbles—the science of diffraction and light—the principles in each context are the same. The class moves from a consideration of bubbles to thinking about the applicability of their ideas to other phenomena. Being able to do this is because a design has both a background and a foreground. The apparent and obvious part of the design is the foreground. That is composed of the things we have been doing: working with bubbles, talking about that phenomenon. We can move though from this design to another by recomposing the foreground from other parts of the background, by rearranging the components of the foreground to accommodate those. In the class and the teaching the progress of this follows the same pattern of our other explorations and conversations: we move between observation, metaphor, explanation, doing things, and use of tools and of the community. These and their interrelationships compose the pattern, the design, of the teaching as well as of the community of the class itself, community because it reflects that the pattern and design can be dynamic, and its focus can shift and move.

THE LAST CLASS: A CONSIDERATION
OF BACKGROUND AS WELL AS FOREGROUND

What This Can Mean In Science
March 26
This is the last class we are going to have about bubbles. Kathy and I have planned a field trip to the local children's science museum for our next class. At the museum, there is a special exhibit about holograms and lasers. I wish the children to work especially with this exhibit and draw some connections to our work with bubbles. For this reason we spend quite a lot of time talking about what holograms look like and discussing examples of holograms the children have seen (e.g. Princess Leia in *Star Wars*, and on credit cards). We examine examples on my credit cards.

I ask what they see when they look at the holograms on the cards. Abeni says that it is shiny and has rainbow colors. Tity says that it's silvery all over. Sueh-yen saw that it reflected light. He also noticed that the bird changed shape as he moved it and that the background reflected his face. I ask the kids who hadn't seen *Star Wars* if they now had an idea what a hologram was. Shumshad says that it looks real and it moves. Emily says that it's *not* real, though.

I ask where they thought the different colors came from. The children say the light. I say that the light isn't different colors, is it? Dan says that yes, the lights are different colors. He points to different lights in the room which are different levels of white. Emily says that the light sort of reflects itself to make colors. Thomas says that we could do an experiment with a prism, the light may not be different colors but the prism can show us. I ask him if he is saying that the white light can be many colors and he says that it can be the colors of the sun. I ask what the colors of the sun are and he starts to list: blue, purple . . . . Other children start to disagree. Others agree and continue to list the colors of the spectrum. I ask Thomas if he is talking about a rainbow and he says yes. He says that the white light can make the rainbow light, and with a prism you might be able to see it.

I ask what other people think—how did the hologram get the colors in it? Paula says that the colors in the rainbow come from white light. Then she says that on the hologram the colors come from the light reflecting on the silver pattern. Emily says that there is "an invisible rainbow and it can go through our school roof and it can go through anything and when it touches that, that silvery piece it would shine 'cause you know how a rainbow is like this and a sun is right up here and it moves around in a circle, it could reflect 'cause if they were on opposite sides it could just go like that and it would still go down." I ask if the invisible rainbow comes from the sun or if it is always in the sky and we can see it 'cause the light goes through. "It's in the sky 'cause the light goes through." Danping disagrees with Emily: "I don't think there's such a thing as an invisible rainbow. I think on the credit card there's sort of like a plastic piece that's cut out like an eagle and they put some kinds of things on it and then when the light shines on it it just comes out like a rainbow." I say, "But the light is white." She responds, "I know, but when the light shines on the plastic I think they put something on the plastic to make it shine, so it makes it shine like a rainbow." I ask her if she is saying it's something in the plastic and she says yes.

Shumshad agrees with Danping "a little bit." He says if they cut out a piece that's silver and put some kind of "medicine or something that's kind of shiny and then they put a plastic piece on the card and then if you move it, it will go. "

Suni gets back to the colors of the sun. He says he disagrees with Thomas, there isn't any blue on the sun. "They have a different name and they're not colors like blue but my dad . . . well actually I really forgot those names." Thomas says that "the colors came through my window and I saw blue." Suni repeats that it might look like blue but that's not what it's called, "it's not really blue." Thomas asks, "Well what color is it?" Suni says that when his dad showed him this that he thought it was blue, too, but it has a strange name. I ask him if he is thinking of indigo. He says yes. He says that there were "some other colors in the blue parts, too." He says that "all the colors mixed make the sunlight, make white light." I ask how the colors get out of the white light. He says that they separate but he doesn't know how they do that. Then he says that the sunlight isn't really white light but is yellow.

Cory says he agrees with Suni and reminds us of what we did last year with the rulers.[4] How he looked up through the rulers and saw rainbows around everything. I let them try out the rulers (Fig. 2.12).

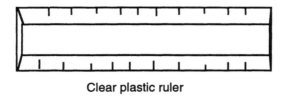

Clear plastic ruler

Figure 2.12

I ask what they saw. Alyosha says that he saw a blue line under the thing that he was looking at. Danping says that now she disagrees with her idea from before "now I know how they make the rainbow, I think on the plastic they just fold a little bit so if they fold over here and over here then these two will be different colors, if they didn't fold any this whole piece of the bird (pictured in the hologram) would be a different color." I ask if she is saying that the rainbow is made because of the way the plastic in the ruler is formed.

Sakti says that she saw different colors when she looked at the light. Meiying did also. Kwanhyo says that she saw a rainbow all across the room. Thomas says that he was disappointed because he didn't see as many colors as he usually does. He only saw red and blue. I say that they aren't very good prisms.

Suni says that he has just figured something out. "If you put light through glass you can see the colors because glass makes the color of the light separate into other colors that are mixed to make that color, that's what I think glass does." I ask him why the glass in the window doesn't do that. He says that there isn't too much sun out and I say that it doesn't even when there is a lot of sun out. He says that it works on his window at home. Danping says that it needs to have corners. Abeni says that she thinks the thickness of the glass or plastic has something to do with it. I point out that the rulers aren't very fat. She says that different parts are fatter or thinner. Emily says that you see the colors only when you look through the places where the thickness changes. Tity says that you can see colors by looking through the edges, too.

Cory saw a prism at his grandmother's house and she told him that if you don't keep it in the light the rainbows might go away. He says that she said this because once she kept one out of the light too long and then when she did put it in the light there were no rainbows. You have to keep them in the light to get rainbows. I ask him about the rulers and he says he doesn't know. I ask him why we don't see rainbows all the time and he says he doesn't know.

Sueh-yen says that the rulers and the prism have three sides and he thinks this is important to make rainbows. Shumshad thinks that the reason he couldn't see a lot of colors with the rulers is because of the little lines that measure. Emily says that if she crosses her eyes everything is outlined blue or sometimes yellow. This also makes it hard to see. Alyosha tells us about a rainbow he saw in Yugoslavia that happened after a rainstorm. He thinks that it is light shining through the water from the rain that makes the rainbow.

I ask why we can see colors in the bubbles. Emily says that the light reflects in it. I make a bubble for them to look at. The children start exclaiming and calling out the colors. Others say that they can't see the colors. I ask why there are colors and Abeni says it's because like the hologram, the light is shining on it and that makes them or it might be electricity. I ask if the colors are the same everywhere or different in different places. The children say different. I ask if they are moving and children say yes. I ask if in some places the stripes of colors are spread apart and in some places close together. The children just stare at this one.

Then they start working with their constructions again.

CONCLUSION

In order to be perceived as a design or as part of a design, an object or an action needs to stand out from a background. We need to be able to "see" it. Such perception is enabled through framing—demarcating and bounding one thing from its background and from other things. A background can be composed of emotions, understandings, and already-constructed ways of doing things. When we enter into a situation (any situation, including one that appears to initiate with our entrance) we are already immersed in such a background of preexisting circumstances and understandings—we *know* how to act, how to interpret, what to do. Heidegger (1962) calls this "falling," and the concept explains how we are able to interpret circumstances and act upon them—nothing is *ever* brand new. Qualities of framing and of the background differentiate a design but without necessarily calling attention to themselves. In looking from the outside, however, as we did in my story of teaching and of science, we should be able to abstract the qualities of the frame. What composes the frame in this teaching—what leads to my decisions as I teach this unit? What leads to the decisions made by the children as they design their experiments? For me decisions emerge from my ideas of the science and of the children which existed before we began the unit but reform continuously as the unit progresses. This is both in and out of my control: it is shaped by the materials and the children as well as by me. Similarly, the children's decisions come from preconceptions they have about bubbles, the subject of the unit, and school, transformed by the discoveries they make as they work with the materials, each other, and me. As Heidegger and also Wittgenstein (1969) imply, it would be a mistake to view decisions as only reflecting what we know. They also represent what we don't know and what we think we'd like to know. This theme—that actions and decisions reflect assertions of knowledge as well as uncertainties—threads throughout the remainder of this book. It will appear many times in the stories that I tell. It is the basis of my assertion that statements of knowing, by the children in explaining the science, by myself when making choices in teaching, are also statements of not-knowing—places where learning can take place.

The act of design is purposeful—it expresses a need, and is symbolic of that need. The actions in this class should be interpreted in terms of needs. The articulation of these needs is again enabled by qualities of the framing background. The things the children and I say about what we are trying to do, what we want to do, are expressions of our interpretations of both the background and foreground. Examining expressions of need exposed to us in the act of design allows us a pathway back to the background. It gives us a tool to explore selected components of the frame. When we examine the things the children are trying to do with bubbles in this chapter we can rediscover the qualities of their knowledge that have been buried, as well as their ideas and theories that are on the surface, that they are working on *now*. The design, the thing within the frame, can act as a frame itself for the elements of the background. It causes their differentiation from the continuum. This is also true of the act of teaching. As I write about what I am trying to do with the science and the children, I expose the hidden assumptions, values, and beliefs which underlie these needs and desires.

Design as a verb—a method—should serve both cyclical, symbolic time and progressive, historical time. As an expression of needs, it serves the former. As we act to realize these needs, it serves the latter. This is interesting because what is actually realized can only partially (if at all) satisfy the needs it stems from. Or it may do something entirely unintended. This very much happens with both the teaching and the soap bubbles. Sometimes I plan for this, but usually only partially so. For example, I planned that in our initial experience with bubbles I would "find" what the subsequent classes would be about. What I actually found was much more sophisticated than what I had anticipated. This happens in teaching because actions do not occur in isolation. It happens in science because acting on one set of variables locates others. So design, and method, are both controlled and uncontrolled. They represent both what is known and what can be known. They are both atemporal and integrally of the substance of time—looking backwards, forwards and at this very moment. Do we have to look at a cross-section of time to see a design or a method or is it also recognizable in particular moments, actions?

I had planned this unit about soap bubbles to also be about design:[5] design in the sense that Schon (1990) defines as an interplay between the materials and the person, which is shaped by metaphorical images of purpose. I picked soap bubbles as a vehicle for this "design process" because understanding soap bubbles as a phenomenon is abstract, nonintuitive, and therefore presents interesting design problems for me as a teacher. How do I design this curriculum and this teaching? How is this design process an evolving one that is interactive between people as well as between a person and things and tasks? I also picked soap bubbles because children can usually be counted on to have had some prior experience with them. But this experience is often very constricted and proscribed. What I do in this unit both is and isn't proscribed. How it is constricted and proscribed by me, the children, and the materials is the point of this being a story about design.

This unit, which I claim to be about design, could also be described as beng about the process of involving children in the scientific processes of experimentation. By saying this I would satisfy the demands of local and national science curriculum requirements. The unit is, however, much more than the simplistic view of experimentation often advanced as science in schools. For example, what is often called "experimentation" in schools is really *demonstration* of what is previously known—it is artificial. To have true experimentation there must be a potential for discovery of new things, for surprise. Experiments are designed—they address particular end points—but still they also represent questions, the unknown as well as known.

In our final class about bubbles, we focused upon one particular aspect, a fundamental aspect, of the science that we have been studying: color. We extend our ideas about color, formed through our interaction with the bubbles as well as from other places, to new phenomenon. Being able to do this reflects the complexity of the initial explorations: they didn't address simplistic and confined questions but rather larger, more fundamental ones. These explorations (I use this word because it contains both what we did—the substance—and how we did it) addressed particular observations and questions in the foreground but always contained the potential to address new things. We can move from one exploration and set of questions to another by recomposing the foreground—what we are explicitly examining—to contain the elements of the background—those parts of the science which were not focal until called upon.

A design, in teaching, in classroom interactions, in science, is composed of a background and a foreground. Our perception of the design is both through a cognitive differentiation of the two but also because of an interplay between the two. They are mutually dependent upon each other to construct our perception of the whole. We can understand and interpret the pattern because the background sets off the foreground. It is the interplay of background with foreground that gives the foreground meaning. How we construct the foreground is really a question of why we construct the foreground. The construction of a pattern or a design reflects the things we wish to do—our needs and purposes. The pattern and design also reflect who we are, what we know right now. It contains the potential to be a tool as we construct our future selves. As we try to realize the future, we can act to reconstruct the pattern by recomposing the foreground/background relationships. Our implicit awareness of the background has to become explicit for this to happen. We explicitly perceive the foreground, but circumstances which cause us to question the pattern can make us aware of the background.

In this unit, the children explore qualities of bubbles. They construct a pattern in the science and in the things they are doing. Because I can perceive the pattern, recognize the science that is useful and important embedded in the things the children say, I can design the teaching, the things that we do together, and also how we talk about those things. I want to do this in such a way that we maintain the potential for reconstructing the pattern. In the background of the pattern is the more fundamental scientific questions and the potential for knowledge of which I must remain aware.

This pattern constructed through the design of the teaching, which contains both the science, the way we are doing the science, and the children's interactions, defines the community in our classroom. It contains all the elements of idealized definitions of community: people working together around a shared purpose, people developing a shared language. and methods of acting in service of this purpose. This community is also vital: it can grow, change, shift focus and direction. This is a manifestation of the interplay or potential for interplay between foreground and background that I am trying to maintain. I will return to the idea of patterns and of communities in the following chapters, where I will develop and challenge the definitions and uses of patterns and communities that I have tried to illustrate here.

NOTES

1. Donald Schon (1990), The theory of inquiry: Dewey's legacy to education.
2. Dewey (1933) in *How we think* suggests a concept of what drives inquiry. (The question is, inquiry into what?)
3. Schon, D.A. (1984), Generative metaphor: A perspective on problem-setting in social policy.
4. In last year's science class I had given the children small, clear plastic rulers to use to measure plants. These rulers have beveled edges so that if they are held up to the light and looked through, objects appear to be surrounded by an aureole of color. Cory is remembering this.
5. This unit was taught in a first and second grade combination class. The classroom teacher was Kathy Valentine. For a full description of the school, class and children, please see Appendix 1 and 2.

CHAPTER 3

Patterns and Understanding

The last chapter was about design; design both in teaching and in doing science. It was about how the acts of design precede science or teaching and act as lenses or as molding agents on what can happen next. But design is also interactive—it occurs as a dialectic process between person, objects, and purposes. It occurs while the science and the teaching are going on. A design is recognizable within a context; it is formed out of that context. The act of design—designing—can't be decontextualized. The trick, however, is that designs give the appearance that they can exist separate from context, can be abstracted. Designs are metaphors for what can be done with them. They are then generalizations, simplifications; they only capture some aspects of the context from which they are derived. They are recognizable as entities because they are abstracted, partitioned. In many instances this is the cumulative effect of patterning. We recognize a design because of the repetitive quality of the patterns it contains. The repetition of a design, however, also creates a pattern.

If repetitions and relationships create a pattern, the choices behind repetitions and relationships define the act of design. In this chapter I will describe another unit of science teaching, this time about patterns themselves, first examining patterns in the abstract and then applying patterns to an exploration of music and sound. This is, at least in initial approach, an inversion of the unit I described in the last chapter. In the last chapter we started by examining design and thought about how the teaching and science came from it. In this unit we start with observations and recognize patterns and then explore the design—the reasons behind the observations we are able to make. A pattern is made up of repetitions and relationships in the science and also in the class—the things we do in class, both scientific experimenting and ways of talking, repeat. This, in turn, reflects relationships between people and science and also constructs relationships. This defines a classroom community, a culture, however that changes as the dynamics of the relationships alter.

The community that develops in this classroom is not static; instead, it changes and evolves as the topic of conversation and the ways of talking change. The medium for the construction of the community is the science that we are doing (Hawkins, 1974a). At different times, this science is being looked at and thought about in very different ways. For example, we start our examination of music through an observation-based study of sound-producing devices. We proceed to an experimentally based exploration. Finally, we intellectually examine what music is and then think critically about this. Each of the modes of acting, thinking, and communicating with each other develop as interplay's between people, people wanting to communicate their own ideas and also hear and understand each other's. This is the essence of a community—people interacting with each other for a purpose, out of a need (Sartre, 1963; Schwab, 1976). The purpose evolves because it develops as people interact; therefore, the ways of interacting evolve also.

AN OUTLINE OF THE UNIT ON MUSIC AND PATTERNS

This unit on patterns and sounds and music had three stages which are separate and also interconnected and interdependent. The first stage, taught in the fall, was about patterns and seeing—seeing patterns and developing language to talk about those patterns. It was at a more fundamental level about discussing what the word *pattern* means— what is and isn't a pattern and why. The second stage began again in the spring, when I started the unit on sound and music. This stage was about exploring how sound is made. It's about patterns, because in order to do this the children looked and listened for patterns in the things that we were using to make sound. It was also about patterns because in order to do this in a way that illuminates the qualities and genesis of sounds, the children had to interact with the xylophones and rubber bands that we were using in a systematic manner, which was a pattern in itself. The third stage was a return to the first stage in a way, although the vehicle was the music and sound, the children discovered the pattern of acting methodically. In the fourth stage, we explored the definitions of the word *pattern* both in music and more broadly.

What this synopsis doesn't capture is that in all of these stages, what was the focus for me and what I was trying to make apparent in the children's discussions and arguments was that a pattern is a manmade construct that captures some aspects of a phenomenon and leaves out others. Seeing, hearing, acting in patterns involves choices—conscious or unconscious that can be articulated and talked about either before a choice is made or afterwards, when it becomes apparent that everyone hasn't made the same choices. This is why talking about patterns is also talking about perspectives—having a perspective, taking a perspective. It is these differences in perspective that drive the development of a community—the children share their ideas about sound and music, both learning from each other and developing the ability to articulate their own ideas.

In the fall the children made patterns using pattern blocks and then talked about those patterns, developing descriptive language which ranged from the simple "it's a red hexagon" to metaphor and statements involving mathematical progressions and relationships. I chose to have this beginning abstract and "manmade," artificial, designed. Then we went on to look at pictures of things made by people, like buildings and bricks, and "natural things." These are only so-called natural things because they are pictures—framed and chosen. To see patterns in these things is a reductive process—seeing some things in a foreground and putting other things into a background. It is selective, just as choosing how to shoot the picture is selective. In looking at these patterns which are both made and not made by whoever is seeing them, there is a new element (as compared to the patterns constructed by the children from pattern blocks). These patterns don't have limits; they extend beyond what we can see. Even when they do have edges and borders in the pictures, it is usually obvious that these borders are arbitrary and chosen—the pattern could extend on. These patterns can be simple repetitions or progressions, but all are created by relationships, relationships between the elements of the design. The idea was to help the children articulate both the content—the "thing" repeated in a descriptive manner (not to name it) and the way it was repeated—the relationships.

When we started with music and sound in the spring, my idea was to use the children's ability to perceive patterns and talk about them in an applied way that enabled and suggested scientific explanations and explorations. So we started by experimenting with a xylophone. I simultaneously asked the children what patterns they could see in the instrument and hear when the instrument was sounded, and invited the children to do things to try to relate observed patterns to other observed patterns. Then we did this again with rubber bands. The children, with my help, quickly began to relate the things that they were able to observe and postulate these relationships as explanations for the phenomena. Because they were also acting on these relationships, testing them, and doing this in a public forum, we together developed systematic ways of going about this. The children suggested that certain patterns of observations were related, and then they tested those relationships out publicly. Through this process of public demonstration, communication, and discussion of results, these explorations got more and more systematic. Thus, the relationships that the children were working on became further reduced—separate variables were located and tested. In some sense the relationships the children held between each other also became reduced—for the purposes of communicating their experiment, the children had to act and talk systematically and unambiguously. The children listening had to suspend their own ideas and think within those of another (connected thinking rather than critical thinking, although in the end there is always an interplay of these).

These variables and the relationships between these variables became the focus because of how the children were interacting with the musical instruments. The children were now talking about how sound made vibrations and these vibrations were characterized by amplitude and different periodicities, and these in turn were effected by thickness, tightness, and length of the materials which make up strings and bars of xylophones. They were also talking about how what they did when playing the instruments effected these variables. This is done by acting systematically on the instruments themselves so that variables can be isolated and studied alone. It also gives you the illusion that you can pretend that you, as the experimenter, aren't part of the system, especially if you can conveniently forget that you made up the variables—extracted them from the continuum—to begin with.

This is, however, one of the reasons I chose a study of music and sound as a medium for this exploration of the power of patterns (rather than just sound). Most people would not mind that the aesthetic choices and criteria, made in creating, listening to, and judging a piece of music don't represent a fundamental. My point is that these same choices have parallels in the criteria—the variables—used in the study of sound. These are just as arbitrary and should therefore be subject to debate and justification. And this justification can be rational or irrational; it can be on a basis of usefulness or on a basis of aesthetics, or some combination. But it ought to be possible to articulate these even though when we do make these choices, they most often haven't been articulated by us—we are just acting on reflex (Heidegger, 1962).

Because of the above-mentioned reason of why we are looking at music and sound, rather than just sound, my next move was to return us to talking about music so that I could work with the children to articulate the reasoning behind their choices. This leads them to specify variables which could be examined empirically. I asked the children what the difference is between sound and music, and also effectively what criterion they would suggest for judging a sound as music. The children all seemed to agree that judging something as music was an interplay of context and the presence of certain components. These components were pattern, beat, and rhythm. In exploring what the children meant by these words in the context of "music" that they created to demonstrate their ideas, we found that these words were, in themselves, intertwined and interdependent—that their meanings overlap and slide into one another. That to differentiate between them was arbitrary, a choice of the user based upon what they were thinking and trying to do. This became a conversation about design—that patterns and music are designs. Both are also arbitrary, made, reflect choices, although it is unclear when the choices have to be made in order to call a design a design. This takes us back to the idea that music is music because of context. We talked about bird song— was that music? The children argued that maybe it was, if they applied their criteria of pattern, rhythm, and beat, but maybe not if they applied their criteria of context, purpose and design. What is the purpose of the bird singing—is it music, or communication? Again we go to perspective—they as listeners might call it music, but the bird who makes it might not.

BEGINNING OUR EXPLORATIONS OF PATTERNS

What Is A Pattern, How Is It Constructed, How Is It Used?

The first and second grade science curriculum focuses in many ways upon the development of observation and classification skills.[1] I thought that by combining these curriculum goals with the study of patterns—both in the abstract and as observed in nature—it would be possible to explore the intricacies of how to describe sensual observation with words and how to link these descriptions to explanation. This is a fundamental component of science as I have experienced it. To this end we started the unit using pattern blocks[2] to construct patterns and then work on developing ways to communicate those patterns to each other. First students developed language to describe the shapes and, then, language to describe relationships between shapes. For example, to build a hexagon out of two red trapezoids the children had to specify both number, orientation, and placement of the pattern blocks. Finally, the children discovered that to describe complex patterns they could use metaphor: a pattern of four yellow hexagons surrounded by red trapezoids could be described as a "honeycomb with the honey leaking out."

The children described patterns often with body movements and hand gestures, which are ways of reducing or simplifying what they have seen. To turn this into words can be thought of as a further reduction (but an ambiguous one—since words have multiple meanings—for example see the final discussions of pattern, beat, and rhythm). Being able to turn the whole into parts that the children can talk about is fundamental to science. Examining these parts, trying to qualify, quantify, and define these parts and think about the relationship(s) between parts, involves thinking about differences and similarities (defining frame and overlaps), and thinking critically about what can be done with those parts and relationships. Many people have written about the links between symbol systems, communication, audience, and purposes.[3] In this literature, the authors talk, in different ways, about tacit knowledge and articulated knowledge and how these are created and used to exist in this world both socially and individually. All of these authors suggest that the way in which knowledge is created has a lot to do with communication, first with the object and then with others, both for a purpose.

After working with the pattern blocks for some weeks, we viewed slides of close-ups of leaves, flowers, bricks—things with repeating patterns. This replicates one of the ways that I learned to do science. As an undergraduate, I majored in geology and did a minor in art history. Learning to see analytically and critically in my art classes has always been very important to me in my science. Looking at things in two dimensions, in a picture, can be very helpful in learning to do this. It seems easier to me to abstract content from form and process in two dimensions. We also worked with xeroxes of Turkish tile mosaic patterns, coloring in different components and talking about the relationships between those components.

Looking at the pictures of objects and then at objects themselves, the children noticed varying levels of articulation of the components of the picture and this is what enabled them to see a pattern. Seeing a pattern involves differentiating foreground subject from background: for example, in the following picture of a Turkish tile mosaic (Fig. 3.1):

Figure 3.1

To be able to describe it, we can talk about it being a series of lines, but that isn't very informative—it doesn't differentiate it from any other series of lines. We can say that the lines form shapes like squares, kite shapes, stars, and diamonds, but that doesn't tell us that it is a pattern. To describe the pattern, we could say that it is a series of squares that repeat along three axes which meet at sixty degrees to each other. The squares are composed of four kite shapes, two large and two small, arranged in a fourfold rotational relationship (two fold rotational relationship to like shapes) to one another around the perimeter of the square. The intersections of the three axes of squares is marked by a six-pointed star made from the vertices of the kite shapes. The overall symmetry of the design is three fold. To make this description I have focused on the squares and arranged my descriptions of the other shapes to help me talk about the squares. By doing this I have defined a foreground and a background. I could have done this by starting with a different shape and building up the picture from it, or I could have started with a description of the symmetry—three fold rotation with three two fold rotational axes intersecting at the threefold axis, and then arranged the geometric shapes so that they became derived from this.

Here is a drawing of one of the slides that we looked at (Fig. 3.2).

Figure 3.2

To describe it, we could say that it is a drawing of bricks and plants, or we could describe a pattern and say that the bricks repeat in a certain way or the plants repeat in a certain way. To talk about this repetition would involve focusing on certain parts of the picture and excluding other parts. The bricks repeat in shape and orientation but not in the number of holes shown. The plants repeat because they are all the same type and are spaced evenly, but each has a different number of leaves oriented in different directions. To make a pattern, to say that something is regular and repeats means defining the characteristics that are regular and do repeat and ignoring the others. This is an example of how a pattern can be seen because of contrast, the repetition of a component sets it against a background—but it is also true that the application of a pattern creates its own contrasts by defining certain features and obscuring others, by taking features out of context, generating a "background."

In order to see a pattern in this picture, we make abstract generalizations about shape. We make an idealization about an observation. This is an example of using metaphor to describe and simplify (to call a plant a plant is an example, recognizing the ideal in the real). There is a tension in this process: A pattern can incorporate more and more detail, making it possible to reduce and/or ignore that detail. Again, we are defining a foreground and a background both by substance and by relationships. Recognizing relationships that are important—ones that mean something, and are not just descriptive— and knowing what qualities of the object can be ignored and what must be included are fundamental judgments in doing science. They are also judgments constructed from our previous knowledge and from our purposes. Seeing patterns is an act of design. Making generalizations has much in common with seeing patterns. Seeing patterns is in a sense generalizing about what I do see—ignoring individual differences. And the purpose of this is so one can see the similarities between the components of a pattern and see the pattern as a whole—see the whole in order to resee the parts in a new way.

The children started to use mathematical relationships to describe pattern progressions. For example, Suni said, "The bricks . . . that one has four holes and that one has three holes and that one has two holes, four minus one is three minus one is two, I think the next one will have one or four and the pattern will start over." The children began to talk about how they could use the patterns to predict how things looked that weren't included in the picture. The children are working on being able to see changes as a pattern because they can quantify—use counting and numbers as tools to describe both the object and the changes in the object. Then they move to predicting through extrapolating. There is also a quality in doing this that is a form of experimenting with ways to include previously excluded qualities of the pattern into the pattern. I said above that in order to say that the bricks repeated we would have to ignore qualities of the bricks that didn't repeat like the holes. Suni is attempting to include those.

This anticipates the next step, in which I encouraged the kids to extend their observations of patterns to talking about how the patterns have explanatory power in science. The explanatory power of patterns, rather than the descriptive, is in correlating what appear to be unconnected patterns and in postulating reasons why they are correlated. The bricks repeat in shape and orientation, and the holes repeat in another sort of pattern. Those two patterns are associated spatially. Is there a meaningful connection and does it tell us something fundamental about the bricks or maybe about the forces that constructed the pattern? Are these in reality the manifestations of one more fundamental pattern? And what about the repetition of the plants—is that linked to the repetition of the bricks?

An observation can be called a pattern because whatever is observed is observed to repeat. Can it be assumed to repeat some more? An important point about patterns is that while many are in reality contained, limited things, an inherent assumption to the idea of pattern is that they can extend infinitely. Although to create patterns we need to be able to generalize and categorize, generalizing and categorizing constructs limitations, what I have been calling borders or edges. But what I think is pointed out in this discussion of the science of pattern making is that in order to generalize or categorize, a pattern must be assumed. This pattern making assumes that the process is uncontained, infinitely extendable. It also assumes the validity of the generalizations used to create the patterns, but in fact the pattern and the generalizations generate each other; are in an interdependent relationship rather that an independently supportive one.

Finally, I used the patterns to make comparisons. We examined a collection of dried leaves—maple, tulip tree, sweet gum, poplar, cut-leaf birch—that are similar yet different.[4] We also looked at crystals and fossils to think about patterns and what they might mean.

STARTING TO EXPLORE MUSIC THROUGH PATTERNS

Constructing Relationships
April 14

I started this part of our exploration of pattern by asking the children to remember looking at the musical instruments at the children's science museum we had just visited. Then I tell them we will explore music and sound for the rest of the year. I say that I want to do this because music is to me "a lot of patterns." I ask the children if they play or know anyone who plays a musical instrument. We have quite a long discussion of this, in which virtually everyone names someone that plays something. Of the children in the room, Thomas has just started playing a keyboard and Sueh-yen is on Book Four of Suzuki in violin. Suni also says he plays the flute. Then we look at the xylophone.

I begin by asking if anyone sees any patterns. Suni talks about the grouping of the bars of the xylophone. He says that there is "one long one and then three and then two." The bars in the xylophone are of the pentatonic scale—this pattern in the way the instrument looks is related to the scale. I take a turn at describing it: "There's one of these, then three, then two, then three. What kind of pattern is that? What would come next if that's a pattern?" I'm thinking about the bricks when I ask this. Suni replies, "One." I repeat this and other children start agreeing or disagreeing and counting sequences. Then Emily says, "two." I suggest three.

There is a lot of debating going on over this. The children seem automatically to assume that the pattern extends in both directions. They don't question that assumption. I ask why the bars might be grouped in that pattern and Suni says that "maybe they just put it like that." In other words, he thinks the pattern is *made* and not something natural or reflecting something fundamental about the nature of the instrument or sound. So I suggest that maybe we could move them around and make different patterns. I do this for a bit and then I ask if the children have noticed that the bars have letters written on them. The children have all noticed this (probably because Mrs. Veenstra, their music teacher, calls the notes by name when the children use these xylophones in music class—music as it is taught at Spartan is very hands-on, and the children get to try out a number of different musical instruments and observe a number of others being played by visitors). I continue, "Maybe we should write them down. Suni, can you write them on the board while I say them. C, a big C, big D, big E, big G, big A, big C, big D, big E, big G." We talk about patterns that the children see in this. Some children think there might appear to be patterns, but they are created by me or whoever made the xylophone. Finally, Emily suggests testing to see how the slats marked with the same letter of the alphabet sound: "Why don't you see if the two C's are different?"

I ask if the children think the two different bars with the same notation written on them sound different. Many children respond that they will sound different, and some call out that one is "high" and one "low." I start playing the pairs, low and then high. I say as I do this "large and then small." Many say that the smaller is higher (implying I think a higher note). The point of this is to demonstrate a correlation between two patterns—in size and in tone.

I go back to asking about what patterns they can observe now. I am also trying to construct a dialectic between observation and experimentation. The children start to note different qualities of the physical design of the xylophone. This xylophone has two rows of pegs, one empty with no bars. This is nice because it lets us examine the sound box without the bars in the way (Fig. 3.3).

The actual shape of the two parts of the sound box are a bit different for each row, and each row is segmented with differing lengths partitioned off, with each partition at a different depth—like the parts of a lock. I don't know why this is or whether it corresponds to the intervals in the pentatonic scale we were just talking about. Maybe it has something to do with how xylophones are often played two notes at a time. Or maybe it's to limit resonance effects. Different children point out the physical qualities of both the xylophone and the keys and finally start observing (or constructing) patterns in their observations: for example, the zig zag pattern of the rubber tubing, the differing number of plastic pegs on different rows. Cory describes a pattern that a number of others have also noticed, and I ask him to try to speculate why that pattern might be there. I do this purposely—this unit is about observing patterns, but not passively; it's about thinking about reasons behind observed patterns and then experimentally testing those reasons. However, the children have to have it in their heads that there might be reasons before the experimenting can start. I am not saying that reasons aren't formulated *during* the experimentation also, because I think they are—as patterns are correlated—but I want to initiate the idea that

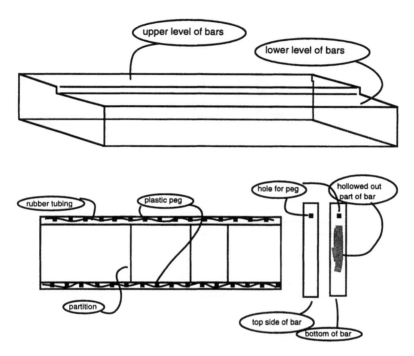

Figure 3.3

we are working on *reasons*, not just observation, now. In the fall we were concentrating on observation and description. Cory's response is to detail his observations further to emphasize that there are two different patterns in the plastic pegs. He doesn't wish to speculate on cause and effect, however.

I return again to asking for observations, now about the sound box. Suni says he sees a pattern: "Well see it's like one big square right there, well like a rectangle, and then like, um, a littler rectangle and then another big square and a rectangle and another rectangle." I ask him why it might look like that and why the top of the instrument is different from the bottom. At first Suni says he doesn't know, then he says that "they made it a little different."

Alyosha directs us to look at the bottoms of the holes inside the sound box (Fig. 3.4).

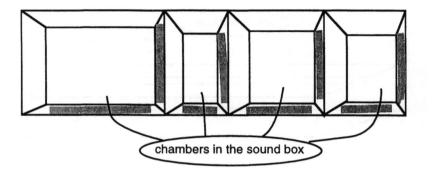

chambers in the sound box

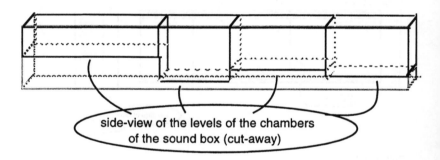

side-view of the levels of the chambers
of the sound box (cut-away)

Figure 3.4

> *Alyosha*: I see a pattern, see there is these two . . . I think there is
>   these two over there too.
>
> *Teacher*: Alyosha said that he thought, he was looking like in this
>   square [*inside the chambers of the sound box*] in here, see there
>   is like a step in here and he thought that that was in there too but
>   it's not.
>
> *Thomas*: Yeah it is!
>
> *Teacher*: What do you mean, Thomas?
>
> *Thomas*: Well there are steps right here that goes like this and then
>   there's a big dam and the water goes higher here and a bigger
>   dam here and the water goes higher. . . .

Teacher: Wait, let me see if I can say it, okay? so that everybody can see. In this one here, it's like a big space here and then a step and then another step, so there's two steps and three, um, things here and then up here, it goes up again to get to here and there's a space and then a step and then it goes up again to get to here and then up here there's a big space and then it goes up like a dam, like this is like a dam of water. . . .

Thomas: Like um . . .

Teacher: To get to here and it's up higher and then it goes up again and it gets to here.

Thomas: So it's like this water would be falling all the way down into here and all the water would be trapped here.

Teacher: What, Shumshad?

Shumshad: But I think this would have the most because it's more deeper down.

Teacher: Would have the most water? [*Children nod and murmur yes.*]

Shumshad: Because it's the most deepest down, see this one is not as deep, it's not as deep as this one, you see I don't know, but if you put these [*the bars*] on there, this is low and this is high, this one makes lower sounds and this one makes higher and those make medium.

First Alyosha points out that the bottoms of the parts of the sound box are of different heights, then Thomas describes them metaphorically like levels and dams in a river. For some reason this metaphor seemed particularly important to me—that's why I repeated it to the class. First of all, I like it when the children use metaphors to describe things that they see—I think it is interesting because it enables subsequent comparative talk. Metaphorical statements invite "why" questions from me and also seem to invite other metaphors. Exploring how those metaphors are applicable in different ways—they highlight different things about whatever we are examining—can then get much more explicit. Second, this particular metaphor was interesting, I think, because it made me think that Thomas was saying that sound is like a fluid, and I thought that was really quite worth thinking about. Often the mediums that transmit sound are fluids, but I also think in a lot of ways that sound has the properties of a fluid. For example, it fills its container, and that seems to be particularly applicable to thinking about sound boxes. I go from Thomas's metaphor to Shumshad's observations and ask if they are trying to correlate the two, "This would make a lower sound and this would make a higher sound because, are you saying because this is deeper?" Shumshad says, "Maybe it would be true. . . . " I ask again, "So would that be true here, this is the lower sound and this is the higher sound?"

> *Shumshad*: I think I need this to tell you. See, if you do this and if you do this and try it, it will be low and if you do it on that and try it [*he does both—takes one bar, rings it in one place, moves it again and rings it*] see that one is more higher.

Shumshad is the first child to have made a conjecture and then formulated an experiment and tried it in this part of this unit on pattern and music. His interpretation of his results, however, is in opposition to that of the rest of the class. "NO, IT'S THE SAME!!!" many children call out. I repeat Shumshad's hypothesis and try it. To me it sounds the same in tone, but different in resonance.

> *Cory*: It's the same because the wood is the same.
> *Emily*: The wood is the same long.
> *Shumshad*: Or maybe you need a little one for that.

I think this is a classic response of a scientist to an experimental result that has not come out as expected. Shumshad has immediately started incrementally to modify his experiment, thinking, oh, maybe if I try it just a little bit differently it will work. Danping makes a new claim by correlating two different patterns of observations: "I think because the wood is the same length it will make the same sound. Not just because you put it in different spaces." I turn Shumshad's conjecture into a counterargument by restating the observation on which it is based: "Well, what Shumshad was saying was that it was the deepness of this. This is shallow, this is deep. You don't think that makes any difference?" Danping has her own, different, observation, which she thinks correlates to Shumshad's: "I a little bit disagree with that because, see, I think that if you have lots of them of course it will make a different sound but if you have one, if you put it over here, like, if you have these space right, if you stacked these space up, I think it will still be the same space even though it's skinnier."

Danping is claiming that the volume of each of the spaces in the sound box is the same, that the ones which have larger rectangles in outline have shallower floors. This is very interesting, but like Thomas's metaphor, we don't pursue it. I think that the reason that we don't is because we haven't gotten to a place in our talking about sound yet where enough children in the class can talk together about these ways of thinking. I think there is a development of this over the course of these classes, which comes about because there is a community that develops through that dialectic process between observation, generalization, and explanation, fed through experimentation and conversation. It's this that I am working on getting off the ground. I think both Danping's and Shumshad's conjectures are very interesting in and of themselves, but the class wasn't at the point yet that they could be acted on.

So I continue on, pushing the experimentation. I say, "Let's listen to it again and see if they sound the same or how they might sound different. Listen to it on the deep one . . . ." I hit the note. Children call out that it sounds lower, it sounds higher, it sounds the same. I ask a couple of the children individually, all of whom say that it sounds the same. I say, "You know to me—and I don't know if I'm right or not—but I do think they sound different but I don't think they sound different lower or higher, I think they sound different louder and softer." Thomas agrees with me and we try it again. This time all agree. Actually I think I am trying to say here that it has a difference in resonance rather than volume or tone, but I really don't know how to express this. With the deeper hole the tone was fuller, but however it is I said it, I purposely introduced another variable.

Cory doesn't agree with me. He also thinks that only the size of the bars matters. Then he adds in a new variable of his own—how hard the bar is struck: "Maybe you're doing it harder over here and softer over here." I invite him to try the experiment, and then Shumshad critiques him, "But he used this part instead of this part [*metal part of pencil rather than the eraser for second try*]." Suni thinks much more along the lines that I was thinking in. "I think I know why, see, this has more of the sound, the sound can go much more deeper and it makes it much more louder, but this is not that deep so the sound doesn't make it so loud it just makes it soft but this one if it was just like this one on this side it would have the same tone, exactly the same tone." Notice that he is again constructing an explanation by correlating more than one pattern of observations. He also introduces a new word, the first that we pursue the meaning of in the context of this unit. I ask, "What do you mean by the word *tone*?" But he doesn't seem able to articulate what he means by tone and I drop it. This is okay—we're just working on starting to develop the language here, and part of this process is introducing new words (concepts), trying them on and maybe keeping or discarding them. The point is that when I hear new words that I judge *might* become important I give them a little air time by keeping the talk on them and not just letting them pass by. The next big word that we will pursue is *vibration*, which is also introduced by the children in this lesson but not chased after for a while.

Next Shumshad takes over the experimenting again, "Maybe this makes a deeper sound, maybe this makes it harder and this makes it softer, let me try this [*raps with knuckles on wooden bars on floor, gets different tone*]." It suddenly occurs to me to wonder if the bars are hollow, and I ask whether or not they seem to be to anyone. I am also quite honestly participating in this experimenting, so I have a lot of questions about this, too. I say, "Is it hollow, by the way? Turn it around—does it look the same or is it flatter?" I am asking about the concave side of the bars. Some say the same, some say different. Thomas responds with a theory: "The tune, this is what makes the tune, how it's carved under here 'cause these two are different, they're different sizes but also these two are cut differently." A number of children engage in this discussion. Again the referent point for their theories (explanations) is the patterns in the things they observe.

In each instance of our talk, the children make statements suggesting explanations for the sounds the xylophone makes. Their explanations relate to things they have been able to observe about the xylophone, the primary basis of their explanations are observations up to now. Periodically, I stimulate observation and explanation by making an observation of my own and then waiting to see how the children use that observation, do they extend it into a pattern? Do they use that pattern to construct or support a theory about the sound? Making a single observation is not enough to construct an explanation; the children have to be able to make the same observation repeatedly in differing circumstances to be able to see a significance in it. In other words, they need to be able to make the same observation about the object in instances where other variables are changing. I try to stimulate this.

The children reach no consensus about what causes the tone changes, however, and we return to that a number of times. Right now Meiying wants to show us something. Meiying speaks very little English, yet her "talk" is quite animated. She hits one bar sitting on the ground, then holds the end of it and hits it again. The results of doing this are really quite dramatic. Lots of children start exclaiming. Danping yells out, "It's dead!" This is the first of a couple of new metaphors to describe the sound. Again, each seems to capture something about both the qualities of the sound and also something important about the physics of this phenomenon. I think this is an example of changing the wavelength of the vibrations in the bar and also causing them to not resonate; it causes them to damp out. First Tity, Suni and Cory critique Meiying's experimental technique. I like this, because I want them to satisfy themselves that the phenomenon that they are observing is real. I encourage them to do this by allowing them to retry the experiment until all are convinced of the validity of the results. Then more children try to describe what has happened.

> *Abeni*: When you hold it the sound gets more [*makes gestures, I say different? she nods*] and when you don't hold it the sound is more [*she makes a face with eyes wide open*].
> *Danping*: Um, I'll, see, see I think when you tap it, it makes sounds, the regular sounds, but when you just hold it, you kind of like kill the sound or something.
> *Teacher*: Huh, interesting word, listen to it again, Cory could you hear a difference in that?
> *Cory*: Um-hum, when you hold on to it, when you went like this, it's like the sound was captured, without it, the sound would just go free.
> *Teacher*: Yeah you're saying sort of the same thing as Danping, Danping used *kill* and you used *capture*, why do you think that would be, why would it sound so different?
> *Andy*: Well because I think when you hit it, the block vibrates but when you hold it and you tap it, it doesn't vibrate.

There, the first seriously, scientifically magical word for this unit. I don't ask for a definition yet; instead I ask Andy why the effect takes place, hoping that he would continue to use this word. This is like fishing: I want them to take the bait. I want them to get into using the

word and maybe have different children use it differently and then start
a discussion of what it means. I ask, "Why would vibrating make any
difference for sound?"

> *Sueh-yen*: Because you're like squeezing its neck or something like
> that and then when you, I can't really say it, but when you tap it
> with holding it, it can't breathe.
> *Suni*: Well the pressure of your, when you have the pressure of your
> hand, you might squeeze it down and when it gets down, it gets
> something, it's something like, when you have a frying pan and
> you turn it over and you hold the metal part and it just sounds
> like it goes dong dong dong but when you don't hold on to it, it
> makes a bell sound.
> *Teacher*: Huh did other people hear that? When you hit a glass too. . . .
> *Cory*: It's almost like that [*points to the classroom bell—one of those
> one's where you hit a button on the top and it swings a clapper
> underneath*].

We do the same experiment with the bell—ding it, then put a
finger on the side and ding it again. I ask, "Is that the same, you killed
it or you captured it or . . . Okay, I agree with you, it does seem to me
that it makes it vibrate when I hit it, but what difference does that
make? Why should it vibrate, does it have to vibrate to make a noise?"
What makes the noise? Ricky says, "I think that there's a little thing
underneath and when you hit the top it hits the side of it." I turn the bell
over so everyone can see the underside. By the way, this bell has been a
source of fascination in the room: when the children think no one is
looking, one or two of them are often trying surreptitiously to check it
out. This is harder than it seems, because if it rings by mistake, or if the
temptation gets overwhelming, everyone gets yelled at. I start to ask
what people think of this, how they think the bell works, when Meiying
suggests a new experiment on the xylophone. Rather than holding the
bar as she did before, she suspends the bar on the tip of her finger. She
tries it first at just one end. When I strike the bar with and without her
finger, the children pronounce the sound the same. Cory puts a finger
under both ends and lifts it off the sound box and we try it. The children
say that it sounds the same. Then Cory puts his fingers on both sides of
the bar. We ring it and he says it sounds the same. Then he squeezes his
fingers, pressing on the bar, and we get the damping effect from before.

Alyosha says, "I think when you hold it, when you hit the wood, it shakes and the music comes out when it shakes, and when you hold it, you don't let it shake, so no music." Now in this statement, Alyosha is connecting the wood's ability to vibrate with the occurrence of the musical tones. He's not saying whether the vibration causes or is caused by the music. That's the trick with correlating patterns—there is the appearance of an explanation when no causality has been established.

An'gele has an addition to this in which she explains how she thinks music is emitted from an object. She explains it as a story: "Okay so there's a house and there's a roof and maybe somebody's playing music inside and then they get it too loud and it sort of vibrates and that makes all the noise and it comes out, I think that's how it works." To me this is a bit like Thomas's metaphor of water and a dam in the sound box. Both involve filling a place up with sound until there's too much and then it comes out. Both are examples of children using their experiences to try to make sense of a new phenomenon.

We return to the children making conjectures about what effects the sound. First Shumshad suggests that it might matter where on the bar you strike it; on the middle or one of the ends. He thinks this might matter because the hollowed out part on the underside makes the center thinner; different parts of the bar have different thicknesses. Some think this will matter, some think not. For example, Suni says, "If you hit it on the thin part, it makes like a sound but I think if you hit it on the thick part, it makes like, just like, um, thunk!" We discuss this some more. Do the children think the sound change is because of where the bar is hit or how it is held?

Then children suggest that the different sounds of the different bars might be due to the fact that they're made of different woods—they are different colors. Some start talking about whether or not the size of the bar effects the loudness as well as the tone. The size of the hollow on the underside of the bars is brought up again. Thomas arranges the bars by size and by their notation and notices the correlation between this and the sound the bar makes. We end the class with all these observations and various ideas about them in the air. I ask the children to return to their seats and write why they think the pieces of wood make noise when they are hit and why that noise is music? I want to see what they got out of all this discussion about how the noise is made and effects on the quality of noise. Assumed in our discussion is that these two things are linked. I also want to know how the children might define the word music, since they are referring to striking a bar of the xylophone as making both a sound and making music.

In this first class, the children make many different sorts of observations about the xylophone and about sound. Oftentimes they are able to make the same observation in different places: for more than one bar of the xylophone, when the bar is held differently, for example. This lends itself to the construction of patterns. This is the first step to attempting to construct theories to explain a phenomenon. Each time a similar observation is made under different circumstances, other aspects of the phenomenon have changed—the other variables, which could be used to describe the whole, have changed. For example, the xylophone has many wooden bars—the children see the same thing over and over. However, different bars sound differently, are in different places, are somewhat different colors of wood, and make new sounds when moved or held in special ways. This lends itself to experimentation: it stimulates the children to try to do things to see if they obtain the same or different results. They can either extend a pattern or limit a pattern in this way. Also, by doing things they are able to try to connect patterns. When two patterns can be connected, or correlated, it lends a great deal of support to an explanatory theory. For example, many children seem to think that hitting the wooden bars made the sound. There are two observational patterns here, one around the bars and sound and one around hitting and sound. They are connected by what the child (or I) do. That's an experiment.

ASKING SCIENTIFIC QUESTIONS INTERTWINED WITH EXPERIMENTATION

Working Within The Emerging Patterns
April 23

I started the April 23 class by asking the question that I ended class with last time: "Why do you think the wooden bars make music?" This question is the foundational question driving the observations that the children are making and the experimentation I am trying to encourage. The children return to the variables they had located in the last class: the length of the bars, the hollow underneath, the way in which it is hit, the construction of the box, whether the bar is on the box and where. Finally Emily starts to try things out. This is my goal in this class: that the children start to take over control of the experimentation. I would like this experimentation to be driven by the children's own questions and ideas. I assume that different children will have different ideas about things to do and different explanations of the phenomenon. These different ideas should fuel the exploration.

Emily takes a bar off the box and hits it. Then she and Cory debate whether or not that results in a change in sound. Cory reminds us of his and Meiying's experiment last time, where he held the bar tightly and hit it and the sound was "dead." Then Cory says, "But it's different with your hand [*claps his hand*] see, hold my hand really hard [*I hold his hand, he hits it again, no difference in sound*] it still sounds, I don't know why that happens, it's not like these [*the wooden bars*]." This is very interesting I think. Why is the sound different when you hit the wooden bar and your hand? And why don't the same things effect the sound? Cory is asking a great question. Also, *he's* asking the question. This is different from making conjectures and then trying experiments to confirm them; and when they don't work as expected, the conjecture turns into a question. I summarize what Cory has done and said because I really want the children to pay attention to this new point. Cory adds this explanation: "[It's] 'cause of the vibration, it doesn't not make the vibration when you're holding on to it 'cause it's not just one whole big, it's not just one whole thing. Like if my arm was cut off it would be one whole big thing."

Cory's explanation for the phenomenon that he has pointed out to us is more an inspirational leap than the children's previous explanations. As I have noted the children's other conjectured explanations are of the form of correlations between patterned observations: for example, correlating the progression in wooden bar size with the tone of the sound the bar makes when struck, or correlating the loudness of the tone with how hard the bar is hit. A similar inspirational leap occurred when the children were talking about the sound box and about the damping process of the sound when the bars were held tightly. In both of those cases the "leap" was both reflected in and furthered by the children's use of metaphor. To say the sound box was like a series of dams and therefore the sound was like water filling that space to different depths and then flowing both caught something Thomas saw in the object and shaped and transformed it through that expression. Cory's idea isn't like that. Cory just suddenly seems to jump between two things.

Children both agree and disagree with Cory. Benjamin says that
the bar of the xylophone is different from one's arm because it's an
"instrument." Meiying points out the difference in size between the bars
of the xylophone and that the effect of holding the bar and hitting it is
larger for the larger bars. Emily disagrees, she hits a bar in the air, on
the xylophone and on the ground, and claims that it makes the same
tone in all three places. I am not sure what she is getting at; I think she
is possibly saying that the difference we hear isn't attributable to the
bar, but rather that the bar has a particular tone which is effected by the
place that it is played. Suni responds, "Well see I disagree with Emily
because see, um, on, um, this part when you put it down here . . .
because something like the ground is kind of hard and it kind of makes
the sound go away, see on this side there's really, it's like the sound is
louder because if the other side is touching . . . like this side, it would
be the vibration, the sound would go like not so high, it would go kind
of not that much, just a little, so I think Cory is right."

> *Emily*: Well but if you went, see that gets higher [*louder*] when it's on
> the ground 'cause it's so small.
> *Suni*: Yeah, but there's a difference between this, isn't this rubber?
> *Emily*: I know but yeah it's got to stay on the rubber to do it but the
> vibration [*hits the sticks together*] 'cause that makes a sound
> too.
> *Suni*: Except you're holding this part, except this part where it makes
> the sound much better and it needs some space. It needs some
> space for the sound waves to come out!
> *Emily*: Yeah, I know!
> *Suni*: Watch Emily, see, see when you put it here . . .
> *Andy*: It has the holes [*the chambers in the sound box*].
> *Suni*: Yeah, on the sides here, to like go inside and make the sound.
> But there's no space here [*on the floor*].
> *Emily*: I know but if I go like this [*she holds it up in the air*] it has a
> whole bunch of space down here.

In this conversation, the children are suggesting ideas to each other
(not to me), both arguing for particular points of view and changing
their ideas as different qualities of the xylophone are demonstrated to
them by each other. This seems very important to me—by taking
control of the conversation, they signal to me that they have found an

aspect of the phenomenon that we are examining that is engaging—the children have found their own purpose for the conversation. Again, developing this sense of a common purpose is central to the development of a community. The conversation is grounded in both what they observe and what they can do—the experiments they can design to try out their ideas—but motivated by their ideas and the sharing of each other's ideas.

We balance a bar in the air on the tips of Suni's and Cory's fingers. Emily rings it. Suni says, "See the sound waves go under it but if—" I interrupt, "It's still nothing like the sound down here, though." The children keep trying different combinations of different sized bars and ringing them in different places—on the xylophone and in the air and on the ground. Shumshad arranges them on his legs so that the hollowed out part rests on his thighs and rings them. Emily tries the largest bar over a deep hole in the xylophone and over a shallow hole. She says that "it would just need a little more space like . . . 'cause this one would be down here and that's a really low one, but if you put this one over here, it gets a lot of space to breathe so it makes a really good sound." Suni again talks about "sound waves." I never do ask him what he means by waves. Too bad. Paula says that when the bar is over a part of the sound box that is deep, it sounds hollow.

> *Danping*: See I have something to say about when Emily put that thing on the floor, see when you put this thing on the floor, the floor's a little bit hard and when you hit it, it's very low and then when you put it back on the box [*she does it*] see the sounds more lower, I mean louder.
>
> *Suni*: Because it has something so the sound can go [*hands to indicate out*] well because it has, like I don't know what to call it, hole, and see if it went, because if it was right down here, it wouldn't make the sound, see when Emily did it down here, it made like, um, a little sound that you couldn't even really hear it, but when you put it here, it sounds, um, higher because most of the sound waves could go inside and make the sound but if you just put it here there's not, there's not enough space for the sound waves and I think that's why it doesn't make a sound so loud.
>
> *Teacher*: An'gele?
>
> *An'gele*: I think I know why it was making a different sound because, like, see, because this one is lower and this one is higher. See,

put your hand in this one and you can still see it, put your hand
in this one and your hand is gone, and you see, probably you
could do this [*I have stretched rubber bands across some of the
empty pegs*], see how high this is and then this one, this would
be low, now if I do this.

She moves some of the rubber bands which I had stretched across the
empty pegs in the top half of the box. Then she takes some of the
rubber bands and moves them to different pegs so they are over other
levels of the inner chambers of the box. She claims the sound change is
due to this. An'gele moves some of the rubber bands and sounds them
over different places and levels of the sound box. She thinks the
differences in sound she gets is due to the differences in the depth of
the chambers. (She ignores the changes in length of the rubber bands as
she stretches them to different pegs.)

An'gele has started to work with the rubber bands. That is what I
had planned that we might do today. I thought that by using rubber
bands we could work more on experimentally thinking about how what
we did effected the quality of sound produced by a thing and also be
able to see the thing vibrate. I definitely wanted to have more
discussion about vibration but I didn't want it to be about something
abstract and without a common experience between the children.
Vibration, to me, is the central concept to talking about and
understanding sound. Defining vibrations and the various variables that
can characterize vibrations is a powerful tool to making sense of the
things that the children can observe about sound. But to do this the
children need a place where they can generate both the observations
and the questions that will lead to those variables. For example,
amplitude and frequency are both components of the vibrations that
they should be able to observe and alter in playing with the rubber
bands. They should also be able to observe what effects changes in
those variables will have on the sounds of the bands. My idea was to
have the children play the rubber bands by holding them between their
fingers of one hand and their teeth. But before we got to that, I wanted
to do a little bit more with this discussion of effects on the sound of a
bar from the xylophone being played in different places. So I ask, "You
know what I did notice was that if I had these just like on the floor, just
the pieces of wood without the hole [*point to the sound box*]
underneath, they still sound different. Listen to the wood, just the wood

without the hole [*I sound it*] you've got to listen very carefully [*I play them again*] the wood by itself without the hole, they do sound different. What do you think, Thomas?"

> *Thomas*: Well I think they do sound different.
> *Teacher*: Why do you think they sound different?
> *Thomas*: Well they're not vibrating as much but there's more places for the sound waves to move.
> *Teacher*: When it's here or down there?
> *Thomas*: There [*on the box*] they can go way down and bounce around everywhere but there, they just hit the ground and bounce up to that.
> *Teacher*: Uh-huh . . .
> *Thomas*: And here bounce out of the hole to our ears.

Now I go to the rubber bands. Each child takes three and goes back to their seat and tries them out.

ENCOURAGING EXPERIMENTATION
BY QUESTIONING RELATIONSHIPS

On April 28 I start the class with the children working in groups. Each child got one rubber band this time. They played them in turn while the other members of the group watched and listened. Then the group compiled a list for presentation of what things they saw, what things they heard, what patterns there were. When the children present their lists, I start to compile a larger list on poster paper at the front of the room. Sueh-yen starts with, "The rubber bands make both sides sound different, the rubber bands vibrate, the rubber bands go up and down, the rubber bands are different sizes." I ask, "How do you know the rubber band vibrates?"

> *Sueh-yen*: Because when you ping it, it vibrates.
> *Andy*: Yeah but you have to stretch it to get it to vibrate.
> *Sueh-yen*: Yes . . .
> *Andy*: 'Cause see it's not doing anything [*if it isn't stretched first*], all it is, is just moving, it's not vibrating.

Now I can ask what they mean when they use the word *vibrate*.
Suni says, "Well see I think they mean you have to stretch it out instead
of like he's, he's just making it fall or something, you got to like make
it . . . stretch it, that's how it makes the sound. Sueh-yen then adds,
"Because when you pull it far and let go [*he wiggles his hand up and
down*]."

> *Teacher*: But what do you mean *vibrate* then?
> *Sueh-yen*: Like it's moving really fast.
> *Tity*: Oh I think I know what he means.
> *Sueh-yen*: Like that [*moves his finger back and forth*].

Then Sueh-yen, with Tity's help, says that it's the rubber band going
fast. I ask if that means that anything going fast is vibrating like me
when I'm driving in my car. I am really just asking anything at this
point just to keep the children talking. Not enough has been said at this
point to do anything with. Children say that no, I'm not vibrating. Cory
says that "what makes the sound is the vibration . . . " I ask again, "But
what is vibration?" Emily repeats Sueh-yen's nonverbal definition by
gesturing with her hand that vibration is movement back and forth.

> *An'gele*: I think I know what they are trying to say, it vibrates when
> you go like this [*does it*], like when your finger goes down and
> then it pops up and then it goes up and down sort of air hits it,
> and then it starts making noises.
> *Teacher*: So it, the rubber band goes up and down [*yeses*] and air hits
> that and maybe that makes noises?
> *Shumshad*: I think they mean, I think they mean, but this is just a
> guess, that it makes sounds, that's what it means, like this [*he
> gestures in the air*].

So is it the noise that makes the vibrations or the thing that makes the
noise making the vibrations that are noise? I ask, "So are you saying
vibration is the same thing as making sounds? An'gele said it's when it
goes up and down, vibration is when it goes up and down."

> *Shumshad*: I don't mean that, see you know what I mean? When you
> pull it, it makes a sound that's what I think vibration is. But I'm
> not sure. You know on the top of houses, like your house but not

on apartments, there's antennas, well maybe there's sort of an antenna that makes the TV go on, I think that's what it means.

Teacher: So the antennas make vibrations?

Shumshad: Yeah. . . .

Teacher: An'gele said that it's when things go up and down like that, Shumshad said that it's the same as sound and it has something to do with the antennae on the top of houses.

Benjamin: I think it's the same as sound.

Sueh-yen: I agree with An'gele.

Teacher: You agree with An'gele, Sueh-yen? How about Cory?

Cory: Um, I think that what like vibration is, like, that something hit it, I can't really explain it real good, but if I hit metal it makes like a vibration, 'cause it makes a sound and I think it's a vibration, it makes a vibration.

Teacher: So if you hit something, if you hit something it makes a vibration, but hitting something isn't a vibration.

Cory: Yeah and you hold on to it and it's going like really fast and it's going up and down very fast.

Teacher: Jiggly. . . .

Cory: It's going up and down very fast!

We go back to the lists that the groups have compiled of their observations about the rubber bands, and Suni reports. This time I have the class discuss each thing Suni reads out from his list. Suni's list is of a form where each statement is attributed to the person who has made it. The first thing he says is about Teton: "I think Teton is the loudest because he's got the thinnest rubber band." I echo his statement and ask if others thought the thinnest rubber bands were loudest. Trying to make a discussion out of this was premature. I had assumed that Suni was presenting claims about the rubber bands that his group had come to a consensus about and I wanted these "claims" to start to appear more problematic—I was assuming that other groups didn't find or conclude the same things. It turns out that Suni's list actually represented an argument among his group members rather than a report of observations agreed upon. This might be why each statement was ascribed to a particular person. Other people in the group were ambivalent about whether or not they agreed or even had shared Suni's report. Cory claims that his was loud, and demonstrates. It is also thinner than other people's bands in his group. But Andy (also in Cory's group) says that Cory is pulling it longer than other people, making it tighter. Tity thinks that his plucking strength or size could be varied.

In other words, the children weren't ready yet to start thinking about one variable at a time. I am waiting for them to be ready for this because then we can start more systematic experimentations around sound. The experimentation that I have been talking about which the children seemed to develop naturally in which they relate two separate patterns by doing something is not systematic. To be systematic, other variables have to be held constant. For example, to "prove" that the tension determines the pitch of sound when a rubber band is played, the rubber bands played must also have the same thickness, be plucked the same amount, and be held the same way. I think that in order to do this what is needed is that the children recognize the variables as separate (or separable) from each other. In other words, they need to set them apart from the continuum of the phenomenon. The fact that the children are not doing this is demonstrated in the following paragraph. On April 30, the class after this, when we discuss Suni's list some more, the children do come to do more systematic experimentation. That is an important step.

I go back to Suni's list. He tells us next what he had added: "I think Suni is the same loud as Teton." I ask if it was as thick as Teton's. Suni says no but demonstrates that it sounds the same. Then he reads what Dan said: "We could hardly hear Dan because he had the thickest rubber band." Shumshad breaks in before I get a chance to: "Dr. Osborne you know why? It's because he . . . " Shumshad indicates that Dan played his without pulling it tightly. I ask him if that is what he means in his demonstration and he adds that maybe Dan didn't hit it very hard, either. Then Shumshad wants to try using Dan's band but playing it differently. Suni breaks in, though, to read the next thing on his list: "We could hear Shumshad better than Dan because we couldn't hear Dan at all." I ask why they thought they could hear Shumshad so much better. Suni says, "because he stretched it out." That was the last on the list, so I summarize what I've written up on the chart: "Suni said that Teton's was loudest because it was thinnest, Suni's was as loud as Teton's but it was thicker, you could hardly hear Dan's because it was the thickest but on the other hand he didn't stretch it very far, so they said two things: a thin one is louder and one that is stretched further is louder." I start to ask children what they think of all this and whether or not they saw anything like that in their experimenting. I ask Andy. First he says that it's interesting and that he agrees with it. Then he says that he thinks that if the band is thinner, it will be louder because it is easier for it to move, to vibrate. Shumshad adds that when they are thinner, it is easier to stretch them. It looks like the debate is about to start up again when I end class.

In the previous classes the children have been working on defining and explaining a phenomenon by constructing patterns. Defining a phenomenon means recognizing it and naming it. Describing it follows. It is described through generalizations—recognizing preexisting patterns in it—but also linking these patterns up in new ways. It means seeing how this phenomenon is like and unlike what already exists. This defining and describing the phenomenon is linked to explaining because of this final construction of new patterns. It occurs through linking observation to question-asking. That process, in turn, causes the extraction (articulation, definition—a second sense of that word) of variables that characterize the phenomenon. To say that these variables characterize the sounds and musical instruments means to define how they are related to each other. Recognizing that there are these variables and that they are related is just the first step. After this comes working out how to act on the variables to elucidate their relationships. Acting on variables in science must be methodical. It is patterned. Method and pattern are linked. In the next two classes the children work on this.

THE DEVELOPMENT OF METHOD

Communication And Community

I start April 30 thinking that we will finish compiling the chart at the front from the other group's lists. I begin by reviewing what we already have and then I ask the class if they can see any patterns in what is written there. We didn't get more than a minute or two into this when Shumshad started talking about the substance of the statements on the list and suggesting things that he also thought about playing the rubber bands. Shumshad starts us out by stating that he thinks that even if you stretch a rubber band tightly you still have to pluck it hard to get a loud sound. He reminds us that Dan wasn't doing that. I question him for a bit about this so that it becomes clear to others that he is differentiating those variables.

I ask the class whether or not they think it makes a difference how hard they pluck the rubber band. Most seem to think it does but also think that there are other factors that might make more of a difference. For example, Andy agreed that how hard you pluck the band matters, but how thin the band is makes more of a difference. Suni also thinks this: "I think it's because of the thinness because if you stretch it too long, it might break but if you stretch it just right it will, um . . . maybe it will make, um, and if you pluck it right it might make a louder sound." I ask Sueh-yen about his violin, whether or not plucking a string hard makes a difference to how loud the tone is. He says that it does make a difference: "When I pluck really hard it goes louder and then when I pluck really soft it goes softer." Then I ask him, "Are some of the strings on your violin thicker than others?" He responds that the thicker ones are louder than the thinner ones. This wasn't what I thought he would say, and it starts us off on a discussion of the difference between louder and softer and higher and lower when describing musical tones. I had felt that there was a little bit of confusion over this developing in our last couple of discussions. This is important because the discussion which Shumshad, Suni, and Teton are about to start hinges on having a shared understanding of the difference between those two pairs.

Shumshad begins, "See can you give me a thick rubber band I'll show you why. See if it's thick it doesn't matter, it will make, I don't know." He does this and then I tell him to do it again so everyone can see and then ask if the only difference is in the loudness and the softness. The class says no. Andy says it depends on how thick it is and Ricky says it depends on its length, referring to the rubber band and not to what Shumshad did or to the results. Shumshad has a new idea before I can pursue this, though:

> *Shumshad*: I'm not thinking about lower or higher but maybe, I'm not sure but if you play a different thing it will make it different sound [*He demonstrates—he plucks first with a finger, then with a pencil . . . he and Teton do this, they move to the front of the room at this point. . . .*]
> *Cory*: I don't hear it.
> *Emily*: It depends on what you pluck it with.
> *Shumshad*: I think it depends on how hard you do it.
> *Teacher*: How loud depends on how hard?
> *Shumshad*: Yeah but it depends, this makes a louder, lower sound, see? But maybe on this side it will make a higher sound. [*They*

> *are trying first one side of the rubber band now and then the other.*] I think it's higher.

I remind them again to be sure that everyone can see and hear them and also ask them to clarify whether or not they are talking about lower and higher or softer and louder. "Shumshad, can you make the claim you just made over again and be careful when you use . . . are you talking about the noise being louder and softer or are you talking about the pitch, the tone being higher or lower?" Shumshad plays the two sides of the rubber band over again, calling one lower and one higher. In doing this, however, Shumshad comes up with a new idea. He and Teton try it out for a minute, then show us: "See it makes a different sound if you play it in a different place [*he is having Teton play it closer and further from his fingers, they have it set up that either one of them holds the rubber band stretched between two hands and the other plucks it*] okay see? Okay this side, this side. See higher higher higher, oh I mean not higher higher higher but lower medium higher." First I get them to clarify just exactly where they have been playing on the band. It's been first close to Shumshad's finger then away a bit, then at the middle of the band. Then I ask them to do it over with a thinner rubber band. I ask them to do this just because I think the thinner ones are easier to work with. This is somewhat more effective, more children can hear what they are doing as well as see it and people start responding to what they are doing and saying. Andy says that it changes to being louder and An'gele to higher. I say I can't hear any difference at all. Tity says she thinks she knows why it might work. Shumshad also has a theory: "I think I know what is happening, see if you hold it like this, see this part of it is different, see it's different, so I think this part is different, so this part plays different and this part and this part, see this different, see this has a different part of this finger and this has part of the different finger so I think it will make a different noise." He is holding the rubber band looped around his fingers. On one hand the band is around the base of one of his fingers and on the other hand it is toward the middle of a different finger.

> *Teacher:* What do you mean it's different, how is it different?
> *Emily:* I didn't understand a word of what you said.
> *Sakti:* Yeah!

Shumshad: Well, see this part, this part is in the middle of my finger, so I think they're different parts!

Teacher: Well, how are they different—what do you mean that they are different?

Shumshad: Not fingers but they have lines that are different ways, like some lines of that goes like this and some are like this so I think that they are different kinds of fingers, so I think it will make a different noise, you get it?

Teacher: No, I don't get it! But I'm hoping that I will soon. . . .

Shumshad: See this blue thing [*points to vein in his wrist*] . . . it's the blue thing in your body that the blood goes in [*children talking and looking at each other's wrists*]. So see?

Teacher: Wait a minute, let everybody catch up with Shumshad, everybody's looking at their veins, now what about veins?

Shumshad: Now see some veins are different, now see this vein and this vein, then this vein? So I think on different fingers there would be different veins.

I ask for clarification and Shumshad explains how his different fingers have different rings (in the skin, patterns of markings in the skin) on them. I start asking children if they understand Shumshad's conjecture and if they can put it in their own words. I think what Shumshad is doing is very interesting: he is demonstrating the dialectic between theorizing and experimentation to us. He has made an observation; that the thicker and thinner rubber bands make different types of sounds when plucked. But he also wants to make a claim that plucking each differently alters the sound. In experimenting with these two observations he comes up with a third, that the sound varies with regard to how hard the band is plucked. In playing with this he discovers that the two sides of the rubber band make different noises. Then he and Teton experiment with playing at different places on one side of the band. Finally he comes up with a theory, that something happens when the band is held between different fingers that cause the sound to be different. He has done a lot of leaping around in this and I want to make sure that the class is with him. Suni says that he can explain what Shumshad is up to. He gets about two words out of his mouth and then runs to the front of the room to try out the experiment for himself. The three of them now start telling each other what to do.

After quite a bit of this, Suni announces, "It's not veins, it's your fingerprints."

> *Teacher*: Okay would you tell me, all three of you who are doing this what it is you are trying to prove by doing that?
>
> *Shumshad*: Oh I'm not sure but I just did something wrong see this side of this wasn't any different, this side of this, which is different, so I think it's the same thing with the thumb.
>
> *Suni*: Well let me explain this, see what we mean is, okay like if you hold a rubber band with two fingers, two thumbs, I mean, and you hold it like this and then somebody plinks it, it will make one sound but when you change a finger and make a sound then you're . . . you plink it and it makes a different sound. I'll show you. Get the stuff together!! Okay watch this, okay it makes that sound [*he plucks the rubber band again*].

Cory suggests that they pluck it harder. They do it and the sound is louder. This gets incorporated in the original experiment, where the fingers holding the rubber band are changed.

> *Shumshad*: See it depends on how hard you pull it.
>
> *Suni*: And it depends on what finger you use.
>
> *Shumshad*: See if this is my finger and this is my finger and this is both [*they do it*] see they're different fingers.
>
> *Teacher*: Okay all of you guys stop, stop. Stand up there in a line and stop fiddling around and don't all talk at once. Okay whose going to speak Shumshad or Suni?
>
> *Suni*: Teton!
>
> *Shumshad*: Teton, say something, you haven't said nothing.
>
> *Suni*: Yeah!
>
> *Teton*: Okay I'll explain it, it depends on the size because if there are like our thumbs are one size and they're both the same size, both of our thumbs and if you change a finger they're not the same size, look [*he shows us his fingers*].
>
> *Teacher*: Now listen to me, I saw what you guys were doing and everybody else saw what you guys were doing. It seemed to me that not only were you changing what was holding the rubber band, you were changing how far apart you held your fingers, you were changing how hard you plucked the rubber band, there

> were all sorts of changes and all of them might have made a
> difference in the way the rubber band sounds. . . .

Science isn't just fun; it's disciplined! In order to make sense of the
phenomenon, their experimental actions have to be patterned. In this
way, variables can be located and isolated. Results can be ascribed to
changes in those variables. All of this hinges on the construction of a
pattern—in the observation of the phenomenon and in the method of
interaction with it. The need to do this in this class has grown organ-
ically out of what the children are trying to do and also to
communicate. The construction of patterned action is necessitated as
much by what they are working on in thinking about sound as in how
they are trying to communicate it to others. The patterns of method in
science and in communication are linked developmentally with the
growth of the classroom community. A community is defined by shared
discourse and activities.

They try it again, trying hard to change only the finger they have
the band rapped around. Finally, Suni announces, "It's different, it's
different, there that proves it." The three of them run back to their seats.
I call them back up front and tell them that they need to explain to the
class what they have done, what they think it shows, and ask people
what they think of it and whether or not they agree and why. I tell them
that I personally don't agree with them, but "I'm not totally sure I know
what you are saying." Suni says that he'll explain, "Well, see we had a
rubber band and then we did one thing with fingers that were the same
and then we plinked it and it sounded like something. Then we changed
the finger except kept one [*only changed one finger*] and we kept it the
same distance. Then we plinked it and it made a different sound, so if
you changed fingers, it can make a different sound but you have to keep
them the same distance." I ask him if they plucked it the same way each
time and they say yes, except for Shumshad.

The manner in which Shumshad, Suni, and Teton are interacting is
a very visible expression of the interactions of members of a
community. They listen to each other and try to think inside each
other's thoughts and then, occasionally, one or the other contributes a
different idea, one that is implicitly critical. This manner of interacting
is fundamentally creative. It can only happen socially when people are
honestly interested in each other and mutually engaged in a common
pursuit. The way the children listen to each other, as well as the way

that they criticize each other, is a measure of respect. I think this develops because of a genuine interest in the subject matter and our explorations and a respect for each other constructed by me and enforced by me. I model this way of acting and after a while the children adopt it because they have found that the things that each does are interesting and of value. The children are responding directly to each other's ideas in a manner which is thoughtful, playful and critical at the same time. This occurs between the boys at the front of the room and between them and the rest of the class. The audience is very interested and quietly amused by their activities.

Shumshad continues, "But Suni, sometimes you pluck it and you do this much and sometimes you do this much, so it would make a different sound, see you pluck it, first you pluck it this much and then... You can not go like this always, the same length, you can sometimes go like this and it will make a different sound."

> *Suni*: Yeah except we want it to be the same so it can make the, so we can prove it!
>
> *Shumshad*: Okay do you have a ruler and I'll hold it and then let's see. . . .

That's exactly what I wanted to hear. Now we are ready to construct a systematic experiment. We get a ruler and they start their experiment over again. They measure the distance between their hands and then the depth of the plucking with a great deal of discussion of who does what. Teton insists on metric. The three of them work out that they will stretch the band fourteen centimeters and flick it three centimenters. They are going to do this first with one pair of fingers, then with different fingers. They explain all this very clearly to the class. I suggest that they ask the class what it thinks before they go on.

Suni, Teton, and Shumshad take questions from the floor. Thomas thinks the flick should be larger, so now it's five centimeters. Suni explains his procedure and the rationale again even clearer. Emily disagrees with their statement of what the experiment will prove. Suni says, "We're not sure we're just testing, we might be right, we might be wrong." Emily replies, "In my opinion, I think it won't make a difference." Suni explains again. An'gele wants to make sure of the experimental design. Finally they try it and I have them talk it out while they do it. We can't agree if it is different so they do it again, this time

twice, because Shumshad thinks that will make it easier to hear. Emily
thought it sounded the same. An'gele thought it sounded different, and
so did Sakti. Ricky thought it was the same; Alyosha and the group
different. I poll, it's about fifty-fifty. Then again, and it was five the
same and seven different. So they try it again. I hold the rubber band
this time—there is no difference in diameter of my fingers. This time
all seemed to think it different.

> *Emily*: I sort of disagree with you guys, I'm going to need the chalk
> board.
> *Teacher*: Okay.
> *Emily*: Okay, here's your thumb and here's your finger and here's the
> rubber band and you pluck it and it makes one sound and then
> the next time you do it, and it even makes a different sound or
> the same sound.
> *Suni*: Well to us it made a different sound.
> *Emily*: Well most people thought it sounded the same. It probably . . .
> well, they were either right or wrong but we don't know that
> right now.
> *Suni*: Right.
> *Emily*: So I have an idea so we can find out . . . well one thing we can
> do [*tries it with two fingers and one finger rather than changing
> the fingers*] let's see if it makes a different sound.

Emily repeats so others can see. This is also the first hint that someone
thinks that it is different diameters of the fingers that matter, and not
just something magical about the fingers themselves. Shumshad
coaches her on how to present this to the whole class. The class
progresses from arguing that one idea *versus* another is right to arguing
about method. The result of the argument about method—what to do
and how to do it—is that the children's methodology becomes
systematic, patterned, and disciplined. When the method is agreed
upon, the argument can return to being about ideas. What are the
methodological variables and how do they effect the sound? I make
everybody go back to their seat and try the experiment in their groups.

   This development of a method for acting and a method for
communicating is very important in the construction of a community.
These developments are the tools through which a common language is
built. They cement a common purpose. A method is a patterned way of

acting; it enables people, observers, and participants to anticipate what will happen, to know what has happened. It is a tool in interpretation. Because a method is purposeful action and because it is patterned, it is a design and it is designed (both senses of the word design). Method, the concept, is contingent upon human agency and human interpretation.

METHOD, EXPERIMENTATION, MAKING SENSE OF PHENOMENA

May 14

On May 14 Thomas brought in a small-bodied guitar with metal strings to show the class. He has mentioned to me before that he might be able to do this, and I encouraged him. A guitar is perfect for us to look at at this stage of our explorations. The guitar strings clearly vibrate when they are plucked or strummed. One can control the vibration and the resultant sound with the keys without worrying about changing other variables (such as the string length). The guitar lends itself to systematic experimentation in which only one variable at a time is altered. He starts the presentation off: "Last time we were kind of tangled up and we couldn't decide whether to pull it tight or not [*he is talking about Shumshad, Suni, and Teton's experiment*], well this I can get to sort of do the same thing [*turns key on the guitar after plucking one string—at low end*]. Okay when I pull this it sounds like that because it's two different ones [*strings, he plucked two strings together*], but if I do this, listen to the same [*plucks them again after loosening key, children laugh say it sounds different, higher, lower, flat*] 'cause I loosened the strings too much." I ask him to explain what he has done and he says that by turning the key he has loosened the string; or the key can tighten the string. He continues to do this until he gets the string so loose, it won't make a noise. Then Tity asks him to pluck a skinny string; he does this and says that makes a different noise because it's a different string. I think he says this because he is trying to make a point about how the tightness of the string effects the tone, and he wanted us to concentrate on what he was doing with the one string. But he does continue on to say (referring again to the last class): "And we were also tangled up with how wide and how thin they were, well I have these and they're different, rats you can't do that one [*he has loosened the highest string so that it won't play at all now*], well this one is real high [*plays the next one up*]. . . . It sounds higher and it's thinner and this big one right here starts lower because it's fatter [*a lot of murmuring*] . . . okay now I'm going to loosen this skinny string so . . . it's a bit hard to . . . I hope I can loosen it if I don't tighten it [*loosens key and plays, children are murmuring*]. . . ." Then Thomas describes to us how each string has a different thickness and each sounds different. He plucks each one as he describes it. So I ask him if he would say that those different sounds come from the different strings because they're thicker or thinner. He says, "Um hum . . . [*continues to play the strings*] . . . and if they're loose or tighter."

As Thomas demonstrates on the guitar, the class has reviewed the variables we had been examining with the rubber bands. Different children suggest trying different things with the guitar, stating what they think will happen. Thomas tries them out and people suggest countertheories to explain what actually does happen. Both the theorizing and the experimentation arise out of each other: theories give rise to experiementation and *vice versa*. They are also grounded in observations about the design of the guitar. There is much debate about various features of the guitar—including the frets, the bridge, and the hole. Different children, as they call attention to their observations, suggest theories to explain their presence and also suggest ways to test them out.

For example, Shumshad notices the hole in the body of the guitar and suggests that this makes the sound loud. (Remember this same discussion regarding the xylophone.) He suggest covering it to test this idea. This in turn causes much speculation on what causes the sound we could hear. There was definitely a correlation between the qualities of the sound and whether or not the hole was covered, but that still didn't tell us what caused the change. This, as well as playing with the strings, returned us to a discussion of vibration, that was now much more sophisticated.

Finally we concentrate on the strings, loosening them with the keys as we play. One becomes loosened to the point that it no longer plays. I ask Danping why this has happened. He responds, "Because I think when you loosen it you sort of just let it go by itself and then when it goes by itself it's sort of very loose and I can't say it . . . I mean when it could go anywhere, it just could go . . . I don't know. . . ."

Teacher: If you loosen it, the string could go any way? Any where? Is that what you said?

Danping: Yeah but I don't know how to say it out loud.

Alyosha: I think, see when you let it go and when you let it go loose, then it goes on the side longer and then it, it can't vibrate very good when it goes on the sides, when you go like this when it shakes, when it goes out, then it looses control of itself.

An'gele: I think I know why it makes that noise. Because when you pull the string it's like, see how straight my finger is, now it loosens up and it gets to do whatever it wants to do, it's like I'll use an example, like if your Mom said you have to stay in your house and then she said you're free to go any where you want.

Danping: Then you just go anywhere.

Teacher: That's very similar to what Alyosha was saying and it's a little like Danping, you're saying that when it's loosened up it's free to move any old way it doesn't have much control, is that what you're saying?

An'gele: Yes.

Danping: I think when you loosen it it's out of control.

Shumshad makes a very subtle point next. He says that it's not really the string that changes the sound, it's the keys—by turning the keys you control the tension of the string, therefore you control the sound with the keys. Then he says, "See if you can loosen it, it can go this far but if you tighten it, it can go only this much [*he indicates the amplitude of the vibration on the string changes*]." I ask him, "Are you saying that if it's tight, it vibrates just a little bit and then when you loosen it, it vibrates a lot?" He says yes, that would be true as long as it didn't break.

I ask about the effect of the thickness of the strings. I remind the children of their conjectures about the thickness of the rubber bands, that they had said that thinner rubber bands make higher sounds. I say that that seems to be true here, too. Why do they think that would be? All of this, about thickness and thinness and length is to work further on the idea of vibration and how it effects sound. I want to get at ideas of amplitude and frequency and I know that both the stiffness or the tension of the string effect this and this is in turn affected by both tightness, length, and diameter. With sound, the amplitude is proportional to the loudness and the frequency is proportional to the pitch (variable and effect). Greater stiffness or tightness of the string will decrease amplitude but increase frequency. Greater thickness increases the mass of the string, and decreasing frequency and pitch. These are the correlations we are working on—the observations and phenomena that are related through patterned action, through methodological experimentation.

Andy says that he thinks that the little ones vibrate more because they're thin, that's how they make high sounds; and the low ones that are thick don't vibrate much, therefore they are low. Now what does "vibrate more or little" mean? Is he referring to amplitude, or frequency? Benjamin adds that the fat ones are heavier and the thin ones lighter. This is proportional to the stiffness. I ask Andy what he thinks of this and he says that what Benjamin has said "has to do with how they can bend." Danping disagrees. She thinks that the thick one vibrates more than the thin one and she starts to draw a picture. Meanwhile, I say that: "I can think of ways that that's true, for instance what you guys were saying about how the fat one is less controlled and it vibrates like that [*I draw*] (Fig. 3.5). . . .

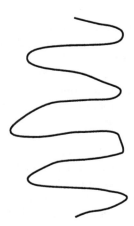

Figure 3.5

. . . and the thin one vibrates like this (Fig. 3.6):"

Figure 3.6

At least I thought that was what you and Alyosha and An'gele were saying about when it was looser." I was trying for a difference in amplitude here, but I also made a purposeful and opposite difference in frequency which is of course a gross exaggeration of what a string on a guitar or violin actually looks like when it is plucked. Danping stops drawing and says that she agrees with my picture. I ask, "Which one is vibrating more?" There would be different answers on the basis of either amplitude or frequency. Danping says the thin one, the one with greater frequency, is vibrating more. Andy grees. No one says the one with greater amplitude is vibrating more.

Alyosha says he thinks the thin one is vibrating more, and also has something more to say. He points out that the fat strings appear to be made of something different from the thin strings. They are different colors, and the thick ones appear to be made of metal. Shumshad shows us by drawing that the fat ones look like little springs (Fig. 3.7).

Of course this doesn't really relate to thickness but to the length of the string—if these little springs were straightened out the string would actually be very long and the resulting wavelength of the sound would be very long. This is why the pitch is lower. This isn't what Shumshad wants to say, however. He wants to tell us that the fatter strings are harder to pluck than the skinny strings. He is relating the thickness to

Figure 3.7

the tension of the string. This isn't really the result of a property of the string, but is rather a result of the setting of the keys. His final statement is that if it is easier to pluck the string, the amplitude is larger. Danping draws Shumshad's idea (Fig. 3.8).

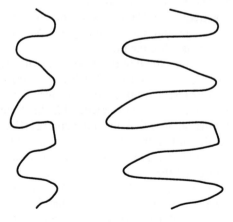

Figure 3.8

Notice that she drew the same number of wavelengths for each string. The result of what she drew would be a change in amplitude in what we hear, rather than a change in pitch. They aren't relating this phenomenon to the sound, but rather to the tension put on the strings by the keys. All these things are linked, but to make any sense of it we have to separate them out, think about each separately, construct an identity for each variable.

An'gele has had her hand up for a while. I call on her and she corrects all of us about how the strings actually look when they vibrate. She points out and then draws a picture to show that they actually vibrate with only the one-half wavelength or multiple of this; she says that this is true for both fat and thin strings (Fig. 3.9):

Figure 3.9

She adds that, "They go all the way down like that, back and forth. That's how they vibrate, then they go in this hole and out that hole, that's why it makes that living sound [*she is talking about the hole where the strings thread into the bridge, not the hole in the guitar body*]. The children talk about this, most agreeing with her observations about how the strings vibrate. Suni says that means that the difference between the fat and thin strings would then be how much they vibrate—their amplitude. That isn't right, but that is the way it stands at the end of this class. The greatest debate is now about An'gele's claim that the vibration goes into the guitar body at the bridge. Most people don't see a hole in the bridge and therefore don't agree with her. Only Sueh-yen agrees. He says that it echoes inside. I remind the children of Shumshad's experiment when he covered up the hole in the guitar body and pluck the string and it sounded differently. Then Suni says that he thinks the hole and the vibrations going into the hole effect the loudness. Then he adds, "It's just like the xylophones, don't you know there was a big hole and you use that xylophone and when you tapped it, it made kind of a loud tune and when there was not that big hole and you taped it, it didn't make that loud tune, so I think the same goes with this, when you pluck it, it makes a loud tune with a big hole and if you used a little hole, it makes not such a loud tune."

That was the end of class. In this class the children continue to define the variables that characterize sound. This is done as an interplay between observation and experimental action. In this instance this is systematic because the guitar, the vehicle for the exploration, constrains the children's actions. Only one variable at a time can be worked on. This is a final repercussion of design—the design of the instrument, the medium through which an experiment is carried out, determines the things that can be done and seen. The design of the experiment determines the result. The act of design is an imposition of meaning. I think a final important point about this conversation is how it contains and makes continuous references to things the class has already done. There is a developing history to this unit and this community and its pursuits. I think this is another important quality of a community—a shared history.

This is the end of the first stage in this final unit in which we explore music and sounds and patterns. In this stage I wanted the children to use the tools we had developed, looking at, seeing, recognizing patterns to "look at" music and sounds and things that make music and sounds. This meant observing patterns passively but then also observing patterns actively, discovering that by doing things systematically, or maybe seeing a system in things that weren't done systematically, they could observe new patterns that correlated to the patterns they had passively observed. This act of correlating lends itself to constructing explanations for phenomenon, or at any rate, apparent explanations. I say apparent because the appearance of causality constructed by the correlation can be an illusion. For example, things that make music vibrate—the two are correlated, but do they have any causative relationship to one another and, if so, what? Does the sound make the vibration or the vibration the sound? Once you've got that kind of relationship, you've got to go outside that relationship to find variables that characterize the two constructs, in this case sound and vibration, that you can fiddle with systematically in order to see how this experimenting effects the constructs. In this way, causality can be established. But does any of this really explain Why? Or does it actually just push the why question to a more fundamental level? Once a relationship is established, you can accept it on one level, but then you have to ask why it occurs. Music and vibration go hand in hand, but that doesn't tell you why something can vibrate in the way that it does to begin with. I believe that this sort of why question becomes a vanishing point in our explorations. With each new discovery that apparently explains an observation, the why question is pushed a step back. I think this is important because I believe a shared pursuit is focal to the development of a community. This pursuit cannot be easily resolved. Rather, it must reshape itself and in essence develop a life of its own to remain compelling.

In the class about the rubber bands we have got our initial correlation, and now we are working on characterizing our constructs with variables. We are locating the variables and seeing what happens when we change those variables. The next class, about guitars, is about this even more so. Doing this is a pattern in itself. Acting systematically to alter one variable at a time means acting within an established pattern. Doing this in conjunction with theorizing is a mental pattern of logic-making, testing, and altering.

WHAT IS MUSIC? WHAT IS SCIENCE?
THE DISCUSSION BEGINS

May 19

On May 19 I decided to ask the children what music is and whether or not they think there is a difference between sounds and music. I am not sure why I did this at this point in our discussions, but I think I had decided that we had done enough systematic exploration of the constructs, sound, and vibration, and we'd done enough locating and working on variables that characterize the two. I had always planned that we should think a bit about some of the more subjective and value-laden thinking that underlies the judgments we had been making or assuming. Thinking within and through patterns should involve an awareness of figure *and* ground, and that periodically the choices made to articulate the figure should come back up for conscious reevaluation. This is important because it keeps us aware of ourselves and helps us to realize the relativistic quality of our choices (Arendt, 1977; Habermas, 1991). It is also a tool used by me to work to prevent the hierarchical development of relationships between people in the class, the people in this community (Foucault, 1980). Both are important scientific and personal values for me.

In the next three classes the children work to define three words: *pattern*, *beat*, and *rhythm*. They do this within the context of defining the word *music*. The choice of defining music through pattern, beat, and rhythm is theirs. This choice of variables very much shapes the definition of music—how it is articulated from the continuum of sound. The children effectively state that music is made up of the three above-mentioned words. Then they work to define those words in such a way that the words themselves become differentiated from each other and it is the relationship between constructs that defines music. Again, there is a pattern being drawn out from the whole of the phenomenon and a pattern in the method generated to work on the phenomenon and communicate with others about it.

This is an example of both the development of a community and a community developing. There is a shift as we move into this part of our explorations from conversations focused upon sharing our observations and our experiments. Embedded in the way that we talked about both observation and experimentation are explanatory ideas about phenomena. This necessitated the development of certain patterns of observing, acting, talking, thinking, and interacting. In the discussions of the question, "What is music?", observing and acting come second to talking and thinking—as the children try to communicate what they think is important about music, they find they have to "show" us. Through the acts of telling and showing us and articulating that in an environment where people respond, the children's ideas change. Portraying what a child thinks they "know" becomes an act of rethinking. Knowing, thinking, and learning become linked. This happens as a new community develops. I call this a new community because the focus—the qualities that the community forms around—has shifted and recoalesced. I would not like to imply here that I could specify what the community was formed about before or what it becomes formed about in this final portion of our explorations of sound and music. It is different, though. Possibly I could say that before we were chasing after explanations of sounds and now we are thinking about the uses of sounds. These two are linked. I do know that the ways in which the children talk about what they are thinking and how they respond to each other are different. There is a different "feel" to this community. A constant, however, is the respect that I require children to show for each other's ideas. This doesn't mean they can't disagree, they certainly do that, but it's a matter of *h o w* they express disagreement. Again, this is a fundamental to the development of the community—a valuing of each other and each other's ideas as they interact in a mutually shared pursuit.

I start our discussion by asking Benjamin if all sounds are music. When he says no I ask him what the difference is and then to help this along I ask him to name a sound that's not music. Benjamin says, "Well this is a sound—dum, dum, dum, dum and music is like when you hit it a lot of times and kind of get beat or it's like rock and roll." This starts immediate controversy.

> *Suni*: I have something to say about that. When you did that dum,
>   dum, dum, dum, I think you are wrong. I think that's a music
>   beat. So, so that is a musical sound.
> *Emily*: When we talk it's a sound.
> *Ricky*: Yeah but it's not always music [*to Suni*].

I ask Suni what he means by musical beat—what is a beat in music? He replies, "Like sometimes when people play drums they go dum, dum, dum, dum and then other people play something and that's how they make music."

I clap my hands once and ask if it's music. Everyone says no. Then I clap my hands three times and ask again. Many say yes, it is. I ask Emily what she thinks. She responds, "Well music is one thing that you, um, it's like one kind of sound that you're playing, it's just like

one kind of sound. . . . " I ask her what the difference between a
musical sound and "the other kind" is.

> *Emily:* 'Cause like music, it has a whole bunch of different things. . . .
> Like different beats and stuff, it's like, if you were a cow you
> would just go moooo and that's just one thing.
> *Teacher:* So lots of different kinds of sounds makes music?
> *Emily:* Um hum. . . .

My interpretation of this is that a sound is musical because of its
context. This is not the answer that I was expecting, particularly. I was
expecting a conversation about the qualities of the sound, that musical
sounds are different from other sounds because of an intrinsic, not
extrinsic quality. Both ways of thinking fit into what I wrote about at
the beginning of this section about my goal in the setup of this teaching.
They do this in different ways, but I think it adds up to the same thing.
My response to Emily's statement was to ask: "So what if you went
moo, baaa, meow, is that music?" Some children thought yes and some
no. Suni says that it's just noises from animals, not a musical sound at
all. I think that he's meaning what I was thinking—intrinsic quality of
the sound—but he goes on to place his thinking within the contextual
definition Emily had started on. "I think a sound that's not music is like
when people walk across the street with their feet stomping, it always
keeps going it doesn't like, um, it doesn't like repeat in the same way,
like they go like this instead of going like this and this and this, so
that's why they make a different sound that's why I think it's not a
musical beat." I ask him about marching, whether or not that's a regular
beat and whether or not that's music. He says that it is because they
"stomp at the same time." Danping joins this but she says that she
thinks music is sound that has rhythm. I ask if rhythm is the same as
Suni's beat. She says yes, that music is "regular."

Now Emily asks Suni, "Is this music? [*claps hand on thigh*]. . . ."
Suni tells her it's a musical beat. Emily says that yes it's a musical beat
but it's not music. "Musical beats are music!" responds Suni. Danping
agrees with Emily. She slaps her hands on the floor a couple times and
says that she doesn't think that is music. I asked her why not, but Suni
both answers me and continues his argument with Danping and Emily.
He says, "Not going like that [*referring to Danping's demonstration*]
you're supposed to make a beat [*slaps hands deliberately on floor, with*

deliberate pauses in between which he indicates with head nods]. . . ."
Then he adds a new phrase which Kathy uses to describe the rhythmic
hand-clapping she uses to get the class's attention: "Now if you would
want a rhythm pattern like our class is doing, now that's a rhythm
pattern, just going like that is music." Now this is different to me. First
of all, a rhythm pattern doesn't repeat the way clapping to a beat does.
It doesn't repeat but it can repeat, it's like the definition of the word
pattern which means a design that can be copied. It also doesn't have
regular spacings between claps. It seems to be different from what Suni
has just said about beat and music.

Throughout these conversations on the nature of music, Suni plays
a key role. His definitions of patterns and the components of music
evolve as he talks and does things. There is a feel in his talk that he has
an idea in his head of what he thinks music is and is trying to find ways
of describing that. There is a sense that he is trying to articulate these
ideas, but there is also the feeling that he is constructing these ideas as
he is going from components of different things that he has experienced
that he would call either music or not music. Anyway, his use of the
words *beat* and *rhythm pattern* to define music is somewhat
contradictory.

I ask Andy what he thinks next. He tells us that he thinks music is
"a bunch of sounds put together in a type of order." I ask him if that
means it has to repeat like Suni said, and he says no. Suni corrects me:
"It doesn't *have* to repeat but it can also be a rhythm pattern."

> *Emily*: I think he means, I think Andy means that this [*hits hand once
> on floor*] . . . that can be—
> *Suni*: That's a rhythm pattern.
> *Emily*: Yeah.
> *Teacher*: Is it a rhythm pattern if you just do it once or does it have to
> repeat to be a rhythm pattern?
> *Suni*: A rhythm pattern has to do the same thing over and over again.

There is much talk going on now about this with children asking
each other whether or not they think various sounds are music or
rhythm patterns. An'gele says that she thinks people walking do make
music. I think she is thinking that she can hear a rhythm listening to
herself walk; Suni, however, is thinking about listening from outside,
listening to others. Larkin raises her hand and says that she thinks that

screaming isn't music (my daughter Larkin was visiting this class and the next; she participated in each class as a class member). Larkin and Andy both say that it's just a loud sound. So I ask, what if someone were to scream repeatedly, would it be music then? Larkin says no, so I say, "Why not? It would have a beat." I am thinking suddenly about experimental music I listened to many years before in which elements of traditional music were separated from others and whole "songs" were composed and played using just one element. I am somewhat more familiar with this "playing" with the elements of art in the study of minimalist modern visual art in which an artist purposely pushed upon the constraints and demands of various components of painting or sculpture, making the subject of that art the components and the play themselves. When I studied art I was taught that the purpose of such art was to cause us to reflect on the question, What is art? I think in the conversations to come about music, the children do something analogous—they break music into parts and then explore the meaning and interplay of those parts in the total phenomenon. I think the children here are getting at whether or not sound has to be purposeful to be music and whether or not it has to be purposefully music to be music. I think Larkin is saying the latter and Suni the former.

Larkin agrees that it would have to have a beat and Andy adds that if you also had a guitar it would be a song. Alyosha says that sometimes screaming is music. He gives an example from opera. I ask, "And that can be musical screaming?" Alyosha says yes but Cory says that that is singing, and Andy adds in that is *loud* singing rather than screaming. Again, a lot of children are discussing this. Finally Suni and Benjamin start to talk about rock and roll music and screaming in that context. Benjamin says that he has heard rock stars scream, and it's music. Emily asks him how he knows it's music and he says because the person was also singing and playing the guitar and he was also singing/screaming words. I think embedded in this was that what Benjamin heard was called music and it was on the radio and on videos on the TV. So a number of different kinds of contexts define this screaming as music. Finally, people seem to agree that screaming could be music sometimes.

Through this conversation and those in the next few weeks the children work on what they think constitutes music. In my thinking, there would be three categories of criteria that we might be playing with—intrinsic qualities of the sound (tone, pitch, etc.), relational qualities between the sound (the beat, pattern, and rhythm that the children are talking about), and context (music is music because it's in a context where it is labelled music). I had thought that the children would focus on the first quality because this would have been the most connected to the discoveries that we had been making in the first part of our explorations of sound. From that, we would work on the second quality because music is an assemblage of sounds. I had hoped that this would be how we would get back to talking about patterns, and what constitutes a pattern, rather than just continuing to use patterns as we had been in the part of this about sound. I had thought that discussions of context would be our vehicle for calling into question whatever definitions we constructed using intrinsic and relational qualities of music. The children skip the first quality, however, and instead debate at length the relational qualities of musical sounds. There is a continuous interplay with ideas about the contextual quality of music although this does not become an overt questioning of the definitions of music, until the very last class. At times various children (particularly Thomas) remind us that musical sounds have intrinsic qualities, but this is not important until the children start to create their own examples of music and they use the different qualities of particular sounds as components of their patterns. But these qualities are still not used to judge the music; it is still the relationships between sounds that is the primary criterion.

Different children define the relationships between sounds differently. They struggle through conversation both to make others aware of their criteria and to define words to describe what they mean. This is complicated by the continuously interactive and social qualities of these classes. The children are trying to explain their ideas to each other as they are formulating them for themselves. Their ideas are a work in progress. In the final parts of this chapter I include a great deal of these conversations. I do this knowing full well that they are somewhat tedious to read and confusing to try to make sense of. The children are changing their minds continuously. It was very confusing to participate in as a teacher. My primary role in this was to keep conversations open rather than focused between two or three people, to continuously invite new people into conversations. In other words I took as my responsibility keeping the community one that encompassed the whole class. To me it is amazing that a conversation like this can go on for weeks and continue to engage so many of the children. I think that speaks most powerfully to the concept of community that I am developing in this chapter.

Alyosha returns us to hitting the floor, rhythm and beat, adding in things that have come up in the discussion of screaming. He hits the floor once and says, "See this [*hits the floor*] . . . is a musical beat but it doesn't have words and it's not a part of a song. . . ." Suni repeats his opinion that that's not a musical beat, and Emily agrees—she says that it's just a sound. Suni then echoes Emily and demonstrates his idea of a musical beat. He hits the ground a number of times with even and deliberate spacings between the noises. Thomas calls that a rhythm pattern. Then Suni says something a little new. He says, "When you do it fast and other people do it, it is a rhythm pattern." Now Alyosha says, "That has rhythm and it sounds like some music, it has rhythm and this is just a sound, it doesn't have any rhythm, when you just hit it."

I summarize this: "Okay, you just hit it once and then the next time you did it repeatedly and then the next time did it an actual (*pattern of long and short pauses*) something that was different, can somebody play something on that?" I am referring to the xylophone. Most children say "no way" for some reason—I really don't know why, because they showed no hesitation to interact with it before. Maybe they thought being asked to play music meant play an already existing piece of music. Emily volunteers. I give her the sticks and she plays kind of randomly different notes, with a sort of progression up in tone yet ending on a down note, but with consistent timing between notes. Danping says that she thinks that is music, and then she amends that to she thinks it's a song. That is an interesting differentiation that I don't pursue. I ask Emily why she would call that a piece of music. She replies that "it has the sound of music, of music, and it was well, it's not like this [*hits the floor a couple times with even spacing between slaps—no change in tone*] . . . it has different beats to it." Suni picks up on her use of timing to call it music but not on her requirement that it have different tones. He says, "Yeah not like this [*hits the floor with random timing*] . . . but like this [*hits the floor with a rhythm pattern*] . . . like that." I point out to him that "you could do that on the floor, but it's different when you do it on the xylophone."

Next Suni says that what Emily played isn't a pattern. I ask him why not. This is interesting to me because throughout the rest of these classes Suni will insist that to be a pattern it has to repeat. The consistent beat doesn't make it a pattern. Again this is at odds with his use of the phrase *rhythm pattern*. Suni says, "'Cause she was doing it in different ways like if you wanted to, it to be a rhythm pattern you'd have to repeat the same thing." Emily responds, "But Suni just like Andy said it's different parts of music hooked together." Now that is not what I heard Andy say, but it is interesting. Suni repeats that it isn't a rhythm pattern. I ask if in order to be music it has to have a rhythm pattern. Suni says "sometimes."

Suni now agrees to play a rhythm pattern on the xylophone. He plays three different notes over and over. I ask him if it was music and he says "a rhythm pattern." I ask other people if they thought it was music and whether Emily's was music, whether only one was music or if they thought both were. Thomas says that he doesn't think Suni's was music because it doesn't sound like music. Suni replies that it's a part of music.

> *Thomas*: Well, sure, but it doesn't sound very nice.
> *Suni*: I know because you have to put different beats in it.
> *Emily*: And you have to play different notes.
> *Suni*: Except you didn't make it into a pattern.
> *Thomas*: You should play different notes if you want it to be a nice thing of music, now that could be a part for a piano because when you're on the xylophone you can't really hit the two at a time and keep them going but when you're playing piano that could be a nice part, you might go [*sings the pattern*]. . . .

Suni and Thomas continue to argue this. Thomas is making the point that pattern in sound isn't necessarily music. To be music it has to have some "song" in it, too. I don't think he ever communicates what he means by song, though.

Suni responds rather defensively that he was "just showing you a pattern, that's all." I ask Thomas if he thought Emily's was music. He says that yes it was because it had different notes, but "it didn't have a rhythm pattern, which it really needs. . . ." Emily says that music doesn't always have to have a rhythm pattern. Thomas says that he can play a piece of music with a rhythm pattern and I tell him to go ahead. He plays two, three note series with the same descending qualities. Suni states, "You have to repeat it over and over again." Thomas agrees, "You go and repeat the pattern over and over again, except it will have different notes." Now Suni adds that then you have to play different notes, however. So next Thomas plays a three-note pattern and then plays another three-note pattern which is the same but at a different place on the scale. Then Thomas changes the pattern. Suni tells us, "That's a rhythm pattern with different beats." Thomas agrees and says that now he is going to "make a rhythm pattern with one beat but with different sounds." This starts a new argument with Suni.

He interrupts to claim that each piece of music is one beat. I take it from this that he means each note. Thomas seems to have something of an idea, very foggy, that a beat can contain more than one note in it. Neither of them is able to communicate what they are thinking to each other. I think this is because it's vague and formative for both of them. They keep arguing about it for quite a while, however, and this working on the definition of beat continues on the next day and then the next week in even more detail. I fluctuate in all this between letting them work out their own definition and trying to communicate my own. My additions come next time.

Thomas demonstrates a beat containing more than one note and Suni continues to insist that a beat corresponds to a note. Thomas tries to explain that a beat has to do with how you divide it.

> *Suni*: No no no no I'm asking you why are you saying that you are going to make one beat with different music pieces 'cause that would be impossible, why'd you say that?
>
> *Thomas*: Well what I mean was [*plays something with three notes*] . . maybe it would be like that, and you'd play all those different notes and it would fit into one beat.
>
> *Suni*: Well how are you going to get one beat and all those different other different pieces?
>
> *Thomas*: One beat and all those other pieces? Well if I cut this into one, maybe sixteenth. . . .
>
> *Suni*: No no you have to play it. . . .
>
> *Thomas*: Play it faster!
>
> *Suni*: But that won't make a beat, that will make lots of beats [*Thomas plays about five notes fast*] . . . see?
>
> *Thomas*: See that is a beat divided up!

I ask Thomas finally why he did what he did. He replies that it would be boring if he hadn't. Larkin offers her definition of a beat and how many notes can be put into one beat—with a slur in which a number of different notes are played with out a break between. Then she talks about timing and notes having different timing so that one or more notes can make up one beat just so the timing stays even. I ask Sueh-yen what he thinks, since I know about his ability to play. He agrees with Larkin. Neither of them are able to communicate this to the others. The children debate this quite vigorously using the xylophone to try things out.

Cory returns us to the question of whether or not music has to have patterns. He says that it does because he has observed patterns in his brother's music book. I presume that he is talking about the way written music looks, that it forms visual patterns. Suni doesn't think that means *all* music has to have patterns. Alyosha says that they *usually* have patterns.

I send them back to their pods with rubber bands. I remind them of all the things that we discovered about the rubber bands and discussed on April 30 and before. They are to play with the rubber bands and think about what they think music is. I had them write on this—what they did, whether or not it was music and why they thought so.

THE MEANINGS OF VARIABLES, DEFINING WORDS

May 21
The class on May 21 starts with me asking again, What is music? For this class I obtained three more xylophones, two made of metal and one of wood, and two glockenspiels from Mrs. Veenstra, the music teacher, so that each pod has their own instrument.

I begin by having the children review the last class for Abeni, who was absent. Emily tells us that we had been talking about what sounds were and how sounds started—how sounds are made. Danping says that we talked about what constitutes music. She reiterates that music involves beat and she recounts Suni's statement that you can't put too many notes in one beat. Suni says if you do that fast, it makes it into a beat (which is what Larkin and Sueh-yen claimed). I ask if there has to be beats in music, and all agree that there does. Emily says that irregular hitting isn't a beat; it has to be regular. Suni responds that is a rhythm pattern. I ask Abeni if that is music; she doesn't think so, but won't define the word herself.

I remind the children of what they had been doing with rubber bands and ask them whether or not they thought it was music. Ricky says sort of, because it has beat and rhythm. Sueh-yen also says it had rhythm. I ask about being able to make more than one sound. Dan says that the two different sides of the rubber band played different sounds. Tity thought it wasn't music because the rubber band just vibrates. Thomas doesn't think it's music because there's only one note, he can make more than one rhythm pattern but not different notes. Tity says that even when she did what Dan described, all she got were different "sounds," not notes. Larkin says she thinks it can make music because the rubber band is similar to a violin string, which vibrates to make music, and so a violin needs strings to make music. Tity thinks rubber bands and violin strings are different. Suni agrees with Tity; music can have more than one sound—it doesn't have to, but it can. Danping thinks that with rubber bands, you can make rhythm and different sounds.

Back to their pods in cooperative learning groups, they work on the xylophones and the glockenspiels. I tell them to experiment with them to think about what music is. Then as a group in their pod they had to decide what music is and what to show us in the whole group on the xylophones.

Differentiating rhythm, beat, and finally pattern is to be the substance of all the conversations until the end of school. That and the role of these three in music. I think these are very interesting conversations. To me, differentiating between these three concepts isn't and shouldn't be easy or stable. The differentiation of these words hinges on establishing conventions. In turn, establishing conventions is dialectically tied to the uses the words are put to. This is a fundamental task of a discourse community. The children in these conversations are working on the meanings of these words as they work on their concept of what music, and finally language, is. They are constructing the meanings of these words in the context of what they are doing and what others are doing and also within a context created by the interplay of the three words. There is an initial assumption, I think, that because these are three different words, they must have three separate and different meanings. In many ways, I am directing the conversation to bruise this assumption. I want the children to look for ways the words are related and similar as well as different and separate. By doing this, I am positioning myself outside the developing discourse community and effectively altering the development of conventions. According to Foucault (1979, 1980) a fundamental quality of the process in which discourse communities are created is the creation of dominance relationships between members of the community. I don't wish for this to happen, and I work to prevent this: I keep our conversational referent external to the personal relationships developing in the class. I keep our questions unanswerable. I think this is an important point and one that keeps this classroom community focused by science, dynamic, and shifting rather than becoming established into a set pattern of thinking or interactions. My fundamental goals in doing this are not about the science as much as about shaping the interactions between people. I want people genuinely to value each other, and in particular value differences between people. Keeping the science answers receding is a tool in doing this. This is not just a social goal or value for me; it is also intellectual. When voices are silenced, then those perspectives are lost. When we lose those perspectives, we also lose the potential of these to help us understand things differently. I would argue that the accumulation of different understandings adds up to a more profound understanding. Those that don't speak often do so for social reasons. The social and the intellectual can converge in a negative as well as a positive sense.

The first and only group that presents what they have done on the xylophones is the "Cheetahs." This group is made up of Tity, Paula, and Meiying. First they play a pattern. (Paula plays two notes—one high and one low and alternating.) Then a rhythm. (Paula plays three notes repeatedly; two are the same, and are both two bars played at the same time. Then she plays a third, which is lower, not in a major scale, and is just a single note.) Then beat. (Paula plays the same note over and over about four times, and then she pauses and repeats that same thing.)

> *Teacher*: So the whole thing with the pause was beat?
>
> *Tity*: No, each note.
>
> *Teacher*: Now what about music, you did patterns, rhythm, and beat but what about music?
>
> *Tity*: Well, I think music is sound and it's something that has rhythm and beat and pattern.
>
> *Teacher*: So all of those were music?
>
> *Tity*: Yeah.

I ask the class what they think. I have Paula play the pattern over again and ask if others would call that a pattern. Everyone says that yes, it is. Then I ask if people think it is music, and again everyone answers yes. I ask Suni what he thinks. He says, "I think it's a part of music, just part of music." Dan says that he thinks it's part of music and music too. I ask Paula to play the rhythm again. She does (the Cheetahs have written each of these out on a piece of paper using the notation carved on the xylophone bars). Suni says that he thinks "it's a rhythm, I don't think it's really rhythm, I think it's a rhythm pattern because it's repeating over and over again." I ask him if he thinks it's music and he replies, "Uh-huh, part of music." Danping says that it is a kind of music. I end the class.

DEFINING WORDS CONTINUED

Comparing/Constructing Similarities And Differences
May 26
I start May 26 exactly where I left off the last class. I ask the Cheetahs to perform rhythm, beat, and pattern over again, and start the discussion. I ask the Cheetahs first, this time, what they thought was the difference between rhythm, beat and pattern. Paula says that they all sound different. So I ask how they sound different; I ask Paula what they were thinking about when they decided what was what. This didn't get much of an answer, so I tried again: "Well, I guess the reason why I'm asking is that what you showed for rhythm could be a pattern, and what you showed for pattern could be beat and I didn't know what was the difference between the three from what you showed." Paula adds that to her they all sound like beat except rhythm and that rhythm sounded like pattern.

The children discuss how they created the music that they played. Finally Suni adds, "A pattern repeats over and over again, rhythm doesn't have to have a pattern in it but it can, it can just be mixed things that make it sound like music." I ask him if he can show us an example of a pattern that's not a rhythm. At first he says, "Sure" but then retracts: "Well it's impossible to make a pattern without rhythm." So I ask if he can make rhythm without pattern.

> *Suni:* Well, yeah [*hits random notes with equal timing*] . . . except it doesn't repeat over and over again.

Teacher: So how is it rhythm?

Suni: It has, like, a kind of beat to it except it's not called *beat*.

Emily: He means like you can put rhythm, you can put anything in rhythm but it has to, it doesn't have to have pattern but then pattern, it won't be a pattern if it's not one thing, well not one thing but it has to repeat to be a pattern.

Cory: Well this isn't really a pattern [*hits notes randomly*] . . . you're just going . . . 'cause nothing's repeating.

Suni: 'Cause that's not a rhythm pattern.

Cory: I know this is a rhythm [*hits notes with equal spacing, all notes are different*] . . . you mean a pattern is [*plays two notes back and forth*] . . . it's got to repeat, this is not a pattern [*hits random notes*].

Teacher: Now listen, there's nothing that repeats in this (*I play the scale descending*) . . . but it goes high, lower, lower, lower, lower, lower, lower, lower, lower, lower, that's a pattern, but it's not repeating.

I introduce this because I am thinking that patterns aren't just something that simply repeat; or rather, the question is, if repeating is the criterion, what is it that does repeat? In doing this pattern, my actions repeat, the change between notes repeats, the timing between notes repeats. Just the actual notes don't repeat. This is a background/foreground kind of argument—what is in the background and what is in the foreground? Defining those two generates the pattern.

Suni says that it's not a pattern. Emily says that it has beat. I have said that I think it is a pattern and ask how could it be a pattern. Suni says that it has to repeat, for music, it has to repeat but all patterns don't have to repeat, just musical ones. Sueh-yen also thinks that music has to repeat. Suddenly Suni seems to change his mind. "Well I never said it really has to, did I? Well it can also make patterns different ways but, um, just rhythm is mixed up things instead of just going one one one, I mean a different way . . . you have to do it mixed up instead of like, you have to make it out like a musical sound." Suni subsides to think a bit. Danping says that pattern has beat in it. I ask her if that means it also has rhythm. She says no but it does at least have to have beat.

While the children are saying these sorts of things, I think about patterns elsewhere. I mean, I think they are constructing these definitions just thinking about music and what they are doing with the xylophones. Whenever they say something like this I think about the things that they are doing and showing to us, but I also think about visual patterns or mathematical patterns or patterns in actions, and think about how the things that the children say apply. That's really the source of my counterexamples. When Danping says this about patterns having to have beat but not rhythm, I am thinking about visual patterns. It seems to me that to apply her statement to visual patterns, rhythm is the repetition, and beat is the substance of the pattern—the design in any one unit of the pattern. Her statement doesn't work with visual patterns, at least as I've defined them. With patterns in numbers maybe it does work. That is the source of my proposed pattern when I played a scale. Here the repetition, "timing"—the relationship between the units—is a constant, the substance isn't. In a scientific equation, say $E = MC^2$ (energy equals mass times acceleration squared), the relationship between the variables stays the same. The content of the variables can differ in some ways—in magnitude—but what is actually being measured stays the same. E is always energy, M is always mass. For example, in the number line, the relationship between the numbers stays the same, and the content differs. But does it? Actually each is always a number. The magnitude changes. But that happens as a function of the relationship. This is very confusing. Maybe this is a matter of where you stand to look at the pattern, what perspective you take: especially whether or not you stand outside the pattern and look at the meanings of the variables or whether you assume the meanings and effectively stand inside the pattern. From inside the pattern you can see the relationships but maybe not the identities. Moving between standing inside and outside the pattern—using the pattern and assessing the pattern—are primary goals of mine in our explorations in the earlier teaching about visual patterns and now with sound and music.

An'gele suggests that if all three were put together, we would have a little song. Emily says that that is what they did in their group, so I ask if they would like to show that to us next. First of all, Emily tells us that her group thought that music was pattern, beat, and rhythm all together. Then she says that they did this because then "it wouldn't be so boring, for a pattern you wouldn't do [*hits two different notes repeatedly one after another*] . . . it's kind of boring but with all of them, it gets more interesting." I respond, "And you think in order for it to be music it has to be interesting." Emily nods yes. Again, this is really interesting to me. This is the reason I embedded this "scientific" exploration of sound in a study of music—to invite aesthetic judgements that we could talk about and examine. I think an overlay of aesthetics characterizes science. The generation of patterns is through the application of an aesthetic (e.g. Chandrasekhar, 1987). Differentiating background from foreground is through aesthetic judgement—judgements based on unarticulated values and relationships between those values. I want us both to explore using such values and also to examine them and examine how we are using them. Constructing music from sound, as well as deconstructing music into sound, is a part of this process. Understanding sound by defining variables—by seeing patterns—is a part of this process. When Emily says that applying a pattern, beat, and rhythm makes it interesting, I think she is really saying that the interplay between pattern and the undifferentiated whole, between foreground and background, makes it interesting. The overapplication of pattern, so that there is no irregularity, makes it boring. Weaving the irregularities into the pattern makes it interesting.

> *Emily*: No, it doesn't have to but it's just more fun when it's interesting, instead of just going like this [*hits a couple notes*], that's not very interesting, you're just hitting them, well the first thing we're going to do is do all of them together and I wrote down a separate of them.
>
> *Teacher*: Okay you're going to show us pattern, rhythm, and beat together and then you're going to show us the separate parts. . . . [*Emily plays first a simple pattern which she repeats twice, then a pattern on a descending scale, then a more complex pattern which she repeats twice, then an ascending scale, and two simple patterns which she repeats twice.*] Okay so that has pattern rhythm and beat together?
>
> *Emily*: [*Nods*] Okay and now we're going to separate them, this is pattern [*plays a pattern of two notes alternating, then goes down the scale and does it again, then back up the scale and again*] . . . and then this is rhythm [*plays two notes in a descending scale with one timing, then tree more notes ascending but with a faster timing, then some other stuff which is more complicated and ends with a descending scale with a slower timing*].
>
> *Teacher*: That's rhythm?

Emily: Um-hum and this is beat [*plays up and down scales with little do da's in them but all with the same timing*].

Teacher: Okay, I don't see how pattern, rhythm, or beat were different, how were they different?

Emily: Well pattern is like [*plays three notes descending, then a different three*] . . . two or three at a time, this isn't really pattern [*plays random notes*] . . . it's not an even pattern it's not close to a pattern but this is pattern playing one or two or three at a time [*plays a scale twice*].

Teacher: Okay, and show me what beat is again?

Emily: Okay this is beat [*plays a little tune with deliberate spacing between notes*].

Suni says that this doesn't really sound like a beat, rather it sounds like a pattern "a little." Emily starts to argue with him. She plays a descending scale, hitting each note twice, and challenges him: "You call this a pattern?!" Suni responds, "Yeah it's a pattern, beat just keeps going, it has spaces, long spaces." Tity agrees, she thinks it's a pattern, too. Emily continues to play and starts to vary the timing in between notes. Suni says that it should have consistent spacings between notes.

Then Emily tells us that, "What we did, what we decided was that we would just do like three or two at a time in patterns [*plays the xylophone*] . . . and then we'd just rest for a minute and then go on and do some others and go like that [*repeats*] . . . and then we'd rest and we'd go again [*does it again*]. . . . Danping comments, "Emily, when you played the first thing, I think the five notes, or whatever, in between the two notes or whatever, the time was a little bit longer than at the end because, see, when you went like, first, when you went like da do la la la and then at the end you went like do do do do do [*fast*] like that, well that didn't sound like beat to me, it sounded like a song." Emily replies, "Well that's your opinion, it's not our opinion." That's true, but I still want her to be able to articulate what she is doing and the base upon which she and her group have decided to do that thing. I think that is an interactive process, however—interactive with other children and interactive as the "music" is created and with the creation after it has been made—purposely creating illustrations and also discovering what they have done after they have done it.

Now Alyosha says that he thought that what Emily played was a pattern, and that a beat is much simpler. He plays the same note over and over with no change in timing. Suni says that he agrees, but then he says that "it's a pattern except it's a beat." Alyosha responds, "It's a pattern because it goes a lot of times, but this is a beat [*hits it once*] . . . that's why I think it's a beat, then it's in rhythm, well that sounds like a pattern to me."

> *Emily:* Well, we decided that a beat doesn't always have to have repeats, you can just keep on going [*plays different notes*] . . . 'cause like every part of music is a beat, music has to have a beat.
> *Suni:* Emily why did you put rhythm in it, when you know you're not supposed to mix things up.
> *Emily:* Well because we decided that a beat doesn't always have to be going like this [*plays something*] . . . we decided that you could go like this and put rhythm and pattern in there [*plays different notes repeatedly.*]
> *Suni:* I know but a beat isn't supposed to go like this and this and this. . . .
> *Emily:* Music has to have a beat, has to have a beat first.
> *Suni:* I know but it has to hit on the same thing each time.
> *Emily:* Not to us!
> *Suni:* Well why'd you think of that?
> *Emily:* To us we think that we can just go like that [*plays random notes with the same timing*].

They keep on debating what a beat is, very much like last class. Emily seems to think it's the timing that defines a beat, and Suni the note. Finally, I ask Cory what he thinks a beat is. He says that he can't really say, a "beat doesn't go anywhere. . . ." I ask Sueh-yen. He says, "A steady beat." I ask him if he means that it has the same amount of time between beats and he agrees. Suni says, "A pattern is when you repeat it with different notes and sometimes you can do the same notes." I think his insistence that beat means hitting the same note is because he is trying out ways to differentiate beat from pattern. Sometimes he says that one is part of the other and sometimes he is working on how they are different and he wants to make them completely different. Finally, he says, "A beat is a pattern except a beat just keeps on going going going just like Sueh-yen said, a steady beat."

Emily thinks that he is trying to differentiate between beats and rhythm patterns, the latter which she calls "pattern beats." I think she is saying that the beat is defined by the repetition of the whole pattern. This gets confusing, because Suni keeps bringing in different criterion to judge them by. This time he says that the tone can't change. I ask Andy what he thinks. He says that he sort of agrees with both Emily and Suni: "The reason why I agree with Suni is because beats do have, um, one note in them sometimes and sometimes they have different notes, that's why I agree with Emily." But Suni repeats, "That's a pattern, beats are patterns too and beats just have to stay on the same bar [*note*] and just keep going and you can add more beats to make it music." Finally, he adds, "You have to keep doing it and add other stuff to it [*I think he is talking about resolving to a tonic*] you can add."

I end class by telling them to write a sentence in their notebooks saying what they think a pattern, a rhythm and a beat are.

DEFINING WORDS CONTINUED

What Is A Pattern In And Out Of A Context?
Playing With Context To Think About Meaning
May 28
On the twenty-eighth we start class trying to write paragraphs together that define pattern, beat, and rhythm. Emily suggests this sentence: "If a pattern doesn't repeat it wouldn't be a pattern." I ask Emily to explain why she said the sentence that way. She explains it by giving an example, hitting on her desk. Suni doesn't agree that a pattern needs to repeat.

> *Danping*: If a pattern doesn't repeat it's not going to be called a pattern.
> *Suni*: Yeah but it could be something else.
> *Danping*: Yeah but it can't be a pattern.
> *Emily*: It wouldn't be a pattern, it would be something else, it wouldn't be a pattern.
> *Suni*: Well what if it's called a pattern.
> *Emily*: Well there's two kinds of bats, one bat and another bat.
> *Suni*: Well see a pattern could have been another thing.
> *Emily*: I know but it could be two kinds of patterns.
> *Suni*: Or one kind but it's not what the pattern . . .

At this point Emily gets up and goes and gets a dictionary and starts to look up the word *pattern*. I ask Shumshad, who has his hand up, what he has to say. He says that he sort of disagrees with Suni and sort of agrees with Emily because "sometimes a pattern doesn't have to be . . . if it didn't repeat, it couldn't be a pattern, and sometime I agree with Suni. I agree with Emily and disagree and I agree with Suni and disagree because, see, you could . . . pattern has to repeat otherwise it couldn't be a pattern and sometimes maybe not." Thomas says that he does think that patterns have to repeat; he doesn't agree with Emily but Emily tells him that she has changed her mind.

> *Danping*: She didn't say that patterns have to repeat.
> *Teacher*: Well she didn't really say it, she just did it.
> *Suni*: Patterns don't have to repeat. [*Many are yelling.*]

Emily announces that in the dictionary there are "tons" of meanings for the word *pattern*. She reads from the dictionary: "An arrangement of forms and colors, designs, the pattern of wallpaper, rugs, and jewelry; a model or guide for something to be made, I use paper patterns in cutting the cloth for my coat. A fine example; model to be followed, he was a pattern of generosity. Make according to the pattern, pattern yourself after her." I reread them and after each ask whether or not that works for music. These definitions appear at first to be unpromising, except that they link pattern to design, to having a purpose, and to human agency. These are important concepts for me— pattern, design, and method are all connected by people purposively doing chosen activities. These activities are chosen with respect to the attainment of a goal. This is something I would like to develop with the class—thinking and talking overtly about this. To do this I increase the time we dwell on the first definition.

For the first definition, the children say that they think it doesn't apply to music. All are thinking about visual designs. They talk, using the word *design* until I ask, "Is pattern a design, are pattern and design the same thing?" Emily says that pattern has different meanings. Cory has said that wood has a pattern so I ask if that pattern repeats. Suni says that the wood is like fingerprints. I ask if this repeats. Suni says, "Well they're a design." An'gele says something about people who are talking on Mars, who are from Mars, that wouldn't be a pattern because it couldn't be understood by us or recognizable as language by us. I summarize the things that the children have been saying: "You're saying that patterns have designs in them, do musical patterns have designs in them?" Now most of the children seem to think that musical patterns don't have to have designs in them. Teton says that some patterns do have to have designs. I ask him if he can suggest a pattern that doesn't have a design. No one can, so I suggest 2, 4, 6, 8, 10, 12 and ask if that's a pattern (I think it's both a pattern and a design; I think they go hand in hand). Some say yes and some say no. Teton says that he thinks it is a pattern, and so does Sueh-yen: "Yeah, 'cause it keeps skipping two all the time." I ask him if he thinks it's also a design.

> *Teacher*: Is that a design?
> *Sueh-yen*: Ummmm . . .
> *Danping*: And they're all even numbers.
> *Teacher*: They're all even numbers? Does that make it a pattern?
> *Andy*: Even even even even . . .
> *Sueh-yen*: And odd odd odd odd odd . . .
> *Teacher*: And those aren't designs or those are designs?
> *Andy*: Those aren't!
> *Teacher*: So Sueh-yen, how about in music, does music have designs?
> *Sueh-yen*: No.
> *Teacher*: Does music have patterns like 2, 4, 6, 8?
> *Danping*: No.

But many others think that it does. Danping changes her mind. Sueh-yen adds that "they have certain kinds of patterns but not the 2, 4, 6, 8s." He suggests that you can play a pattern like hitting two bars and taking turns between them. I do this and ask whether or not it is a pattern like two, four, six, eight. Everyone says no. I play an ascending scale, skipping every other bar. People say that is like two, four, six, eight. Ricky says, "When you skip each one . . . it says out the name, like when you skipped the first one, to me it says, um, two and the other one says four." Danping adds, "When you write a piece of music, you could use numbers." I ask her how she would do that.

She comes to the board and writes three, five, seven, then she plays those bars on the xylophone. After doing this, she explains that you could do this same sequence at different places on the xylophone and the notation for describing this would involve putting "dots" above or below the numbers. If you wanted to sing something along with this you could write the words under the numbers. I suspect this is from one of those little books that come with simple keyboards that teaches children to play songs. I remember something like this from a present Larkin got when she was four. Sueh-yen has a different suggestion; he writes "do re me fa so la te do." He calls this the scale, and equates the words with Danping's numbers and the actual notation written on the bars of the xylophones. I ask him if it's a pattern and he says yes. I'm not sure if we are trying to find ways to describe the same pattern or even the same idea of the meaning of the word *pattern*.

I go back to the definitions in the dictionary. I read the first one again and ask whether or not it has anything to do with music, but this doesn't get anywhere because Emily wants to talk about more notation for the music. She suggests that when using numbers, the numbers should correspond to the relative positions of the bars from one end. Then letters above or below the numbers could be used to refer to tones that aren't really on this particular xylophone (ones with larger ranges of notes). I ask how any of this could be a pattern because I don't see how using numbers leads us to patterns that repeat and they have defined patterns as repeating. I ask Danping how hers repeats. Danping says with the dots. Danping, Andy, and Emily debate the qualities of their different notations. They get into working this out on the xylophone. Danping seems to be quizzing Emily on whether or not she wants the numbers to just keep on going or if there is some beginning, and ending. Danping's scale seems to have implicit recognition of an arbitrary beginning and Emily's doesn't.

Cory asks Emily why her scale is descending rather than ascending. Emily says that it could go either way, it's just what she likes best. The two of them start playing with the scales. They start discussing which of various patterns sounds better and then the two of them together begin to do different incremental changes to one pattern of four notes. Cory seems to want the pattern to end on a descending note. I ask them why the final choice sounds better to them. Emily says because it's not boring. This goes on a lot longer with different children adding in what they think of the piece or how they would alter it.

> *Teacher*: I don't understand what any of that had to do with patterns.
> *Benjamin*: Nothing!
> *Cory*: It had to do with patterns.

Teacher: What?

Cory: Well it didn't have anything to do with patterns but if me and Emily kept on, the last one that we made up, that we said was good, we should have kept on, kept on doing that.

Teacher: So this is a pattern (*they play their bit again a number of times*) . . . that's a pattern (*yeses*) and is that a design? (*yeses and nos*) Who said yes? How is that a design?

Thomas: It's a design in music, well that wasn't just theirs, somebody designed it, they couldn't have just said we'll make D D E or something like that, they had to design the music, to make it, they had to make up the notes.

Teacher: So a design is something somebody made?

Emily: They had to go, let's try D C C and see how that sounds like.

Teacher: What's the difference though, Thomas, between your idea of design, which is something somebody makes, and a design in the wood on the table?

Thomas: Well they're designing music not a table, I mean somebody didn't really design it, but they designed the shape of it, of how it would look.

Teacher: Oh I see, so somebody had to decide how that would look and somebody had to decide how that would sound.

Thomas: They designed the wood!

Emily: They had to decide what they were going to do to make this and how they were going to make this, what they were going to do.

I summarize Thomas's definition of design as "something that someone has made so if you play a piece of music like [*plays it*] . . . that's a design because somebody made it." Then I ask what people think of that. Cory says that he disagrees, a design has writing. Suni doesn't think that has to be true. Different people suggest designs like the school, the color pattern that the cubbies are painted, carpets. I ask again if designs are things that people make.

Tity: Yeah!

Teacher: So if I write a book, is that a design?

Suni: Yeah, you designed the book.

Tity: If you designed a book . . .

Andy: If somebody else made it, if somebody else invented the book and you put the book together that would, that wouldn't be your design.

Teacher: You have to invent it too as well as put it together?

Andy: Yeah.

Danping: Yeah.

Suni: But army people, they design their faces with paint!

Cory says people are designs. I ask him how, and he says that "somebody made em . . . if nobody made em then there wouldn't be any of us right now." Some children respond to this by saying that God made people. Some start to disagree with this. Sueh-yen says that people are designs because they choose what to wear, how to look.

Then Emily returns to talking about designing the school. She starts to draw on the chalkboard and says, "A design is, well, if someone said, "well, let's build a school," they'd have to design it . . . how they were going to build the school, they'd say, "well how are we going to build the school?" and they'd probably go like this [*draws a school*] . . . they'd make a school building and they'd make a school and stuff instead of just going like this [*draws a scribble*] . . . it doesn't really look like a school." So I ask her what she would think if somebody just took a whole bunch of wood and started to put it together to make a school. She says that it wouldn't be a school. Suni says that it would be a building, at any rate. I ask the same question again. I am thinking that the act of designing could occur, does occur as the building is going on. I don't think you can really separate out design from building. Also, what about building something and then naming it, where is the design in that? What is interesting is how the children have linked design and pattern through the idea of purposeful action. I would define the word method as purposeful action that mediates between object and subject. I think this is exactly what they are doing, also. This time Suni responds to my question about just starting with wood and building until you got a school: "Just because you did that— you designed it— so it is a design."

Teacher: It's being designed as I do it, is that what you are saying?

Suni: Yeah but you designed it, you wanted to make it, then you made it.

Emily: But if you were planning on making a school . . .

Suni: That's designing, but you don't always have to plan on it, you can just think it over.

Emily: But if you designed it on a piece of paper and you said, this is what my school's going to look like . . .

Teacher: What do you think, Teton? Do you think that you have to design a school, if you're going to build a school, you have to design it on a piece of paper first, or do you think you're also designing it if I just go out and start banging pieces of wood together and call it a school?

Teton: I think you have to design it because, um . . .

Teacher: On a piece of paper?

Teton: Yeah, well you could . . . just if you had lots of people and you do it and each of you had an idea and if you make your idea and if it's at the same place, it's going to be different.

Exactly my point—a design represents a plan, it enables purposeful action, it necessitates methodical, disciplined action, it gives meaning to action. Ricky adds, "They have to do that on a piece of paper because usually they have like a big piece of paper and then they design what they are going to make and then they, when they make it, they bring their paper with them and then they look at the paper so they can design it like they drawed it on the paper." I think he is talking about making sure the outcome matches the design, but that's not really what either I or Teton are suggesting. Finally Andy says, "Maybe if you just start banging wood together and you didn't know what it was and you were just banging, like you didn't shape it before, and then when you were finished before you know it, you had a school made."

WHAT IS MUSIC? USING PATTERNS TO EXAMINE A FUNDAMENTAL QUESTION

June 2

June 2 is the last science class. I start class with a hand clap and ask if it is a pattern. All seem to say yes, but then I ask if it's rhythm and they also say yes, and Danping says it's rhythm but not pattern because it only happened once. To be a pattern, it would have to repeat again. Suni agrees with this. So does Meiying, but she does a simple repetition, and someone argues that this is a beat. Cory says whether or not it's a pattern depends as much on the "rests in between." There is a lot of argument about this. Alyosha and Suni say it depends on the regularity of the rests. Ricky and Thomas say that if there is at least two, it's a pattern.

An'gele suggests as an example of a pattern that a person grows from a tiny baby, larger and larger and larger, and then when the person is very old, they start growing smaller again. This is important, and we get back to it in a minute. For now, however, the children continue debating whether or not a beat is part of a pattern or *is* a pattern. Finally Cory says that pattern repeats and so does beat, therefore beat is a pattern.

Sakti has had her hand up for a while, and I call on her. She says that she disagrees with An'gele, she says that she doesn't think that as people get old they get small again. Danping and Emily both say that they do. Paula says not all of them. Cory says they shrink, and giggles. Shumshad says that he doesn't think that they go as small as a baby. I ask An'gele to repeat her claim. She says, "When you are a baby, you are maybe about this big and then you get bigger and bigger and bigger and bigger, when you get older, you sort of you loose your balance and you go like this [*hunches over*] and it looks like you are shrinking a little bit." Sakti and Emily continue to disagree. Sakti refers to her grandmother, who hasn't shrunk. I ask Sakti if it would be okay if we amended An'gele's pattern to *some* people. She nods yes. Emily, however, still disagrees, "It can't be a pattern if you're born about this big and you get bigger bigger bigger bigger until you get old and then you just shrink a little bit . . . ." I remind the children of an old pattern we talked about in the fall, of the bricks in the slide. I sketch it on the board to remind everyone. Then I continue, "It went bigger bigger bigger and you called that a pattern . . . you said that was a pattern because it went bigger bigger bigger, bigger? So how come it couldn't be a pattern, as a child gets bigger bigger bigger you know that's a pattern." This is like the two, four, six progression. I ask Sakti what she thinks. She says that it takes a long time for a baby to grow. I'm not sure if she doesn't want to call this a pattern because she thinks it takes too long to see a change or if her point is that the change is continuous—there are no discrete "bits" to form the units of the pattern. Suni says that taking a long time doesn't matter; it can still be a pattern. Emily says that she still disagrees with An'gele because even if old people do grow smaller, they still don't return to the size of babies. I ask her if she thinks that a person would have to return all the way back down to a baby's size for it to be a pattern—does it have to be a complete cycle? "Yeah she'd have to go small bigger bigger bigger bigger small bigger bigger bigger bigger small bigger bigger bigger small." I ask again about the pattern in the bricks or just about a pattern that continues to progress. Cory and Tity both don't think it's a pattern. Tity says, "It just goes up up up up." Suni and Danping do think it's a pattern. Danping says, "Well I think it's a pattern 'cause it keeps going up though." Abeni thinks it has to go up and then go back down.

> *Suni*: Well, um, what Abeni . . . well when it grows up and up, it doesn't have to stop, just like a new baby doesn't stop, see just like numbers, they always grow, they grow and they don't go smaller.
>
> *Emily*: They go one two three four five six seven eight nine ten but if they were to grow smaller, then they would go one two three four five six seven eight nine ten ten nine eight seven six five four three two one!
>
> *Teacher*: Right, and they don't they just keep one getting bigger and bigger, is numbers just getting bigger and bigger, is that a pattern? [*Yeses and nos.*]
>
> *Cory*: No, 'cause they never get smaller and smaller.
>
> *Suni*: Yes they can if you count them backwards [*different children are doing this from different starting places*].
>
> *Teacher*: Um, I heard what Emily said, she said it would be a pattern if you count backwards forwards backwards forwards, but is it a pattern if you just start at zero and count forever? [*Nos.*]
>
> *Suni*: [*Suni shakes his head.*] 'Cause you're just repeating it, repeating, just repeating it and that's a pattern 'cause it's repeating.
>
> *Emily*: Repeating what?
>
> *Suni*: Repeating like growing . . .
>
> *Benjamin*: Numbers.
>
> *Suni*: They keep going and that's a pattern too [*many are talking about this*], well that's a pattern too, numbers are patterns going backwards and forwards.
>
> *Shumshad*: I agree with Suni because see they're growing and growing . . . first it grows a little, then it grows a little more and then it grows a little more and that's a pattern.

Sueh-yen: Well I think the numbers . . . when you just go zero and up and forever is a pattern because every time, when you get to one thing, there's always a zero and then one two three four five six seven eight nine and then a zero and then one two three four five six seven eight nine and then a zero and the numbers are five or six or seven.

I end this part of class. I feel that through talking about pattern in such a number of different contexts we have come to examine quite thoughtfully what we mean by the word. We have done this also by examining examples of patterns—what the word means for different sorts of pattern's, whether musical, visual, or numerical—and by seeing how we could use patterns to construct other things. Examples of the latter are when the children composed music, when they worked on musical notation, when they talked about building a school.

I have one final place in which I would like the children and me to think about patterns and music. I had planned that today, the last science class, we would listen to birdsong. My idea in this is that birdsong varies in pitch and loudness in very complex ways which are hard to describe. I want to see first of all if the children would call these patterns and then how they would articulate the components of the pattern. I don't think this is a simple task, but it seems important, given the way that the children up to now have been defining pattern, beat, and rhythm. l want to know whether or not the children would call birdsong music, and what the criteria for music might be. We start by looking at some feathers and I tell a story, then we listen to birdsong. The birdsong is from the Peterson *Birding by Ear* (Walton & Whanson, 1989) tapes, out of which I have edited the talking.

The first song I play is of the cardinal. There are both the call and the song, and each is repeated three times. I ask if the children think that is music. Andy says yes. Emily says, "bird music." Other children are saying both yes and no. Thomas says that it is music because, "Well some people might think it's not, some people might think it's pattern or beat, I think it's music, it sounds good, it has beat, it has pattern and it seemed like it to me." I ask what music has that pattern and beat don't have alone. Thomas says that music doesn't have really big spaces. He uses an example from the tape, "At the beginning they have a peep peep peep; that was not music that was just the beginning."

Danping says that she thinks it was music because it had a pattern. I ask her if that is all it needs and she says no, it also needs rhythm and beat. Suni says that it doesn't have to have beat, "I don't think it had to have beat, but it did have a kind of pattern, it went chewww, cheww, chew chew chew, but it went like chewww, chewww, chew chew chew chew, chewww, chewwww, chew chew chew chew. When it went like that, I think that is a pattern 'cause it's repeating."

We listen to a meadowlark next. Tity says that she thought she could hear a pattern. I ask her what the pattern was, and she says that she can't say. So I ask how she knows it is a pattern then. Sueh-yen says because it repeats. I stay with Tity and ask her if she needs to be able to say how it goes to be able to call it a pattern. She says that she doesn't know. Suni does think it's a pattern and he articulates the sound that he thinks repeats. Alyosha doesn't think it matters if you can describe what repeats, just so that it does repeat. Abeni thinks that it is just beat, not music: "When they repeat that pawwk pawwk pawwwk pawwwk over and over again, I think that's a beat but I don't think it's music."

Next I ask how the children think birds make their sounds. Danping says that you'd have to test them to find out. Shumshad says, "I think that's their language because we have a language, because if there was a giant and we spoke their language and it was just like the birds . . . so those would be words that they are speaking, so it might be just like our language." I ask how we make sounds. Shumshad says from our brains. I ask if it's made in your brain: "You can't talk but you know what you talk about and your brain helps you a lot." To me this is a lot like the discussion of design as purposeful action last time. Birdsong, or language, is the result of design. Emily, Alyosha, and Ricky disagree with Shumshad. They claim that bird song comes from various parts of the mouth and throat—Alyosha, the uvula; and Ricky, the tongue.

Many start to talk about that. So I ask if you can make sound without talking. Thomas and Emily say yes, and Emily adds that she knows a person who has had her tonsils taken out and she can still talk. Alyosha says you need the thing in the back of your throat and your tonsils. An'gele says that you can't *talk* without your tongue but you can make noises. This is interesting—it's not what *you* mean by your noises, it's whether or not others can interpret them that constitutes talk. Andy agrees, and I ask him, "Where the noise come from, then?"

He says from your throat, but he indicates in your neck. Suni says that when you talk you can feel something in your neck but he can make a click with his tongue that he can't feel in his throat. Sueh-yen says that when he talks he can feel what he says. I ask him if he means he can feel the vibration. He says yes and then he does Suni's click. Everybody starts experimenting with that now and seeing if they can feel it in their throat. Some say they can, some say not. Andy says you can't because "it doesn't have anything to do with your neck or throat, it only has to do with your tongue and mouth."

I remind them that they had said that sound happens because something is hit and it vibrates; How does that relate to sound coming from us or from birds? Cory says he can feel it vibrating when he talks in his throat. I ask how they make it vibrate; they don't hit anything. Abeni says that her voice is vibrating. Alyosha says that the thing in the back of his mouth moves, when you scream it goes up and if you aren't so loud it goes up just a little bit. Andy says that he thinks when you scream your neck vibrates. He points to his voice box but calls it his tonsils. I ask if that means it's making the noise, or is it vibrating *because* of the noise? Andy says because it's making the noise. Suni says that "air waves push through your neck and then when it goes through this part, it makes a sound."

> *Teacher*: So the air waves moving though your neck vibrate and when it hits that part, it makes a sound.
>
> *Suni*: Uh huh.
>
> *Shumshad*: See, um, I don't think we should talk about this anymore, we are talking about birds we aren't talking about humans.
>
> *Teacher*: Okay do you have anything more to say about birds? How do you think birds make noise?
>
> *Shumshad*: Maybe same thing.
>
> *Teacher*: Like what Suni said the air moving through vibrates and . . .
>
> *Shumshad*: I think when you scream in your throat, it's not loud, see when you do it, it's not loud but when it moves [*he indicates out through his mouth*] I think it widens and then it makes the voice louder, that's what I think.
>
> *Teacher*: And is that how birds work?
>
> *Shumshad*: Um, maybe.
>
> *Teacher*: Do people think that birds make noises the same way that we make noise? (*Nos.*)

Abeni: I don't think that birds make sound the same way that we do because birds, you can't understand their words.

Danping: Yeah I kind of agree with Abeni because maybe they're not singing, maybe they're communicating.

Emily: Okay say this was our throat, it has a whole bunch of stuff in it like the bones and stuff, then there's a little thing here that helps you talk and then this is a bird's throat and it doesn't have anything circled so it can't speak, so they have a certain thing that makes them talk but they don't talk like we do 'cause it has a different thing than we do.

Teacher: So the inside of their throat is different, is that what you are saying?

Emily: Yeah 'cause if they talk different from us, then they've got to have something different in their throat.

CONCLUSION

In this last class the children argue about three possible examples of pattern and design—a child growing, numbers, and birdsong. In all three instances, they apply and therefore test their working definitions of pattern, beat, rhythm, and design. Within the context of the child growing and numbers, they seem to be continuing their contemplation of the meanings of the word pattern. There is a sense of their weighing meaning against example and thinking critically about both. In thinking about birdsong, my attempt to get them to think about pattern in this context seems to cause the children to juxtapose music to language. In this instance, through being asked to think about the meaning of pattern and music in this new context, they thought about the phenomenon— the context itself, birdsong—and argued that it wasn't music at all, but rather language. They reassessed the phenomenon, the context.

Many people, in writing about science and about doing scientific research, write about patterns and the role that patterns play.[5] Patterns are constructs that arise through descriptions. They are characterized by variables, constants, and operations. They make connections, see similarities, describe relationships, create regularities. They are made: created, imposed, manipulated, by people through selective vision. Seeing patterns is a simplification; it dichotomizes reality into the regular and the irregular, the explained and the unexplained. Using patterns involves an interplay between the regular and irregular. Explaining phenomena is often done through correlating patterns, in which case this interplay is especially important. It becomes a test of the patterns: every use (application) of a pattern is a test of the validity of its simplifications.

Patterns order observations, and can be used to explain those observations. The function of correlating multiple patterns is to explain. Because they contain variables, patterns can be applied to other observations in the hope of ordering or explaining them. However, to write about the role of pattern in science presupposes a role for irregularity. Both seeing and making patterns is compelling in science because patterns cause one to see the totality of a phenomenon in new ways. The parts of the phenomenon that don't fit the pattern become both invisible and are thrown into sharp relief. I think pattern is compelling because the act of bringing order to disorder is infused with romantic mystery and with power. But the parts that are left in disorder are even more mysterious and maintain the phenomenon's own power! The phenomenon asserts its own reality through its irregularities: the components that exist and which we can't explain. We assert *our* reality through the imposition of patterns, the recognition of regularities, and the creation of explanations. The dialectic between the person and the phenomenon, the pattern and the irregularities, the explained and the unexplained drives the scientist. The imposition of theories— generalizations, patterns—enables seeing the phenomenon in new ways because of the abstracting qualities of the process and the fact that the process is situated in the flow, the activity of applying the patterns. When the qualities of the phenomenon that don't fit the pattern become important, the assessment of the phenomenon or the pattern itself should be revised.

It's because pattern exists as an overlay on the surface of the real phenomenon that irregularity and regularity coexist. There is more to the phenomenon than can be described by the pattern. Recognition of that causes a scientist to apply existing patterns to new phenomena and to discover new patterns. The scientist is the creative agent in the dialectic between pattern and irregularity which intersects within the phenomenon. There are two different ways that patterns are looked at and used. A person can look at the pattern and the object through the pattern, using the pattern to give one new ways to see that object in order to continue contemplating the object. The pattern is a tool to enable seeing the object itself. Our use and creation of pattern in the fall is for this purpose; or the pattern is a tool for doing something with the object. Our exploration of patterns in the spring in looking at sound and music involves this. This means that the irregularities, the features of the object that don't fit the pattern or have been generalized so that their particulars are lost are probably not looked at again. The first stance suggests that the irregularities will sooner or later *be* seen and will cause the pattern to be revised, reformulated, thrown away. We return to the first way of using patterns when we embed our exploration in an examination of music—what do patterns tell us about music, what don't they tell us that we want to express? I think this is contained in the writings of Dewey (*How We Think*), Dewey and Bentley (*Knowing and the Known*), and Levi-Strauss (*The Savage Mind*) on common-sense versus scientific ways of knowing and thinking: Imposed patterns or generalizations in common-sense ways of being are used as tools for doing things, rather than as sources of contemplation in themselves— neither contemplation of the pattern nor of the new way that it presents of looking at the thing that it's applied to. This is also described by Polanyi in *The Tacit Dimension*: when an object or an idea becomes a tool used to do something else, the tool is no longer examined for itself. There is in fact a dialectic between the two which, in effect, causes the continual reassessment and reevaluation of the pattern itself.

If there is an interplay between the two ways of using patterns, this interplay is framed by, and caused by, a person's purposes. A person's purpose causes him or her to *use* the patterns as tools. This use of patterns for a purpose forces the continuous reevaluation and evolution of those patterns. I weigh the qualities of the phenomenon that I've used to structure my actions, through an examination of those actions against the results. The results are framed by the assumptions of the patterns, but also those qualities not contained within the pattern—the irregularities. This is a sort of a statement of the experimental method. I think it is demonstrated in what the children do in the second part of the unit on music, particularly when they are asked to explain some observation. They apply patterns experimentally in an attempt to predict outcomes and hence to explain those outcomes.

I also think that generalizations in science are a form of metaphor. As such, they define comparatively, by saying something is like something else and unlike something different. They act to highlight certain features of whatever is being classified but obscure other features. Any phenomenon is a continuum of qualities, but in order to name these qualities they have to be separated out, pulled out of the context of the whole. But because these labels are in reality only a facet of the whole out of context, the act of labeling refutes itself when seen within the whole again. In other words, other features of the whole contradict this partitioning, if you can see them. But the creation of the categories with which we "see" phenomena or even people is the source and fundamental of hegemony, of manifesting a power structure/relationship between phenomena, and it's only by developing a sense of critical consciousness—recognizing the partial quality of those categories—that we can "see" anything else in the continuum. The point is that these categories and generalizations can be inclusive metaphors—defining what is within to exclude what is without— but they also have the potential to be generative metaphors—helping us to see in new ways, to be starting points in our explorations of the phenomena—that enable science to be a creative act (Schon, 1984).

The children in the course of this unit have engaged in seeing patterns (in the xylophones, rubber bands, guitar, and the sounds that each makes). Seeing patterns in these contexts means reducing the whole of the phenomena into parts—seeing variables that can be correlated. Because seeing these variables was intertwined with seeing the patterns and correlating the patterns (these last two are fundamentally questions), the children became engaged in developing patterned ways of interacting with the music and sound and with each other. They developed a method—a patterned way of acting and interacting around a mutual purpose.[6] This is at the core of community: shared purposes, shared ways of acting, shared ways of talking. It also comes about through knowing each other: another aspect of acting in patterns—for example, when Suni or Emily speak others know to an extent what to expect.

When asked to examine sound within the context of the question, "What is music?" the children again reduced music into variables and began to argue about the meanings of those variables. Defining the meanings of those words—the variables—meant defining what they are and are not, what different words share with each other and what they don't. Finally, it meant weighing the developing meanings of the variables against the phenomenon, music. To define music with solely the variables the children explored—beat, rhythm, and pattern— excludes many qualities of music, tone, and aesthetics, for example.

The children debated the usefulness of their variables to capture what they thought was important about music. Often by trying to apply just their variables they found that this did not describe what they wanted. They thought about both how music is composed of their variables and also about how it is more than just those variables.

Through these discussions, the children worked on both the development of a language as well as "ways" of talking—acceptable ways to present and debate their ideas. Aspects of this process parallel those of a discourse community. Unlike a discourse community, however, I saw my role as teacher to be one of preventing the development of conventions and hierarchical relationships of power between the children. I try to keep the conversations of the community from reaching closure by keeping the referent point of discussion external to the relationships between the children—the referent point was what our discussion tells us about the phenomena, not just what use can we put our knowledge to. In this way the community remained dynamic—its purposes, questions, methods evolving. In effect, the community formed through the medium of our exploration of science. The science was not an end point to the community, but rather the opposite: the science was a tool in the formation of the community. This, of course, was not my intent. My intent was that the children acquire "habits of action for coping with reality" (Rorty, 1991). This, however, can be regarded as at the core of a community[7] and expressions of, conversations about, this activity, its result.[8] The development of patterns of acting—of method—is a manifestation of and a tool in the construction of community.

In the course of their conversations about music, the children came to discuss as noun and as verb the meanings of the words *pattern* and the word *design*. I felt the children reflected on the meaning of the word "method," although this was never explicit, in a number of contexts. The discussion of method—purposeful action—grew out of the discussion of design, which in turn grew from the discussion of pattern. The three are linked.

Finally, in the context of a discussion of the physical growth of people, numbers, and birdsong, the children used their ideas of the variables of music and patterns to assess whether or not those three things were patterns or music or designs. In doing this, they again thought anew about the definitions of those words and about the classification, the nature of the phenomena themselves.

NOTES

1. The teaching in this chapter occurs in the same first-second grade combination as the previous chapter. For a complete description of the school and class as well as a list of the children's countries of origin and pseudonyms, please refer to Appendix 1 and 2.

2. Pattern blocks are plastic or wooden geometric shapes which are sized and proportioned so that they fit together nicely; it is possible to make one shape, for instance the red trapezoid, out of a number of other arrangements of the other shapes—one triangle and one diamond, for example.

3. Lakoff, G. (1987), *Women, fire and dangerous things: What categories reveal about the mind.* Lakoff, G. & Johnson, M. (1980), *Metaphors we live by.* Polanyi, M. (1966), *The tacit dimension.* Derrida, J. (1976), *Of grammatology.* Moi, T. (1985), Helene Cixous: An imaginary utopia. Norris, C. (1982), *Deconstruction: Theory and practice.* Kristeva, J. (1986), The system and the speaking subject. Moi, T. (1985), Marginality and subversion: Julia Kristeva. Moi, T. (1985), Introduction.

4. Stevens (1974); Thompson (1961).

5. For more information on the explanatory and comparative powers of patterns in science, the following books are particularly helpful: *Patterns in nature;* Stevens (1974), and *On growth and form;* Thompson (1961).

6. Note that this is a different way of viewing the meaning of method in science from that commonly cited in philosophical works about the nature of science, for example, Rorty (1991), *Objectivity, relativism and truth: Philosophical papers,* "methodical: . . . to have criteria for success laid down in advance" (p.11). In a social sense, I am agreeing with this definition, however: to successfully communicate with each other, the criteria for interaction must often be laid down in advance.

7. For example, see Marx (1983), Theses on Feuerbach.

8. "Dewey. . . *any* philosophical system is going to be an attempt to express the ideals of *some* community's way of life" (Rorty, 1991).

CHAPTER 4

Knowing

The focus in this chapter is, in a sense, on me—the things that I do in the class and why I do them. That is not to say that the previous chapters were not also about that. I think that in the stories that have preceded, I wished to communicate that my role was both proactive and reactive. I chose the science that we were exploring in class, and I responded to the children's ways of shaping that science. However, this rarely meant a fundamental alteration of my original choices. In this chapter, I have to choose between the science and maintaining the classroom discourse. There are many fundamental choices that I have made, moral, emotional, and aesthetic—about how I manipulate the children into interacting with each other as well as with the science. I hold those values more important than engaging the children in the science. In many instances in this chapter, I recast the science so that I can maintain my values about the discourse.

In the other chapters, I make the argument that the classroom community is shaped both by the ways that I encourage the children to interact with each other (respect for each other and each other's ideas) and by what I feel is a genuine engagement the children have with the science. I have emphasized the latter until now—that it is the sense of shared purpose that enables the construction of ways of interacting. This is not entirely true, since the community of the classroom is dynamic, and its purposes and focuses shift and reshape themselves as our explorations evolve. The constant is the way the children interact with each other. Because I require the children to act in a certain way, the focus of the community can change without the community dissolving. The children value each other and so they value expressions of new ideas, which become new purposes as more and more children participate in exploring them. (Remember, these ideas are expressed primarily as questions and assertions—this enables exploration and discovery, method and purpose.) In the classes in this chapter there is a greater tension in this choice for me between the science and the discourse. Often, in order to maintain my ideals about the discourse, I reshape the science radically so that we can respect each other's ideas. In order to maintain the sense of a community with a shared purpose, I abandon the science that I want to be doing (exploring simple machines) and allow the children to shape a new topic (the solar system). Finally when I want to stay with one particular topic in the science and not allow the children to reshape it, I invite conflict in the class, either by introducing discrepant theories myself or by allowing children to argue ideas out. It is a measure of the strength of the children's valuing of each other that this conflict does not disrupt the community. I do this rather than explicitly telling the children science. To do otherwise seems a violation of my ideas and goals about the development of a community in the class. I am also uncomfortable with the role of manipulating the children into acquiring knowledge that I have already pinpointed. This seems a violation of my ideals about respecting and valuing the children. It makes me feel that I am not a member of the community with the children. I think the tension this induces is, at a fundamental level, the source of my discomfort with the classes I teach.

A DESCRIPTION OF THE UNIT ON THE SOLAR SYSTEM

In this chapter I write about a unit I taught in third grade on the solar system. This unit developed because of the line of inquiry that the children and I evolved during an exploration of simple machines. We went from machines to the solar system because of an experiment that we had done from the children's science textbook using inclined planes. In this experiment there was a lot of confusion about why the weights of objects being pulled up inclined planes of different slopes would differ. From this we started talking about gravity—what gravity is, where it comes from, what its effects are. From gravity we moved to the moon and planets, thinking about gravity as we talked about the motions of the planets intertwined with talking about the planets, themselves because that was what the children wanted to do.

If I think about *content*, this unit had four stages. The first was its beginning, working with simple machines. That was when we started talking about gravity. In the second stage we started to talk about the bodies of the solar system, but this was so that we could understand gravity better and could then get back to machines. In the third stage I realized we weren't getting back to machines, so I let the children take over choosing the direction of the class explorations of the solar system. I would call this part of the unit "developing a shared body of knowledge and language and ways of talking about the solar system." It enables the final stage: the children's conversations and sharings about the planets in the third stage make the conversations about the workings of the solar system possible. In these final conversations the children return to talking about gravity.

Talking about *content* as the only expression of what actually happened in these classes obscures the emotional and intellectual groping that shaped this content. Writing about this unit is writing about curriculum construction; a construction by me and the children. As we construct the curriculum I articulate my beliefs and values— through this process I give shape to what was ill-defined, amorphous, part of a continuum. The first and most important statement that can be made about these beliefs is that this construction/articulation occurs while we were acting, embedded in that context (Heidegger, 1962; Schwab, 1976). The beliefs articulated are done so reactively—in reaction to the things that happened in class—as well as proactively— in order to shape the things that will happen. They are defined by a historical and projected context. What is done in class is not an *illustration* of preexisting values; what is done in class *is* those values. I am stating this strongly on purpose. Let me give an example to explain why.

To say a teacher respects children has no meaning without giving substance to that respect; without illustrating how the teacher acts on that respect and the children are able to act within that respect. Giving substance to an amorphous statement like "I respect children" involves instantaneous choices and actions made emotionally as well as intellectually and which appear rational and intellectually defensible retrospectively because they leave historical artifacts—the content described in the previous paragraph. Values and beliefs such as respect for children are *known* things, but this knowing often isn't articulated until suddenly their embodiment appears before a person.[1] I am not saying that this knowing is without intellectual qualities—it has those, but it also has intimately intertwined emotional and even sensual/ aesthetic qualities.

WHAT DO YOU MEASURE WHEN YOU WEIGH SOMETHING? FINDING THE FUNDAMENTAL QUESTIONS

February 27

I started this "unit" in third grade[2] on machines at the end of January. Up until the class before the class that I am about to describe, we had been exploring the terrain of simple machines and definitions of the word *machine*. In the class before this, we did an experiment in the science textbook about inclined planes in which a weight attached to a spring scale is pulled up a short inclined plane and a long inclined plane. The height that each plane is raised to is kept constant, as is the object weight being pulled, but because the length of the board varies, the steepness of the slope changes. This means that the effective weight being pulled changes—the shallower slope gives the lowest weight, the greatest weight is from pulling straight up. This change in apparent weight is a measure of the work being done to lift the weight—more work for more weight or, conversely, the efficiency of the machine at helping decrease the work that you are doing. Of course, all of this neglects frictional pull on the thing being dragged.

This experiment is, I think, pretty confusing because of the use of the two different boards—it's not obvious that what you have done when you change boards is change the slope—rather, children say that they've changed the length that they drag the weight along. Also embedded in making sense of this experiment is understanding what you are actually measuring when you measure the weight of something—where that weight comes from. Weight (of something moving at the same relative speed to its surroundings) is derived from the interaction of the object's mass and gravity, and gravity is also a function of mass. So the object itself has its own gravitational field, too. Gravity is a measure of an attractive interaction between two bodies determined by mass if the bodies are stationary with respect to each other. At least that's the way that I think about it (I think about the relationships $F = MA$ and $F = G(M_1 M_2 / r^2)$, in which F is force, M is mass, A is acceleration, G is the gravitational constant and r is the distance separating the two bodies, and think about the way those fit together in pictures I construct in my head. I do think about how space around a body is warped by a gravitational field and how objects with less mass fall down the contour lines of that warped field as analogous to a glass of milk spilling in bed—these three images fundamentally shape the science for the next month.

It occurs to me here that I should say something about my background in thinking about the science that is about to come up in this story. As a child, I was absolutely fascinated by astronomy. I read anything I could find on this subject, primarily the sort of "popular" science books written by Isaac Azimov or George Gamow. I think in this I had a lot in common with some of the little boys in this class, particularly Yong Sun. In college I continued to take a number of classes in astronomy. My very favorite class in college was in astrophysics. Astrophysics was the place were classical physics finally started to make sense to me, I think primarily because in that class there was an assumed understanding of differential equations and because of the kinds of understandings mechanics were used to construct. For example, it never made sense to me to think of acceleration as velocity divided by time, but it does make sense to me to think of it as the *change* of velocity over time. Then constant acceleration becomes a special case. And this made sense to me, because I could think about it in terms of orbits of planets, or more accurately, I could deconstruct what I knew about the orbitals of planets and come up with equations from mechanics and suddenly I could see how they worked. I really liked this feeling.

When I went on to teach, especially teaching in my field, in crystallography and optics, I taught a course on Earth Science that was a "service course." It was a full-year course with extremely high enrollment, and it was the major way our department funded itself, so every professor taught it. It was roughly divided into a half-year of geology and a half-year of atmospheric science and astronomy. I always taught the atmospheres and astronomy half.

At the end of the last third grade class, I had asked which experiment was easiest. Most people replied that pulling straight up was easiest because it was the simplest experimentally. We started with a recap of that. Although most children thought that pulling the weights straight up was easiest, Selamawit thought the short board was easier because the distance pulled was shortest, and Yong Sun thought the long board was easiest because it required the least amount of work. He knew this because the numbers for this experiment were the smallest. The trick here is what the numbers mean and that's what I ask Hamal. He replies, "It means whatever you weigh, the number, it means that's how much it weighs."

I ask John and Daniel what they think. All agree with Hamal that the number signifies the weight of the object lifted, so I ask, "But when you did it on the long board you got a different number from the short board and it was different again when you lifted it, do you actually think it changed how much it weighed?" This to me is the key question to seeing how they are making sense of the experiment and also leading them on to try to work on making sense of what they have done. It's my confrontation of what I suspect is a place where they have *stopped* having it make sense, where they are either being passive or trusting or are invoking magic. The children answer my questions with both yeses and nos. Yong Sun yells out, "Always weighs the same!" I choose, however, to call on Joey to comment on this rather than recognizing Yong Sun, and then quiz Joey to push the class on this. I chose to ask Joey to speak for two reasons: I am checking him out, I would like to bring him out in class more since I think he knows a lot. I also don't want Yong Sun to talk yet—Yong Sun is recognized as knowing a lot and I want to hear more of what everyone is thinking before I focus the argument. That is how I use Yong Sun: to focus or redirect an argument. To excuse my not recognizing Yong Sun, I remind the class about our hands-up rule. (This is a convenience, this rule, in which children need to have their hands up and be recognized to speak; I use it as a controller in many ways involving social interactions, content, and personal relationships with the different children. It's rare for me to cite it for Yong Sun.) Then I call on Joey. He says that it always weighs the same, but I push, "So why are the numbers different?"

> *Joey*: Because when you have to pull them up different heights, 'cause when you lift it, it goes all the way down [*the pointer on the spring scale*], as much as it weighs, but if you pull it up something, it won't say as much as it weighs.
> *Teacher*: So if you pull it up different heights it weighs more or less?
> *Joey*: Um . . . less.
> *Teacher*: But it actually doesn't weigh more or less, it stays the same weight?
> *Joey*: Um-hum. . . .

Teacher: Why does it seem to weigh different?

Joey: Because you're not pulling it up the same thing every time.

Teacher: Oh, so it has something to do with what you're pulling it up. . . .

Joey: Yeah.

Teacher: What do you think, Kristin?

Kristin: I disagree. I think it's different, 'cause I can prove it. . . .

Kristin points to the numbers that her group has recorded on the chart. For one experiment, they are very different; her group measured 150 grams and when she did it alone she measured 250 grams. I had watched this group do the experiments quite closely, because Kristin presents a social problem in the class and in particular in her group— Kristin wants to be "in charge" and her group won't let her. Anyway, they got very different numbers because they measured differently. This is obviously a valid issue in scientific experimentation. I let Kristin explain what the group had done and then I asked for comments. Ricardo responds that he knows that the object keeps the same weight and the apparent weight change in this case is "a mistake." I table this (we return to it at various times later because it is important: knowing whether or not to think about or reject an unexpected or out-of-the-ordinary answer is really important in experimental science) and redirect the conversation back to comparing the numbers *between* experiments.

Teacher: So the difference . . . when you weighed it on the long board it weighed 70 grams and on the short board it weighed 110 grams and when you lifted it straight up it weighed 160 grams and that was just because you made mistakes?

Ricardo: Uh no, 'cause like with the first time we got three ounces but it was really supposed to be two and a half ounces.

Teacher: *That* was a mistake. But what about the difference between on the long board you got three ounces and on the short board, I can't see, you got four ounces and lifting you got five and a half or six ounces? What about the differences between the different experiments?

Ricardo: Oh 'cause one takes the most force and one takes the middle and one takes the least force. So . . .

> *Teacher*: So the numbers aren't just weight, they are also a measure of the force? Do the numbers have something to do with the force?
>
> *Ricardo*: Yeah.

Now suddenly we have here introduced an *IMPORTANT* word, but whenever this happens I know that it's also a magic word, and suddenly I get all stressed out trying to keep the conversation centered on examining *that* word in *this* context. It's like when Bullwinkle pulls a rabbit out of his hat and it's a lion. In one sense he's pulled off the trick, but it's starting to go completely out of control. I feel like with this conversation, which is flowing and has its own rhythm and which I am shaping by following, I suddenly have to stop the waves, hold it in one place. But this isn't all true, because we would work on what the word *force* means as it is applied by the children—the class is still moving and evolving. So there is this *tension*, and in some sense *force* is a truly magic word. What does it signify, anyway? It is a word we invoke to silence questions: a rabbit in a hat that makes relationships between other real data, measurements, and observations work. Forces aren't *things* we can talk about directly. We can only talk around them.

Rather than going with the flow and letting Ricardo keep on talking, I call on Joey for comments. Joey is of course in a different place, "Um it can't change its weight because it's not a thing that's living," which is a wonderful statement that I would normally draw out, but not now because we've *got* to talk about force now. I recapitulate the question-answer dialogue: "What do you think about what Ricardo said about why the numbers are changing?" But I get no real response. I try Mwajuma. She responds that the object pulled did weigh differently on the two boards; not because it really was a different weight, but because "you pull it more [*on the short board*] and [*on the long board*] you don't pull it so much." The key phrases in this statement are around pulling the object and around differences in magnitude of pulling. That *is* a definition of force, but rather than relating this to the change in slope of the two boards, Mwajuma connects it to the length of the boards and again Hamal restates this, "When you pull it on the long board you pull it longer and when you pull it on the short board, um, you pull it um, in not that much time and when you lift it, all you do is lift it up."

I stop the conversation at that point and have them redo the experiment just using the long board and dragging the weights up a slope constructed with different numbers of books (six, three, zero—pull along the flat board) and also lift them straight up. Between this experiment and the class having a conversation about the results, a week has passed. This happened because Sylvia Rundquist, who teaches subjects other than math and science, wanted to have the children read in their textbooks about simple machines, and she also had one class period with them to talk about wheels. In the middle of this class on wheels, I started to think about how hinges are very similar to wheels, so that I didn't understand how they were different. After class I tried to tell Sylvia about this and said that I thought the difference was around the perspective you took on what was moving relative to what was stationary. After talking about this for a while I went home and had this insight that both wheels and hinges were reducible to inclined planes. That's why they seemed so similar to me. Then I started thinking about the other simple machines as reducible to inclined planes. This was getting me very excited, because all those vector diagrams I used to just memorize were starting to seem like they might make sense. I had always thought of each of the simple machines as unconnected before this. This seemed to me what I *really* wanted to do with the children in class—explore this idea of connectedness.

So finally in class we come back to talking about this second inclined plane experiment a full week later on March 10. I start by reviewing the problem with the children and then having them take a couple of minutes to discuss their results in their groups before starting the conversation. Dembe is the first to present her group's numbers, "We got 100 grams and 3 and 1/2 ounces, oh, we got 110 grams or 4 ounces with six books and three books we got 80 and we noticed that each time we used less books we got less ounces or grams and so it doesn't weigh as much. . . . Lifting it weighed more because you have to pick it up and lifting it you used energy and the weights are very heavy . . . because when you're using a board you can just lift it up on the board and you can lay it on there instead of having to pick it up yourself." Ricardo, however, continues to argue that it's easier to pick the weights straight up: "I think lifting is still easier 'cause all you have to do is wrap a spring scale 'round the things, put it on, and then lift it."

Timmy clearly disagrees and starts a discussion with Ricardo. I remind them again about the hands-up rule—this happens a lot in this class and is a measure of the level of animation of the discussion going on—and then call on Kristin. She says that she agrees with Ricardo, that it's easiest just to lift the object rather than drag it up any of the inclined planes. But when I ask her for her reasons, she is back to talking about the experimental conditions rather than the actual results of the experiment itself. So again I ask, "But how come if it's easiest it weighs the most?" Kristin starts to answer but Dembe cuts her off, "It uses more energy!" [*Another magic word!*]

> *Teacher*: It uses more energy to lift it?
> *Dembe*: Yeah, because like for example on the board you can just slide it instead of having to lift it.
> *Timmy*: Yeah, but . . .
> *Teacher*: Hands up, . . . Timmy?
> *Timmy*: Yeah, but you have to get all the stuff ready with that after you've done the rest you just pick it up . . . now you don't have to lay anything down, you just do it!
> *Dembe*: She's not talking about that she's talking about how come it weighs more when you lift it.
> *Timmy*: Because, because you're just pointing it down you're just pointing it down, that's all you're doing!!

Timmy gets very excited when he talks in science class. He also gets all tongue-tied with his ideas. He does a lot of thinking out loud— he seems to come to class with quite a good store of outside knowledge on the various topics that we talk about but not to have thought about them in the ways that I like to try to encourage in the class, where connections between ideas and between ideas and observations are important. I put quite a lot of pressure on him in many classes to work to reconstruct his knowledge and understandings to enlarge their applicability and the connections between the things that he knows. I do this primarily for two reasons. He does do his thinking out loud so that other children can participate in it, and he does this quite happily. He seems to enjoy it when I push and pull on him and his thinking and to enjoy it when the other children join in. I don't mean to imply that he is playing a game with the discourse and the content in the class, because that would be far from the truth. He is very passionate about his ideas but he seems to enjoy the stimulus of the class' discussions and challenges. I feel that my relationship with him is quite special. We like each other a lot. One thing that is interesting is that while I really value his chance-taking and mistake-making in the class, Sylvia, listening to the conversations in the class, labels his ideas "misconceptions." I respond to her that I think that those are things that are constructed in the class through the discourse that Timmy and I engage in in the class. I think this is interesting because it illustrates the subtlety of what it means to participate in the loops of logic that the children are articulating. I am detailing this right now because of Timmy's big role in the next few classes.

I should also probably say some things about Yong Sun, because in this particular class he says some very surprising (to me, anyway) things. Yong Sun does a great deal of reading and talking about science outside of class. He has told me that he and a number of other little Korean boys apparently get together after school and read books on science. He seems to know a lot about chemistry—atoms, planets, and astronomy, but with big holes in their understandings. For example, he seemed to know about stellar evolution, but not what the sun was made up of or how it generated heat and light. Those concepts are rather intimately tied. I normally count on using him in class discussions to feed in bits of scientific information when I need them to goose a conversation along. In this class, he plays a role much more similar to Timmy's usual role—he takes a stance that is only partially okay and I generate a discussion which challenges it. However, he responds in ways that are very different from Timmy. He is clearly accustomed to being "right" in science.

> *Teacher*: Because *what*, Timmy? I didn't understand that.
> *Timmy*: You're just bringing it down, like bringing the spring down. It's not sideways [*he indicates movement along the board with his hands*], it's not like this, it's just going straight down. . . . [*He is talking about the spring in the spring scale and also about the pointer, a part of the scale which indicates the weight. This is the first hint of a connection to the concept of gravity. I had planned class discussion to include this.*]
> *Teacher*: So then you could just pull it up the board, if it weighs less you can pull it easier. . . .
> *Timmy*: No, gravity pulls it down and it will weigh more.
> *Teacher*: Yong Sun?

> *Yong Sun:* I think Timothy's confused 'cause gravity doesn't pull it
> down, the weights pull it down.
> *Jin:* *Plus* gravity!
> *Teacher:* What did you say, Yong Sun, say that again?
> *Yong Sun:* Gravity does not pull it down, the weights pull it down.
> *Timmy:* Yeah but plus it, plus gravity does, and those aren't weights
> [*they're washers in plastic bags.*]
> *Yong Sun:* Gravity makes you fall or something like that. Gravity, it
> doesn't pull things down. . . . [*Children start yelling, "Yes it
> does, yes it does."*] *Look!* Is gravity pulling this down [*pen in
> hand*]?

Timmy yells out, "You're holding it!" and others chime in, "Yeah!
Yeah!" Dembe and Timmy make the connection back to the experiment
and claim that it's the scale that's holding the weight and gravity is
pulling it down against the scale. Everyone continues to yell at Yong
Sun until Jin says, "If there isn't any gravity then if you drop it, it will
just go in the air." Everyone agrees but Yong Sun, "We're not talking
about gravity, we're talking about how much it *weighs*." Jin counters,
"But if there's no gravity when you lift it . . . then it will weigh less!"
At this point Yong Sun starts to get offended. So I interrupt and ask,
"So why does it weigh anything? Why does it . . . what are you
measuring when you weigh it?"

> *Yong Sun:* You're measuring how much it weighs and how much
> force it uses.
> *Teacher:* How much force it uses to do what?
> *Yong Sun:* Like if you pull something that's heavy then it just will use
> more energy and that's using more force.

Of course, what Yong Sun just said is a description of gravity, he
just isn't connecting his "force" with the force of gravity. I suspect this
happens because of the way books talk of gravity as if it were another
property of an object, as if it were a "thing." I could have chosen at this
point to work with Yong Sun to make that connection, but instead I
return to Timmy. I do this because both children are saying correct
things and both of them need to connect what they are saying together.
I need to keep them engaged with each other and also work to have
their ideas converge. It is important for me that members of the class

work together on making sense of this topic. This means using children who have interesting things to say to stimulate others. In this process holes in their thinking are often exposed and the "working together" becomes increasingly genuine.[3] I ask Timmy what he thinks now, and he responds that he still thinks that gravity has something to do with it, that " gravity is helping it to stay on the floor, it's not just the weight that is on it." Then the class starts talking about how if there were no gravity the desk would float. I turn this to a discussion of whether or not this would mean that it would have no weight. This is an important concept—to differentiate between weight and mass. I think the root of the confusion in this part of the conversation is that the children are unwilling to say that something that exists, that is and remains an object, has no weight because they have not learned to differentiate weight from mass.

> *Timmy*: Yeah, no I'm not saying that it wouldn't weigh anything I'm just saying that gravity's helping it to stay on the ground, it's when it's hanging down, it's heading toward that way so . . . just like when you drop something, like when you drop it, the gravity's pulling it down, you don't feel it pull it down but it's pulling it down, if there were no gravity when I dropped it, it would stay right up.

Now Alice makes an interesting comment. She says, "You know how Dembe is standing up? That's gravity that's helping her stand up." This seems to me to be similar to the observations about how a person can hold an object up despite the force of gravity, that there is a balance between the things that we can do—moving, standing, picking things up—the force of gravity and properties of ourselves, the ways that we are constructed. This gets picked up and amplified when Dembe and then Amina start talking about gravity as a tug-of-war and will again be returned to (by Alice) in a subsequent class in which she will ask "How can birds fly?" I turn to her and ask, "How is gravity helping her stand up, I thought gravity would pull her down?"

> *Alice*: Well I mean help her stay on the ground because if she wasn't on the ground then she would be floating up in the air somewhere.

Amina: I have a comment for Yong Sun, Dembe, and Jin . . . Jin and
Timothy. I agree with them and I have something . . . I agree
with them because if I jumped up, I would be up in space, I
would be up and floating, I would be, well actually, your cup
would be floating, the book would be floating, everything would
be floating and we would be like doing our studies up there and
Kristin would be drawing. . . .

Timmy: She'd be drawing upside down!

Amina: And there'd be no way for us to stay on the ground we'd have
to have something hold us, like a rope or something.

Teacher: So are you saying that if there were no gravity that things
wouldn't weigh anything?

Amina: They would just be floating up in the air.

Ricardo: They'd be floating . . .

Amina: I don't understand what you're meaning, Yong Sun, I mean if
you, if I just hold a book, you're holding the book, you're
holding it, but if I don't, if you just drop it . . . your book, it
just . . .

Yong Sun: Wait a minute, wait a minute, are you saying that without
gravity this doesn't weigh anything?

Timmy says that yes this is true; in space, things don't weight anything.
There is no gravity and they weigh nothing. He read this in Florida at
the Kennedy Space Center. Others, however, think they will still weigh
something, it just might be less.

I summarize, "Okay, it seems to me Yong Sun is saying that if
there was no gravity, things would still weigh something? Is that right,
Yong Sun? And other people are saying that if there were no gravity
things wouldn't weigh anything. Is that true are people saying that?"
The children yell both yeses and nos. I call on Dembe, who has very
patiently had her hand up through all the yelling. Dembe states that she
agrees with Timothy and Yong Sun. Kristin turns in surprise and asks
her why.

Dembe: Because gravity is part of this because you know when we're
lifting this it [*the weights on the spring scale*], it's pulling it
down and also because if you're holding it, the gravity won't be
pulling it down that much because it's still going up, but gravity

is still pulling it. It's like um, tug-of-war? When you're pulling it
and the gravity is pulling it. . . .

Teacher: You're using force against it?

Dembe: Yeah!

Amina: You can't do that, you can't have a tug-of-war with gravity.

Teacher: Why do you say that?

Amina: Well if there's a rope and there's one side, well there's just
one person against gravity . . . the person would win . . . so that
you can make things go down, you can make things go up, like
hold it, that makes it go up I mean but if you let go, it will fall
but gravity just lets things go down, it doesn't let things float, all
it does is make things go down, all it does is let things go down
and it can't move the rope unless you throw it up in the air.

Teacher: So are you saying that if you hold something up in your
hands, gravity is no longer working?

Yong Sun: Yeah, it's working.

Teacher: Dembe, why did you say "tug-of-war?"

Dembe: Because tug-of-war is like you're, if you have a rope and one
person is pulling it, okay, for example, one person is pulling on
my right hand and the other person is pulling my left hand and
of course Kristin would win because gravity is pulling it down
but she's pulling it up and she's a lot stronger than me. . . .

At this point Dembe and I have to stifle some interruptions. I remind
everyone that they need to put their hands up to talk, and then finally
Dembe continues, "I mean that, I'm not even done, Timothy, I mean
that like gravity if you're pulling . . . okay, for example, you have
Joey's shoe and then somebody is pulling it but gravity is pulling it
down and you're pulling it up and you would win, of course." Suddenly
I felt that I had had enough—I think the idea of gravity as a piece of a
tug-of-war is extremely important, but there are too many other things
going on. I also don't like it when the children seem to be just arguing
in general rather than arguing ideas. Other children are not a part of
this. I want the whole of the class focused before we continue with a
central idea to the concept of gravity. When Timmy started to respond
("Then why'd you just say—") I stop him ("Hands up!!") and change
the subject, "Kristin, are you ready? [*Kristin has been drawing a
picture on the board that she wants to use to present an idea to the
class.*] Can you show us what you drew?" (Fig. 4.1.)

Figure 4.1

Kristin: Well see on the moon here, a man can walk and he can jump
   up and down but on the moon there's no gravity so if he went to
   the bottom of the moon and just stood there he wouldn't fall
   because there he could just . . . he would not fall because there is
   no gravity and gravity makes you fall.
Timmy: No, gravity makes you stand!
Teacher: Hands up, Timothy. . . .
Kristin: Okay, Timothy! Okay here here's some chalk, okay, now this
   is the moon but it goes back onto the earth and it's got gravity,
   now watch . . .
Jin: It's still on the earth.
Kristin: It makes things fall, gravity makes things fall.

Kristin has been a delicate problem in science class since we
started the unit on machines. She has reached the social level that I
sometimes see in third graders where all discussions take on personal
overtones. I am uncomfortable with this facet of children. I am very
aware of children's abilities to exclude and wound each other, and am
not very good at handling it. In the first part of the machine discussions
Kristin turned out to be very knowledgeable—more so than Timmy or
Yong Sun. This was, I think, due to to the fact that she spent weekends
working with her father in a garage rebuilding cars. She also seemed to
possess a better intuitive grasp of how machines worked than the
others. I spent a lot of time in those classes reaffirming her knowledge

and encouraging her to share it with us in class. I made sure that she had enough room to speak whole thoughts without interruption, and then I would often organize ensuing discussion so that people were talking in response to what Kristin had just explained to us. I made sure that the (apparent) antagonisms between Kristin and some of the little boys like Jin and Timmy were suppressed. I wanted Kristin to have a chance to exercise a knowledgeable voice in my science class—this was often difficult because Timmy, Jin, or Yong Sun would just *assume* that they knew more. Things are different in these classes on gravity and the planets. The children argue until I stop the class and have them write in their notebooks what they think gravity is.

At this point I felt like there was a huge amount of stuff out on the table, all of which we needed to deal with in order to make sense of the experiment. There were so many ideas in the air because each child was in a different place, coming from a different perspective or source of knowledge and experience. I wanted to center the argument on gravity, and to do this I took it back to the abstract—to a definition. I chose to do this because I wanted a common point to end class on. I wanted to have *everyone* cognizant that this was what we were talking about. I needed time to think about the children's different examples of gravity and think of an example of my own that would catch something "common" to each of theirs. In this way, they could think through their own ideas within this one, common idea, and I would have children thinking convergently as well as divergently. So I felt I needed to think through their ideas and their abstract definitions in conjunction to do this. I also think this is a valid approach to science—as a conjunction of abstract ideas and concrete, personal, experience-based sense-making. I started the next class (on March 12) with this.

In many ways, the nature of the explorations in this unit are different from those described in the previous chapters. We started out unfocused—our explorations were about simple machines, similar to the work with sound and music described in the previous chapter. This, however, became focused as we tried to make sense of how a machine worked. This is very different from my usual teaching—there is a particular goal here that I am maintaining. I am shaping and manipulating the conversation in service of this goal—first to understand the machine and then to understand gravity. For this reason the conversations the children participate in are qualitatively different. Rather than sharing ideas which listeners first try to understand and critique only secondarily, the children have been engaging in argument with each other in which they are making claims and attempting to convince others of their validity. I am fostering this; in the subsequent classes, I even introduce conflicts in logic to further this process. However, it is problematic to me—this sort of argument is a part of the activities of a discourse community in the Foucauldian sense, and I am uncomfortable with the hegamonic interpersonal relationships constructed in such a community. For example, I will not allow Kristin or Amina to be silenced by more conventional scientific thinkers; I believe in the validity of their ways of thinking and in their right both to speak and to be heard respectfully. It is stressful for me to be playing these multiple and conflicting roles—of scientific expert (in shaping the conversation so that it stays focused on first machines and then gravity), of being *so* controlling of the class, and of being respectful of others ideas, beliefs, feelings, and desires.

WHAT IS GRAVITY? OUR GOALS AND OBJECTIVES EVOLVE

I start the next class by asking the children to open their notebooks to the page where they had written about gravity. "Would somebody like to read what they wrote about gravity? Karen?" Karen reads, "Gravity is a force that tends to pull something [*I start to write her definition on the board*]. . . . Gravity is a force that intends to pull something down that has gotten off the surface." Next I add Ricardo's, "Oh, something that keeps you down." Then Alice's, "It's a force, it's something that holds things down." I finish writing and read the three definitions, emphasizing the verbs, "*Holds* things down . . . *keeps* things down, *pulls* things down. . . . Anybody have anything different than that? Amina?" Amina responds not with a definition, but by stating that she disagrees with Kristin's argument from last time. I stop her for the time being because I want more definitions. In particular, I am looking for one that connects the idea of gravity to the earth. I have decided that today we are going to play more with the difference of weight and weightlessness and environments where this occurs. So I ask Jin if he has anything different from what is on the board. He adds, "Gravity makes you stick to something." And Mwajuma asks him to explain.

> *Jin*: If we jump up, it still makes us come down!

> *Teacher*: Why's that . . . you just said it makes you go down; I don't understand how that's "stick to something. . . . "
> *Jin*: I mean it makes you stick to the ground.
> *Timmy*: I know what he means.
> *Teacher*: Mwajuma?
> *Mwajuma*: You don't really stick to the ground. . . .
> *Jin*: I know, it's like it's stick to it.
> *Ricardo*: Then it would *stay* on the ground!
> *Jin*: That's what I mean. I found it in the glossary. . . .

We go to their textbooks. This almost immediately becomes different children looking up different things. We had started this pattern of textbook use when we were exploring plants. One of the things I did when we first started to use the science books was to teach them how to use the index, because I regard the textbooks primarily as references. I find that letting children chase after things in their texts by using the index is a provocative initiator of bracketed wanderings. I found this very useful in discussions—different people would find different things and then we would share and discuss them all with a common referent.

Finally I call the class together to listen to Jin read the definition of gravity given in the book, "The force of one object pulling on another object, gravity pulls things toward the earth." (Wrong, I think; gravity is the pull. The measure of gravity is how much the object is being pulled, the degree of pull.) I start asking different children what they thought that definition meant. I start with Amina.

> *Amina*: Um, that means that, well I don't understand the first part, the force of one object pulling on another object . . . um, um, *OH,* one object is pulling on another object, this is an object [*she holds up a pen*], so if I jump off with the pen gravity pulls both things down at one time.
> *Teacher*: Is the pen pulling on anything?
> *Amina*: No. The pen can't be pulling on anything, 'cause it's not living.
> *Teacher*: When you jump up in the air with the pen in your hand, what's pulling on you?
> *Amina*: Gravity, gravity it's not like something, it's white like air, you can't see it, it's like clear.

Teacher: But the definition says that gravity is a force, from one
object pulling on another? The force of one object pulling on
another object . . . oh, if gravity is pulling you down it must be
pulling *you*, something is pulling you. . . .

Amina: I'm jumping and then gravity is pulling me down, like this. I
can't fly like a bird, but I don't know why gravity can't pull a
b—well, gravity can't pull down a bird because it has wings.

We're going too fast; again there seems to be just too many ideas
out on the floor, and in particular the children are using the idea of
gravity to explain different phenomena rather then focusing on talking
about what gravity is—I still want more talk about that. I move back a
step, "Where is gravity coming from?" Timmy answers, "Gravity is
coming from down in the earth." I repeat his answer and he adds that
gravity can also be on all the different sides of the earth. So I ask him if
the earth is also pulling on him. He replies, "No, gravity's from the
middle of the earth." I ask him if this means gravity's pulling on him
and he says yes.

Jin: I think gravity pulls birds down cause, well, 'cause when they're
flying and they're trying to pull it down and then they're still
flying and it makes them more tired and it makes them have to
go down.

Teacher: They're working pretty hard to stay in the air, is that what
you're saying, and then they get really tired and they have to
come down?

Jin: Um-hum, yeah, 'cause if there wasn't gravity then they could fly
like for over an hour in the air with-out stopping.

Sook Chin and John both think gravity comes from the earth. Kristin
wants to return to Jin's statement about birds. "I have a comment for
Jin, um, Jin, if there was no gravity wouldn't people, flowers, things be
flying up in the air?"

Jin: Uh-uh, not trucks!

Kristin: Uh-huh!

Jin: No, because it's like, people going to the moon then there's no
gravity but they're wearing very heavy boots so they won't fly
'cause it's very heavy.

Kristin: They can't wear very heavy boots 'cause then they couldn't walk.

Jin: They could 'cause there's no gravity.

Kristin: Then I'm saying they could fly!

Jin: If they don't wear heavy boots they can!

Kristin: So you're . . . they can't walk!

They start to argue seriously, so I interfere, "I don't understand, what's the point of what you're arguing about?" Kristin responds (with Jin breaking in repeatedly), "Well I think that anything could fly up in the air if there was no gravity [*Jin interrupts*] . . . and um, but Jin said, "but not a truck" because um, because it's too heavy because um, the gravity [*Jin interrupts again. I ask, thinking about the talk of birds, if she means fly or float. She answers float.*] . . . and um, the people on the moon they wear boots that just make them, they don't quite fly but they jump up really high but they do come down." Jin really doesn't like this. He says again, "No they wear really heavy boots that make them stay on the ground if they don't wear those boots like um, I think if you're on the moon then I think things weigh six times less, I'm not sure but it was much less so, so if like, if you have, if we were running right now and we were on the moon then we would be floating because our shoes are not heavy enough!"

Teacher: Is there gravity on the moon?

Jin: No.

Teacher: There's no gravity on the moon? But you do have a weight on the moon?

Jin: Yeah, 'cause if you have boots or like heavy boots like six pounds or something really heavy, well not six pounds but like really heavy, then, then you'll stay on the ground and, but, you can still hop really high you can still jump really far and high the boots just make you stay on the ground.

Kristin: How?

Teacher: How do they make you stay on the ground if there's no gravity?

Jin: 'Cause they're heavy.

Teacher: But if there's no gravity what difference does it make how heavy they are? If there's no gravity doesn't everything just float?

Jin: No.

Timmy: No!

Teacher: Gravity's the thing that makes things stick together. . . .

Yong Sun: But there's a . . .

Jin: Then if there's no gravity on the moon, then the things on the moon would go up. . . .

Teacher: So why would heavy boots make any difference?

Jin: They'd make you stay on the ground.

Teacher: But there's no weight, I mean there's no gravity, they're not going to help.

Jin: Some boots make you stay on the ground. . . .

Teacher: But you said there's no gravity.

Jin: I know, that's why they made gravity boots!

Teacher: You mean the boots have their own gravity?

Timmy: Yeah they give it out, that's what I just told him, they're gravity boots!

Jin: That's what I'm trying to say.

Timmy continues, his enthusiasm mounting, "The gravity boots can make you stick on the ground where there's no gravity. That's why they have them, but they have to jump or else it's too hard just to walk in the gravity boots but if they jump they can't float away the gravity will bring them back down but they'll jump!" The children in the room are *very* interested. The room is full of huge round eyes. I can hear wheels turning. *Now* I ask Yong Sun what he's thinking. Yong Sun, though, is also thinking real hard, "I don't know if they actually can, if they can jump real high, higher than we can . . . then how can they stick to the ground?" Timmy, Jin, and Amina start arguing about how high they could jump on the moon. I stop this with a summary—I want us to talk about what *I* think are the main points rather than the repercussions of this theory. "So Jin and Timmy are saying that on the moon there's no gravity so people would float away except they wear these gravity boots that make them stick to the moon's surface and then they can jump up in the air and then they come back down and it's all . . . they come back down because they're wearing gravity boots. Is that correct, is that what you're saying?" Timmy says yes. Joey, who I think of as a conservative, careful thinker (that's why I call on him here) also agrees with the theory. However, he does so by applying it elsewhere; to images he has of men in spaceships who *don't* seem to have control over themselves like astronauts on the moon do. Timmy adds, "They have something that they put on each thing that they take up, they make their own gravity." A major argument starts about this and about the moon. The class talks especially about things they see in pictures in the book. Finally I stop the talking and call on John.

> *John*: If there was gravity on the moon they would stay on the moon, and if you jumped you wouldn't start flying around or floating you would jump and then you wouldn't do that and Kristin's saying that there's gravity on that [*remember her picture*] then you would fall off but I don't think so, if you fall off there's nothing to go on to, you'd just sit there.
>
> *Teacher*: So are you agreeing with Timmy and Jin that because they wear their boots they go back down? [*John nods.*]

I ask another question which I hope will turn the conversation back from examining the effects of Timmy and Jin's idea to looking at more foundational assumptions. "Can I ask a question? Why does the earth have gravity?" Daniel answers, "Maybe it was made that way." Then Karen, "'Cause people need to live on it, 'cause that's where people live and where all the air is, so they can breathe, I don't know why the air is except the gravity is where all the people are and the air and if there wasn't any gravity everything wouldn't be, it wouldn't be organized, it would be hard to do things." This is a common sort of response to this kind of why question. A sort of inverted logic or causality that makes me think a lot about Habermas and Arendt and the nature of moral claims. It's also horrifyingly realistic scientifically. For example, scientific evidence and arguments for differences between men and women, the superiority of the white race, the mating behavior of birds . . . I respond, "Well, maybe if the Earth didn't have any gravity, we wouldn't be here."

> *Alice*: True, we'd be up there, maybe. . . .
>
> *Teacher*: Floating around . . . Ricardo what do you think, why do you think the earth has gravity?
>
> *Ricardo*: The people need gravity to because um, what if they need—
>
> *Teacher*: No that's not the question. It's not if people need gravity. It's why does the earth have gravity?

Ricardo: Because so the people can live on it and then they can
    walk. . . .
Teacher: If people didn't live on it would the earth still have gravity?
    [*People nod their heads and murmur yes.*] Why does the earth
    have gravity?
Ricardo: I don't know.
Alice: Well I think the earth has gravity well I have two reasons, I'm
    sure about the second one. The first one is because . . . maybe it
    was made that way. And my second reason is, I'm not sure this
    is right but, ah, space doesn't have any gravity. . . .
Teacher: Space doesn't have any gravity?
Alice: I don't think so.
Teacher: You don't think so. Why do you think space doesn't have
    any gravity?

Alice and then Amina just repeat that there is no gravity because things
float there—they have no weight. I think that for me the difficulty I find
in shaping this sort of discussion is in the sort of cyclicity of the
children's logic in the statement that the earth has gravity because it
was made that way. It does have the gravity that it has because it was
made the way it was. It was also made the way it was because of
gravity. You have to step outside this cycle to make sense of it, or for
that matter, to think differently.

Sook Chin has been drawing a picture to show us since I asked the
question about where gravity comes from. Finally he is ready to present
his picture. He is only recently becoming competent in English, so he
talks a little English then goes to Korean and Yong Sun translates.
Notice, on his diagram, the direction of the arrows. The way he has
chosen to draw his arrows has important repercussions for the rest of
the month in our continued discussions of gravity. Arrows indicating
the direction of the force of attraction would go the other way (Fig.
4.2).

Yong Sun: He thinks there's gravity everywhere so um [*it's from*]
    under the earth, there's gravity but we can't feel it.
Teacher: So everywhere on the earth there's gravity even if you're on
    top of the earth or on the bottom of the earth there's always
    gravity so you . . . that's why people on the bottom of the earth
    don't fall off.

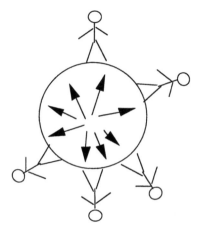

Figure 4.2

> *Sook Chin*: Yeah and they don't feel that [*he gestures to indicate upside down*]. . . .
> *Teacher*: They don't think they're on the bottom of the earth.
> *Sook Chin*: Yeah, they can't, but I think they can't fall because outer space is very large.

I decide at this point to tell the children about gravity and then see what sense they can make of it rather then seeing if they can "discover" it. I do this because I think that the children (and I think this is borne out again in the next class) are postulating theories which are more or less spontaneous bright ideas (or insights, if you'd rather). They are based on almost nothing; many are constructed on the spot. I think the gravity boots is an example of this. Jin was saying that they held the astronaut down because they were heavy. When I pointed out or when he recognized that this is inconsistent with his claim that the moon had no gravity led to the claim that the boots *made* gravity. The children who liked the idea were busy trying to apply it to other things to see if it would work there. This is in line with the manner that Kuhn (1970), for example, describes the testing and assessing process that scientists put new theories through. In the same vein, I suggest a theory and invite them to see whether or not their data makes sense analyzed within it. My theory, I know, has the advantage of greater simplicity and consistency. It has greater explanatory power, and it can be extended beyond the immediate phenomenon. I rarely do this—tell the children a scientifically more correct answer. I choose to do it in this instance in a particular manner. I am careful to portray what I say as another theory, because I don't wish to make an authoritative statement that would stop the sort of weighing and assessing Kuhn describes. I wish to keep my idea with the preexisting norms of our classroom conversations in which people share ideas and then they are discussed and weighed. I want them to think about my theory in the same way as they have the gravity boots—weighing its usefulness in explaining what they know about phenomena. I do this because I respect both that form of the scientific process and I respect the children—their theories (gravity boots, like any other scientific theory, is discarded only when it proves not useful) and their ability to think critically and creatively. I don't actively disprove of their theory; rather, I present another theory that's more powerful for them to try out. I feel I have to be extra careful in doing this (and in describing it here) because I do feel the children may attach more weight to my statements when I make them, and I wish in this instance to minimize this.

> *Teacher*: Listen to me, let me tell you an idea, the reason why the earth has gravity is because it's a great big thing. . . .
> *Kristin*: Bigger then the moon?
> *Teacher*: (I nod.) The bigger the thing is, the more gravity it has, everything has gravity, everything has gravity like you said at the beginning, Amina. . . .
> *Timmy*: Except—
> *Teacher*: Wait! Everything has gravity, but how much gravity it has is because of how big it is. [*This makes me very uncomfortable, using the word* big *rather than* mass *but I didn't want to introduce a new word at that moment.*] So the earth has gravity and it has a lot of gravity, the moon has gravity but the moon is smaller than the earth so it doesn't have as much. . . .
> *Jin*: One quarter. . . .
> *Teacher*: It doesn't have as much gravity as the earth.
> *Timmy*: So it's not easier to get around?
> *Teacher*: So it's easier to jump in the air. I have gravity but I don't have nearly as much gravity as the earth but if I was in outer space where there is no gravity, there's no gravity in outer space because there's nothing there, but if I'm in outer space, I have

gravity and if Amina was to bring a pen up there and let go of it,
just let go of it so that it is floating, it would be attracted to me, it
would be pulled to me because I have gravity. [*Many children
start murmuring to each other.*]

Timmy: Dr. Osborne, I have a question.

I repeat my theory before I let the children talk. Ricardo says that both
the sun and the planet Jupiter must have a lot of gravity, then. I agree
with him and emphasize that it is because they are so large.

Jin: I think it's interesting that if you were in outer space and if
someone gives you a, maybe if someone would hold a pen and it
will stick to you.

Teacher: You think that's interesting? Okay, Timmy?

Timmy: Um, I have a question. Does that mean if something's bigger
than you, you would be attracted to it?

Teacher: Uh-huh.

Timmy: Oh, then I say the same as Jin.

John adds his own interesting idea, "What's interesting is if a
spaceship were to fly too close to the sun it can't get away 'cause the
gravity of the sun is pulling it towards." But Amina disagrees with the
new theory. She draws a picture and then states, "The moon has
nothing on it because it has no gravity, right?" I tell her that no, that's
not right, or at least that's not what *I* had said. I emphasized the "I." I
reiterate that according to my theory the moon has gravity because of
its size. But Amina insists that it doesn't have gravity—at first because
the book says it's in space, which has no gravity, and then because
"Well I think I'm sort of revising because I thought if you think it's the
moon, the moon could have gravity because I thought if this is the earth
there's lots of people, 'cause there's lots of living things on it, that's
why it has gravity. But the moon it has *nothing* on it." On that note I
end the class.

CONSTRUCTING AND TESTING SCIENTIFIC THEORIES
AND THE DEVELOPMENT OF A COMMUNITY

Out Into The Solar System

We start the next class, on the seventeenth, in the same spot we left off.
Kristin disagrees with my theory: "I don't think the moon has gravity

because it says it in our own science book." Amina also still disagrees and goes to the board to redraw her pictures. It is very important that these two were the particular children who started the conversation in this class through disagreeing with my theory of gravity. These are the two children I am most focused on in my worries about discourse. They alter the shape of the ensuing conversation so that it feels more like those portrayed in the chapters on the first and second combination class. They tell us their ideas and we listen to them and work with them and through this process become critical.

I ask Kristin to find in the book what she is thinking about. Meanwhile, Amina explains her picture (Fig. 4.3): "Now this part, just pretend it's flat, um, the moon has no gravity, some people think it does but it doesn't. These lines are the people [*on earth*] and the moon, it has nothing but bumps on it and that's why the moon has no gravity."

Figure 4.3

> *Teacher:* So in order to have gravity you have to have living things; is that what you are saying?
>
> *Amina:* Yeah um, I don't think I should say this, but whatever one you believe in, God, well God, um, he thought that there should be, well, I don't know but maybe this, but maybe it's just because the moon doesn't have to have gravity because there's nothing, why should it have gravity because there's nothing on it that *should* have gravity.
>
> *Teacher:* Oh, so the earth *needs* to have gravity *because* there are living things?

This is very interesting: would the concept of gravity exist without us needing it? Mightn't there be another way to visualize the whole relationship that doesn't require pulling out or defining a concept like gravity? This is on a continuum with Karen's explanation of why there is gravity (because we are here and we need it). Amina's linking this to her concept of God and what God's plans are is also a part of this sort of teleological argument; arguments, either stated or unstated which hinge on a higher authority or a greater purpose. In traditional science the higher authority is the rule, "This must make sense!" It doesn't have to be that way, either, or it can make sense in multiple, often conflicting ways. Both Amina's and my conceptions of gravity arise because of different qualities of the abstractions we make about what we sense in the external world. Concepts such as gravity or God arise because our articulations of reality are partial and incomplete. God and gravity are different because our abstractions are different. Amina's way makes sense to her as does mine to me but how we can *use* that sense-making is very different. That's how I like to think I approach this sort of argument in class—asking children questions so they can try out their arguments in different places and contexts, with different data. That's also the approach I think you can see the children adopting. When Amina talks about God as an explanation, no one challenges her right to do this. They listen to her argument, then present their ideas. In a much later class (where we were discussing theories of the origin and end of the solar system) Amina asked me privately whether or not she could tell about her religious beliefs. I asked her to think before she did it whether or not she would be comfortable with children challenging and discussing her ideas as problematic. She chose not to share.

A funny thing about Amina and my interactions is that I don't feel the same sort of moral dilemma in encouraging her to question and think in this way, in which science and spirtual questions are intertwined, as I did in other classes with different students, such as Farzoneh (a child from Iran that I had in first grade in the year before this—I will talk more about this instance in the next chapter). I suspected at the time of this series of classes that these children were from the same sort of conservative Muslim background, however. This is actually not true, but it is what I was thinking and acting on at the time of this conversation. Maybe this difference in my response is because Amina is older, which gives me opportunities to talk with her *about* the discourse and what we are doing in class that I didn't have in first grade. Amina acts extremely feminine and very silly, but is very perceptive about the discourse of the class. She writes to me in her lab notebook commenting on the kinds of questions that I ask and why I phrase them the way that I do. She is the only child who does this.

We continue the conversation:

Amina: Uh-huh gravity, um, people would be floating . . .

Jin: Yeah we couldn't breath!

Teacher: Hand up! Um, but how does the earth make its gravity?

Amina: Well it comes, I'll draw a picture right here . . .

Dembe also wants to draw a picture at this point. While the two girls draw, Ricardo has a comment, "I think without, without gravity the sharks wouldn't be able to live because without gravity, the ocean would fall into space." This is a classic Ricardo sort of comment, in my opinion: right on target but warped by his own unusual thinking. I never know what to expect from Ricardo except that it will be perceptive. Many children make comments like these in all my classes. I have included many of them in these transcripts. They are said too loud to be side comments, but they never become central to our classroom talk, or if they do it is at a very later date. I feel that these comments are important because they indicate something about the playful atmosphere of the class—they are usually said in a humorous way and connect to the topic at hand in a peripheral or even eccentric manner, but indicate (at least to me) the child is connecting to the topic. I usually smile at the speaker or laugh a bit, but don't respond directly to the comment. In this instance, I respond, not about Ricardo's statement about sharks but just to Ricardo in general, "So do you think the earth has gravity because there are living things and therefore the moon doesn't have any gravity?" Ricardo says that he thinks the moon needs to have at least a bit of gravity. When pressed, he can't say why, though.

Amina explains her new picture. She tells us that gravity comes from the center of the earth and out the north pole (Fig. 4.4).

Then she changes her mind, "Well wait a minute that wouldn't make sense because I don't think I agree with my picture 'cause that would mean down here [*she points to the south pole*] . . . I don't know what it would be down here . . . but it might not have no gravity." She decides to draw another picture. I suspect she is confusing magnetic field drawings into her sense-making about gravity. We never return to this, however, so I don't know. Now Dembe shows us her picture (Fig. 4.5).

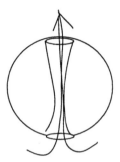

Figure 4.4

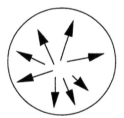

Figure 4.5

Dembe: I think that the moon does have a little gravity.

Teacher: What's your picture of?

Dembe: Um, the earth and the moon, and I think that the moon does have a little gravity because if the moon didn't have gravity, well it should have gravity because it's a little smaller than the earth, and it should have gravity and like you said, well, like the earth is big, but the sun would have more gravity 'cause it's bigger than the earth and the moon and, um, I think that since it's still a size, and it's kind of big too, and so it has gravity and also the earth because it's big.

Teacher: 'Cause of the size.

Dembe: Um-hum.

Teacher: Okay, Ricardo?

Ricardo: I think the moon does have a little gravity. If there wasn't any gravity on the moon it was, um, if the astronauts, even with heavy boots, they won't be able to touch the ground.

Amina: Remember . . .

Teacher: Yes, Amina?

Amina: Remember when Timothy said they have gravity boots?

Timothy: Well I disagree with myself now because when I heard what Dr. Osborne said and I agreed with her.

Amina: Dr. Osborne, what did you say?

Teacher: I said that the moon had gravity but it had less gravity than the earth and the amount of gravity that it has is dependent upon—

Amina: Oh, I think that it doesn't . . . doesn't have any, the [*moon*] doesn't need it because it doesn't have anything on it except bumps, it doesn't have things, it doesn't have space creatures.

Joey also thinks the moon has gravity. When I ask him what gravity is, he replies, "Something that helps you stay on the ground." Yong Sun adds on to this an extension of the theory from something he has read, "Well, I was kind of thinking that some stars are bigger than the sun and um, if you're out in space, if something was really big, then it would pull you to it, it would pull you to it." I get back to Amina and ask her what she's doing. She is musing over her drawing of the earth with people and the moon without: "I know the mountains should have gravity; I mean they're bumps." Dembe reminds her, "You said the earth doesn't have bumps. . . ." and Joey adds in, "Or doesn't need bumps." Amina says, "No, no, no, no, what I meant over here was all there is on the moon is bumps, bumps is not living things!" Dembe says, "But when you were over there you said that the earth does not have bumps and I think it does." Amina answers, "Well, yes, the earth does have bumps like the rocks like in the roads, um, I'm gonna revise." I think this is an example of Dembe and Joey trying to think inside Amina's theorizing. But their approach to attempting this is critical. I don't think their statements should be interpreted as counter-arguments. Rather, they were trying to think along with Amina, and these were problems they saw in the theory through this process. This is much more similar to the workings of the community in the conversations in the last chapter about sound and music.

Finally Dembe says, "I think the moon has to have gravity." I ask her, "Why?"

> *Dembe*: Because if it doesn't have gravity, how can you go to the moon? Like the space rockets and stuff when they're going to the moon, do they just glide right—
>
> *Amina*: Dembe, Dembe! I think you're getting a little carried away, see their space-suits, they *have* in their space-suits to carry gravity, there's this little plug goes in, there's air and there's gravity.
>
> *Timmy*: No, it's just oxygen.
>
> *Kristin*: No, it's *for* oxygen.
>
> *Amina*: Oh, then I think it's the boots that helps them.
>
> *Timothy*: It's those boots you saw how they have gravity on the moon, you saw how they jump, it's because they, the gravity's not real big so the gravity's not real strong, so you float up but then you come down because the gravity pulls you down but then you float back up because the gravity isn't very big. . . . I made a mistake because now I don't think there is and I don't and all they do is they have oxygen packs on them and that's all.

The children have seen these things in pictures and books and in movies or on television, and they believe there has to be reasons for their observations so they try on theories, to see if they work, for a while, then either keep them or cast them aside: a testing process. Amina does this for herself. She adds on addendums to her theory, tries it out for its explanatory power and coherence, then throws it out: like epicycles in pre-Copernican astronomy.

> *Amina*: Air and gravity are opposites.
>
> *Teacher*: Air and gravity are opposites?
>
> *Amina*: Uh-huh. [*Many children start asking her to clarify.*] Not opposites, well they're not opposites actually, but they're sort of the same, they're not really the same but—
>
> *Timmy*: Opposites means different.
>
> *Kristin*: Like yes and no are opposites.
>
> *Amina*: Yeah but I think they're sort of the same, gravity and air.
>
> *Teacher*: You said that last time you said that, air and gravity were the same because you can't see either one.

Amina: Yeah, it's true. . . .

Ricardo: Um, ummm . . .

Amina: 'Cause they're like the same like, Dembe, may I erase this?
It's clear and it helps people . . . air helps them breathe and
gravity helps them stay on the ground.

Teacher: Is air like something that you can hold in your hand? Am I
holding air in my hand? [*All respond yes.*] Okay, can you hold
gravity in your hand? [*Amina says yes, but all the others say no.*]

Amina and Yong Sun argue about whether or not you can feel gravity.
Amina seems to be claiming that you can feel gravity because you can
feel the effects of gravity. I'm inclined to look at it this way also,
although she is also saying that gravity is located just on the floor—we
feel gravity because we are held to the floor. I don't agree with that
part, so I ask the children, "Let me say something about a way you can
feel gravity, if you pick something up, you pick it up and it weighs a
lot, is that feeling gravity?" Now everybody agrees with me (while they
didn't with Amina). So I ask why they think that is feeling gravity.

John: It has weight and it, um, pushes down on your hand.

Joey: Um, I disagree with her [*Amina*] because if gravity is just on the
floor because right now I'm not touching it [*the floor*], if it's just
on the floor I felt it all over.

Amina: That's not what I mean. [*Lots of arguments start.*]

Teacher: Wait, wait, wait, stop, hold it, I'm not totally sure I even
heard what Joey said, Joey you said gravity's all over, it's not
just on the floor, so you wouldn't just feel it on the floor, you'd
feel it any old place?

Joey: Yeah, or I'd just be floating up right now.

Teacher: Okay any comments to what Joey just said? John?

John: Um, I agree with him 'cause if it was just on the floor then
you'd be half floating and half on the ground right now and if
you'd want to stay on the ground you'd have lie down on your
back or something or your stomach.

Jin: I agree that gravity's all over 'cause then you'll be sticking,
you'll be like . . . your one arm will be going like that and your
other arm will be going like that and—

Ricardo: Then your head may rip off!

Teacher: That might be true if—wait a minute, you're saying that might be true if gravity were all over, not just on the ground. Are you saying gravity's just on the ground or gravity's all over?

Jin: It's only on the ground 'cause if it were over there then it will stick.

Dembe: If, if I agree with Joey because gravity is all over, if you um, if gravity wasn't all over your hair would be going like this and everything.

In the last ten minutes of class, Kristin reads a page in her textbook on experiments in outer space while Timmy struggles for words with Dembe to describe how space is nothing. Ricardo says that space is different from the moon—the moon is in outer space. Joey joins the word struggle to describe space (words like *air, night, nothing*). Karen takes us back to Amina's drawing and points out that it makes no sense for the south pole, also where would the gravity go at the north pole? Kristin talks about the ozone layer, that it would hold gravity in and spread it around the earth. Yong Sun thinks this is a mistake, and I define ozone as part of the atmosphere. I ask Kristin if she means that the atmosphere, the air keeps the gravity in. She replies, "Nothing can get out except rockets and I think the rockets have a special thing that makes them able to get in and out of the earth because the ozone keeps everything from getting out of the earth, helps the gravity to work." Yong Sun says this is a mistake; he draws the earth with the atmosphere around it, explains the greenhouse effect, and says it has nothing to do with gravity. Finally I ask them to write in their notebooks where they think gravity comes from. At the last minute two children (Timmy, Daniel) want to bring something in to share next time—I invite this, and it becomes very important in shaping the subsequent classes.

In this last class the children construct consistent theories. I give them new material to do this with—theories, phenomena— which cause the children either to revise old theories to accommodate the new ideas or to throw their theories out. Amina is attempting to do this revision—she is unwilling to release her own theory. Others (e.g. Yong Sun) are testing the new theory by whether it has self-consistency and by its ability to explain phenomena they are familiar with. Again, these are all examples of the workings of a discourse community. Describing the workings of a scientific community upon the publication of a new theory, Kuhn (1970) argues that the scientists weigh the theory against the phenomenon and accept or reject it on the basis of whether it explains more and whether the new theory is generative. According to the ideas of Foucault (1980), this process is mediated by the abilities of the members of the community to communicate with each other—there must be shared language and shared understanding of that language. The latter is developed by the use that the language is being put to. This comes about in a scientific community by the process that Kuhn describes.

GRAVITY AND THE SOLAR SYSTEM CONTINUED.

I Realize We Have Changed Direction
We start March 19 with a short review of what has been going on about gravity for Alice (who missed the last class). I thought for sure that this was going to be a short process and that we would return to the inclined plane experiment today. The actual class starts when I ask Alice what she thinks of our discussions.

> *Alice*: I agree with Dembe [*Dembe has just defined gravity as something that keeps you on the ground and as proportional to the size of planets*] and I have a question for her, if gravity keeps things down and it helps you stay down, well why aren't you laying on the ground, because it's pulling you down?
>
> *Dembe*: I mean like gravity holds you, I mean, like on the bottom of your leg, you see when you jump, it pushes you back down on your legs. . . .
>
> *Jin*: It pulls you. . . .
>
> *Dembe*: It pulls you on your legs!
>
> *Teacher*: But why aren't you lying in the ground ? That doesn't make sense. . . .
>
> *Dembe*: Well because that, you're up, your feet are on the ground and that's why gravity comes from the ground.
>
> *Teacher*: What do you think about that, Alice?
>
> *Alice*: I don't really understand.

I see this as a chance to revisit Alice's and others' questions about birds, and find a place to explore how we "feel" gravity and work against it—the tug-of-war idea. I say, "Remember we were talking a couple days ago about how birds can fly? I mean how *can* birds fly if there is gravity, Kristin?" Kristin responds that birds have no bones. Everyone disagrees. I say, "Well if they do or don't, what difference would that make? I mean, shouldn't gravity work on someone without bones?" Kristin tries again, "Birds don't have weight." This again is shouted down. Everyone is debating my question. I stop the conversations and call on Yong Sun. He says, "They don't look like they have any weight, but they do have weight and they use their own force to keep them up."

> *Teacher*: How do they do that?
> *Yong Sun*: By pushing the air to the floor and lifting them up.
> *Teacher*: By flapping their wings? [*Yong Sun nods.*]

We start talking about how they are able to flap their wings. Yong Sun says it's because they have a skeleton. I ask the class, "Is it just the skeleton or something else that helps them?" Timmy says they have muscles and Jin says feathers. I push it further, "Okay, let me ask this: if birds know there is gravity and birds do have weight but they can fly because they have wings and they have muscles and they have skeletons and they have feathers so *we* have weight but we aren't lying flat on the floor, why are we not lying flat on the floor? There is gravity and we do have weight but we aren't lying flat on the floor." John says, "Bones, if we didn't have bones we'd be flat on the floor."

> *Alice*: Well I agree with John and because there's not enough gravity
>   to pull us down on the ground.
> *Jin*: Yeah there is!
> *Teacher*: There's not enough gravity? What's that Jin?
> *Jin*: Yes there is because if you don't have bones then you'll fall
>   down.

I ask, "Can you think of any animals that don't have bones?" My reasons for asking this are because I want them to think that the children have to work to stand up and that their bodies are constructed to facilitate this. Animals without bones are supported by the ground, water, or exoskeletons. I want them to see that the morphology of living things is related to the things that they can do—a functional morphology argument. The danger of functional morphology arguments is that they are often discovered to be the inverted forms of logic and causality that I talked about when Karen suggested that the earth had gravity because people needed it.

From Ricardo we hear about worms and where they live. Karen talks about snails and slugs. We talk a bit about snakes and remember that they do have skeletons. I suggest jellyfish and Ricardo adds shrimp. At last, Amina says, "I have a comment for Kristin and Dembe and also for you, Dr. Osborne, not only your bones hold you up but also your muscles and your force." Everyone seems to agree this time, so I summarize, "Sometimes your muscles don't work and you fall on your back but you don't lie on your back because you can't get up like because what Alice was saying about gravity, if there's gravity why doesn't it just hold you flat on the ground? I think the reason why it doesn't just hold you flat on the ground is because, as you guys have just answered, because you have muscles and you have bones and you use this force and that keeps you up, that allows you to stay up. Does that make sense to you, Alice?" Alice says that it does.

Then I return to the moon, "Well what would happen to us if we were on the moon, is there gravity on the moon?" All but Kristin and Amina agree that there is. We talk some more about how people move on the moon and in outer space. Timmy looks the moon up in an encyclopedia he has brought in to show us. It talks about the calendar, the phases of the moon, and craters. Sook Chin defines these by drawing a picture. I talk about my early research on lunar rocks and soils.

The children effectively planned out next time and probably a number of days after with the things they wanted to share about the planets. I was still not happy with what they were saying about gravity. I really wanted them to understand weight as the manifestation of a dynamic tension between two bodies. I wanted to get back to the machines. I didn't want to do more on gravity or the solar system. I didn't like the feeling of manipulating them into knowledge that I'd already got. On the other hand, they really wanted to do this. The only children I really didn't think were very interested were Mwajuma and Selamawit. I wanted to respect the children's desires to shape the science we were doing.

This was the last class in which I thought our primary purpose was exploring gravity to get to weight to get back to machines. After this class I let their explore the solar system (and gravity) for themselves, although in my head I still kept the idea of relating things back to what I thought were underlying concepts in making sense of the machines. In other words, in my head the organizing theme of the children's explorations of the solar system was an exploration of gravity—its meaning and effects.

I let the children lead the way on a superficial level by letting them control (introduce) the materials we would discuss. I made no attempt to ask why particular children chose to share the things that they did. I think there was an interplay of children bringing things they had that they thought were pertinent to a discussion going on (I think this because often we didn't get to a child's offering for days and when we did, the child would say things like, "Oh let's not read this now, we aren't talking about it anymore"), were points that they would like to make to support their views of an argument, and that were very interesting to them. How that which the children brought in was played out in class was something I manufactured though.

CONNECTING GRAVITY TO MOTION

Connecting To Each Others Ideas

So we started class on Monday, March 23 with me recapping the children's plan from the last class. I had asked Sylvia if I could teach on Monday that week (normally I don't) because I had thought that one long class and then the shorter classes that I normally taught on Tuesday, Wednesday, and Thursday in which they shared things that they had brought from home would end their interest in planets. The Monday class is an hour and a half long. My other classes are forty minutes. First I poll the room for who brought things in, then for who else planned to, then of the children who had things to show, what they had. This is how I arranged the conversation. I also explicitly said we were going to end talking about planets on Thursday. (This would not happen, however.)

I start with Timmy, who has information in his encyclopedia to share. But before we get to his choices I ask him to look up gravity. Then he asks me to read the selection. The paragraph I read defines gravity through Newton's law, which states that any two objects are pulled toward each other with a force that has to do with the amount of their mass and the distance between them. The closer they are together, the more they are attracted to each other. I define mass for the children as having to do with size, as I was telling them before. Then the encyclopedia talks about how in order to escape the earth's gravity an object has to be moving very fast, at an "escape velocity." So this is where I suddenly get the idea that exploring the revolution of one body around another would be a way to start thinking about gravity as a dynamic interaction between two bodies; another version of Dembe's tug-of-war. I bring this up later in class.

Timmy asks for questions or comments. I have established this procedure so that children lead discussions in my classes. A child who wishes to share something—a book or a drawing, for example—presents it to the class, explaining why they thought it was important. Then they take questions from the class. Children who ask questions must raise their hands and be recognized by the speaker. To an extent, the speaker controls who talks and for how long. The speaker also responds to the questioner. When the topic seems particularly fruitful or becomes important as the question/response progresses, I often step in and interfere with what is talked about and who does the talking. I also step in to make sure certain people whom I suspect have something important to add get their chance and I step in with these people to increase the time spent on their ideas. In other words, I don't rely on the speaker to know what is important scientifically. I feel it is my role to keep these sessions focused on the science, and I break the norms of this type of conversation to do this. Timmy calls on Amina first. Amina asks about another experiment that the class did on static electricity. In this experiment, they rubbed balloons on their hair and tried to stick the balloons together or not, depending on whether the other balloon was also rubbed. Timmy and Amina argue about whether discussing this is applicable to a discussion of gravitational attraction. Timmy thinks she is arguing that gravity and electricity are the same thing.

I feel that Amina is pointing out the similarity in the descriptions of the attraction between two bodies caused by gravity and that caused by electricity, not saying that these are the same thing. I think this is very perceptive. The equations that describe this are of the same form. The difference, though (and it's a fundamental one), is that while gravity can only attract, electricity can both attract and repel. I want to know if the children see this similarity also as well as the difference, so I continue polling the room. No one seems confused by the two as different and Alice does point out that most fundamental difference between the two. This is a nice, short exploration of similarities and differences that adds to the understanding of both concepts, I think. A similar sort of discussion will happen between Yong Sun and Daniel about definitions of the word *satellite* in the next class. These two conversations are different in substance, although the form is similar— here we are exploring the differences and similarities in a phenomenon, whereas around the word *satellite* we are discussing the meaning of a word, a humanmade construct. It is important to think of Wittgenstein's ideas (1968) about meaning and language in these contexts and ask whether and how words have meanings outside the use they are put to, the contexts they are found in. How do we construct meaning and how is that meaning shaped by the social context in which it is formed.

Next Timmy has me read from his book on planets. His encyclo-pedia defines planets as bodies moving around a star, each in its own orbit. It lists the planets in our solar system and I show the children the picture the book has of the planets, labelled, in orbits around the sun. I ask the children what they have in their textbooks. Karen starts us by talking about a picture of the orbitals of the planets about the sun. I ask Karen why she thinks the sun is in the middle. She answers, "Because all the planets have to move around it, like planet earth, then one half isn't warm while the other half's cold." This is very true. The only planet that only presents one side to the sun is Uranus, a gaseous planet, that can convect and even out the temperature differential. But Karen's answer really explains why planets rotate, rather than why they revolve around the sun. So I ask her why they have to go around the sun, why can't they just sit? This question returns us to the idea that planetary motion represents a dynamic tension between gravitational attraction and centripetal force. My reason for pushing on this as a means to try to develop an understanding of gravity with the children relates to my own understanding of gravity. Remembering the equation that describes gravitational attraction, $F = G(M_1M_2/r^2)$, in which F is force, M is mass, A is acceleration, G is the gravitational constant, and r is the distance separating the two bodies, there is a force of attraction between any two bodies. They must work to stay apart. We work to stand upright on the earth, but because we do it constantly, we aren't aware of it. The fact that the planets revolve around the sun is a manifestation of their gravitational attraction toward the sun. It is hard to understand gravity as a force if you can't recognize the work (the motion) being done to counteract it. Karen replies to my question, "'Cause they'd burn up in the same spot." Dembe adds, "Well, I think it's in the middle because [*they can't share the same orbit 'cause then they'd*] share the heat." Then I interrupt and draw this picture (Fig. 4.6):

Figure 4.6

I also want to know why the children think planets can't share orbits.

> *Dembe*: That wouldn't be a good idea because, 'cause if they were too close to each other you would just have to jump to get to one and another thing, the sun would only be on the one side and it needs to get on the other side because then on that side there would be something and on the other side there would be nothing and it needs to be around.
>
> *Teacher*: Karen, didn't you have your hand up?
>
> *Karen*: Um-hum, if it were to stay in one spot and the sun is in one spot, um, the people that was on the half that was cold they would get kind of tired of having it freezing all the time, and the people where it's warm they'd get real hot. . . .
>
> *Ricardo*: Not if you live in Florida or California, you're used to it.
>
> *Yong Sun*: All the planets have to do is spin around instead of go around it.
>
> *Teacher*: Oh okay let me see if I can draw, so like here's the planet here and so it would be just spinning around like that (Fig. 4.7)?

Figure 4.7

Yong Sun: Yeah then everybody could get sun.

Teacher: But it still would just be sitting here, it wouldn't be um, going around the sun. It would just sit right here and spin around by itself?

Yong Sun: Yeah but the bad thing would be um, then astronomers, I mean then people wouldn't know how long a year would be 'cause every time the earth spins around the sun, one time is a year.

A debate starts up about what is a day and what is a year, about the difference between rotation and revolution. We spend a lot of time trying to demonstrate different people's ideas of how you could get a day through revolution and whether or not that kind of thinking makes sense using globes and people walking around each other. Timmy takes the globe and revolves it around the sun once and says that's what makes a day. Yong Sun, though, says that is a year.

Alice: I think I know how it gets dark and light and um, the days because when the world turns around, like Timmy was doing, see, when it turns around then on the other side of the earth, the sun is on that side so if you are on the opposite side of that, then it would be dark over there.

John: The earth doesn't go around the sun every day. . . .

Timmy: *It has to*!!

Teacher: Timmy . . . let John finish.

John: It takes the earth a year to make one revolution around the sun.

Teacher: So when it goes around the sun like this line, the white lines that are in your book . . . those are the revolutions around the sun, and it takes a year for that to happen?

Both John and Yong Sun agree, but other people are still all tangled up and Timmy keeps arguing back and forth. So we do more demonstrations with globes. Finally I summarize again, and Timmy agrees to the logic behind a day and then *he* asks my initial question. He asks why if it is spinning does it have to travel around the sun also.

Teacher: Okay good question, why does it go around me, why doesn't it just spin? And the reason why different people are saying it just spins I think, like Karen said if it didn't spin and I

think Dembe said this also, if it didn't spin then the sun would
always hit the same place and then it would burn up, is that what
you guys said? Or it would get very very hot.

Karen: I still think it goes around [*the sun*] and at the same time, it,
it's turning and then it's also going around [*the sun*].

Teacher: You think so? Why, though?

Ricardo: Why would it do both?

Karen: I think it does because if it was turning in one place then it
would be hot and then it would be cold and then it would be hot
and then cold, I've changed my mind, in one day then it would
be hot then cold, so I think it just goes round the sun.

Teacher: You think it just goes around the sun, it doesn't spin too?

Karen: You see while it's going around the sun, it's heading this way
and it goes, the sun is pointing this way and then it's like that.

Teacher: So are you saying that it goes around the sun once a day,
every day it goes all the way around the sun?

So now Karen has argued herself back the other way. We
demonstrate Karen's theory with the globes and Karen revises her
theory. Timmy says, "I think that I agree with Jin but I'm just not sure,
I don't know if either one is right, I'm not sure I'm not saying Jin is
right and I'm wrong or I'm right and his is wrong, I'm not sure . . . "

We debate this some more. I am letting this talk go on for so long
because of two things. I think this talk recapitulates a long debate in the
history of science and is a good place to try working on making sense
by theorizing with "data" that we "know" for sure. First, we know there
is a year and a day: where do they come from, what causes them?
Second, we can't make sense of gravity using these concepts without
making sense of the concepts first. The earth must revolve around the
sun or fall into the sun. The earth's orbit is the result of the
gravitational attraction between the two and the earth's tangential
velocity away from the sun. That's why I started us in on this in the
first place.

Kristin suggests we look at a picture she doesn't understand in the
book. This is a drawing of the earth going around the sun and the moon
around the earth. I name them.

Kristin: I always thought the moon was bigger than the sun.

Yong Sun: The moon is always smaller than the planet.

> *Teacher*: Who said the moon is always smaller than the planet? Why
> is that? I happen to agree with you, but why is that?
> *Jin*: I don't know but um, in a book I have that has all the planets and
> the moons, none of the moons were bigger than the planets.

We'll come back to this on the thirtieth. Again, this is a place to make sense of gravity as dynamic but right now we go back to revolution and rotation. We go back to my picture on the board (Fig. 4.8).

Figure 4.8

People are questioning it. Jin and Amina found my drawing of the arrow indicating revolution only halfway confusing, so I complete the diagram (Fig. 4.9).

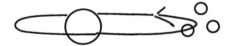

Figure 4.9

But Amina has more. She goes back to Dembe's comment about being able to jump between planets. She doesn't like that idea. She is talking to Dembe:

> *Amina*: The part where you said that um, you're not allowed to touch
> the sun, you're not allowed to be that close to the sun and Dr.
> Osborne said something about the planets, and you have to
> jump, and Dembe said if the planets are real close together you
> have to jump . . .
> *Teacher*: And you [*Dembe*] argued that that couldn't possibly be
> because they'd be way too close together, and also because—
> *Dembe*: Well maybe if they turn around and they, if there was a
> planet right here and another here and it's turning around, it
> might bump possibly.

Amina: I disagree because, if the moon or if this was, well, if this was
here and another planet was here, you couldn't jump, if you did
you'd probably be floating between, just because they're close
together doesn't mean you could jump from each one.

Dembe: I said you *probably* could.

Amina: But you, but you can't . . . well those two big ones right there
um, they're close, but if you put the one on the right, if it was
close, well the one on the left, if you were on that one, the one
on the left and if you were going to jump off to get to the next
planet you'd be, you wouldn't get to the next planet because
they're really not close together.

Teacher: Why do you say that?

Amina: Um, that's just there, um, a picture, it's really the planets are
not close together, they're far apart.

Amina often brings this sort of thing up. It's like she wants to
reaffirm and make sure everyone agrees that diagrams illustrate ideas,
not reality, and what we see in them can be misleading, therefore we
have to remember the way things *are*. Again, I think this is important in
science and how we represent scientific ideas. When the discussion
about this ends I take us back to my original question, which is the one
in which I hope to expose gravity some more.

Teacher: Now I have a question I've heard lots of good arguments
why this should spin around and around so it doesn't get too hot
and burn up and so we can have days, I don't understand why it
has to revolve around the sun, though, why couldn't it *just* spin
round and round and round in one place, wouldn't that keep
it from getting too hot on one side or too cold on one side,
wouldn't that be enough? Why does it have to go all the way
around the sun and come back every year? What do you think,
Jin?

Jin: I wouldn't know how long a year is.

Teacher: Oh so it needs to go all the way around the sun just to tell *us*
how long a year is? Is that right, the earth circles the sun just to
tell you, Jin, how long a year is. Why does it need to do that,
why does it need to tell us how long the year is?

Alice: Well, I think I have a reason and I have a comment for Jin.
What my reason is maybe so it can tell you that a year is and

there's another way something could tell you a year is, well you could tell by the months you could count how many months there have been and see if that's the number of months and that would be a whole year.

Teacher: Okay it's almost recess time and before you go out could you please write about this question: "Why does the earth go round the sun and doesn't fall in, if there's gravity and the sun is this great big huge thing, the sun is a great big huge thing and the earth is a little tiny thing and if there is gravity, why doesn't the earth become attracted to the sun and go crashing right into the sun and burn up.

I revised the question to be somewhat more startling and also to give something of a lead in the direction I want. I start the next class, on the twenty-fourth, with this question. Yong Sun tells us he wrote, "It doesn't because if it did it would get out of its orbiting system." I write this up on the board and repeat it. This is a key statement if we are going to work on orbiting as a resolution between competing forces (gravity and centripetal force). Then I ask Kristin what she wrote. Kristin reads, "Because there is a force field that keeps gravity inside the earth and that's why there's no gravity in space, 'cause if the earth lets out gravity then there would be gravity in space." I write it on the board and question her. This is why it's essential to think of gravity as a warping of space rather than a "thing." If you think of space as "nothing," how can things interact across it?

Teacher: Now why does that stop it from going crashing into the sun?
Kristin: 'Cause if there was gravity it would go straight to the sun.
Ricardo: If there was gravity out in space then *boom*!
Kristin: Right.
Teacher: Ricardo, what did you write?
Ricardo: I thought that gravity keeps the earth from the sun.
Teacher: Gravity keeps the earth from the sun?
Ricardo: I mean gravity keeps the earth back so it doesn't go crashing into the sun.
Teacher: The earth's gravity or who's gravity?
Ricardo: The earth's.
Yong Sun: The sun's.

> *Teacher*: Ah, so the sun and the earth have gravity and the earth's
> gravity keeps it from crashing into the sun . . . but the way I
> understood gravity was that it was something that pulls things
> together; how does it keep it back?

To understand Ricardo's statement, think of this diagram of Sook
Chin's (Fig. 4.9):

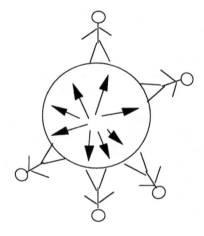

Figure 4.9

He either means the side of the earth away from the sun is pulling away
from the sun or the side of the earth away from the sun is pulling the
other side of the earth toward it; or (invert the arrows in the picture) the
earth is pulling in on itself and this is strong enough to counteract the
sun's attraction.

> *Ricardo*: Um, because gravity pulls, pulls real hard.
> *Yong Sun*: But the sun has more gravity . . . and the other side of it the
> earth would push it this way but the sun goes here.
> *Teacher*: What do you think, Ricardo?
> *Ricardo*: I still think that it keeps it from . . . 'cause the sun is far
> away from the earth and if it's real far away the sun's gravity
> would hardly reach the earth.

Teacher: And what about the other thing that Yong Sun said about gravity on the other side of the earth, did you say gravity on the other side of the earth would push it, is that what you said?

Yong Sun: Um-hum . . .

Teacher: What do you think about that, Ricardo?

Ricardo: Only one, I think only one part of the earth would pull it.

Yong Sun: Well you think that on one side, the side, where the sun is facing, it pulls it, it pulls um, into the sun but on the other side it's pulling around.

Ricardo: That's not what I mean.

Yong Sun: Then I didn't understand it.

Ricardo: Well what I mean is that 'cause gravity in the middle of the earth is pulling and pushing from . . . from the sun so then we won't go into the sun. [*The third of my suggestions above.*]

Teacher: What do you think, Yong Sun?

Yong Sun: [*To Ricardo.*] You haven't answered my question yet, what about the other side's gravity.

Ricardo: Well it's the gravity goes from the middle of the earth and one part of the gravity stays where it was and, um, then the other side goes on the pulls from the other side.

Yong Sun: Well, I think like the sun is here and then the earth is here and this side of the earth is pushing this way and the other side is pushing this way.

Ricardo: One side is pulling and one side is pushing away from the sun.

Yong Sun: So you mean one side pushes and one side pulls and it just stays here.

Teacher: Does that convince you, Yong Sun? What about what you said about the sun being a lot bigger and having a lot more gravity than the earth?

Yong Sun: Well I can take what Ricardo says.

Teacher: You can take what Ricardo says? You think that it convinces you?

Yong Sun: Well actually a little.

Teacher: Actually a little?

Yong Sun: But he does have a good point, though.

Teacher: I think he does too. Dembe?

I really liked these arguments and the reasoning of both are correct in themselves. The only resolution that I can think of would be to put numbers to it. This is the kind of thinking I like to leave hanging. I was really pleased with the form and content of this conversation. Dembe, though, introduces something new to consider—there are planets, Mercury and Venus—between us and the sun. She also makes the point that the earth and sun are far apart. She recapitulates Ricardo's and Yong Sun's argument about the earth staying in its orbit. Dembe makes a drawing of her interpretation of Ricardo's theory (Fig. 4.10):

Figure 4.10

I ask her about this, using the children's definition of gravity as an attractive force, "Well gravity works so that it's pulling towards another thing, one thing towards another thing, why can it pull that way?" Dembe cites magic, "Let me revise about that I want to say that, I, you see the ozone on the sun?" I tell her the sun has no ozone, so she revises to the earth's ozone. I think it is interesting how the children have latched on to ozone as the universal explanation. Dembe seems to want to say the ozone keeps the earth together. Yong Sun tells her ozone has nothing to do with gravity. Dembe starts to amend her theory—this is similar to what Amina did a couple of classes back—and drifts off in her talk. So I call on Kristin, who again has a problem with a picture in the book and a too literal interpretation.

> *Kristin*: On one of the pages it looks like we are really close to the
>   sun, right here, here's the sun and here's the earth.
> *Dembe*: It looks quite close but it's really far. . . .
> *Amina*: Well it's like up there the sun looks real close and the moon
>   looks real close, like one time I was outside and the moon it was
>   so so really close and I jumped for it and tried to get it . . . and I
>   saw the bumps and everything . . .
> *Jin*: It's impossible to jump all the way to the moon.

Amina: I know but it looked that way, really, really close like I could reach it.

Kristin: Well I have something else to say, in another picture in this book on page 230 where it shows the rotation, the orbits of the earth and the moon, um, I think that it only takes twenty-four hours for the moon to go around the sun too.

Teacher: Why do you think that? For the moon to go around the sun or for the moon to go around the earth?

Kristin: Well I might be wrong but for the moon to go around the sun.

Dembe, Jin, Ricardo, and Amina all interrupt to point out she is misinterpreting the picture. It shows the earth orbiting the sun and the moon orbiting the earth. I ask them to let Kristin finish what she is saying because buried in this is what Karen was talking about with Mercury and Venus, orbits within orbits; and also the true statement that the moon does take the same amount of time to go around the sun as does the earth. Kristin states, "I see that the moon is going around the earth and if the earth is going around the sun then the moon has to go around the sun too." I ask, "You guys who were complaining understand what she is saying?" I also ask if the people who wanted to argue with her now understand what she is saying. Finally I repeat Jin's statement for everybody. We will come back to this.

We look up facts about the distances of the planets from the sun for a while in their textbook and in the encyclopedia. After a while I ask again why they don't crash together. Jin and Joey respond, "Because the earth's orbit keeps the earth in its place, the earth can't go any other place." Yong Sun agrees and I end the class with, "For next time write about how did the earth get into an orbit where it goes around the sun, how did that ever happen?"

What Jin, Joey, and Yong Sun are saying is really no different from what we started out class with, but I feel like we've given it a lot more meaning in this discussion. I phrased my final question the way I did because I think it pushes on the idea we've been working on all along about orbits being the result of a dynamic between gravitational attraction and tangential velocity. I'm searching for something that causes us to think about orbits in terms of these two components. I wish I had tried asking about why orbiting spacecraft didn't crash to earth instead, because of course in the question I did ask I'm asking the children to construct a false argument—that the earth-sun system was always in orbit, always in motion.

The next two classes are not transcribed. They were further explorations of the things children brought in about the moon and other bodies of the solar system. The question of orbits was really tabled until the next Monday, March 30 when it returned. Obviously we didn't end talking about planets at the end of the week, as I had planned. On Wednesday, March 25 I thought things were petering out, but then on the twenty-sixth they got going again when people started talking about the evolution of the solar system. A couple children shared books with pictures of Jupiter's and Saturn's moons from the flybys.

DEFINING WORDS, MAKING STATEMENTS OF KNOWING

The Development Of Uncertainty

On the thirtieth, two really interesting things happen. The first is a discussion in which the children define the word *satellite*. They have done this type of discussion a number of times in this unit; about the meaning of the words *orbit* and *astronaut* for instance. This conversation about the word *satellite* is quite long and shows a nice interplay of defining a word by what it is, what it represents, through its intersection of meaning with other words, as well as comparatively, by how it's different from other concepts (defining through difference and through similarity). This sort of conversation, like the one between Ricardo and Yong Sun, could only happen, I feel, between children who want to understand what the others are thinking, not just push their own ideas. This sort of connected thinking, which leads to critical thinking, is quite different from the creative tension which is the result of a Foucault-style discourse community. These conversations are based on a respect for each other rather than a desire to dominate.

The second thing that happens is an interesting return to questions about planetary orbits. The two children talking in this conversation, Jin and Joey, are arguing from positions of certainty—they both argue that they "know" what they are claiming about the manner that planets orbit around each other. When I say "certainty," I mean as defined intellectually in the Wittgenstein sense—the children *think* they know and believe they can defend their ideas logically, but also emotionally or tacitly in a more Heidegger-like manner. Each child *feels* that orbitals must work a certain way. This feeling is not seated in the intellect, but in a more spiritual place or emotional place, like Amina citing God. The Heidegger and Wittgenstein forms of certainty are brought into play with each other because the children are making claims in their attempts to communicate to each other. Because each child has to try truly to understand the other's argument in order to argue against it, certainty is recast as uncertainty. This is an important quality of my community. It is an illustration of how I try to use conflict to strengthen the community, strengthen the need people with different ideas and opinions feel for each other. Because certainty can be recast as uncertainty, the children can value their differences. This is a community based upon differences between people rather than on likeness.

We start the class with me reading something of Amina's about the moon. In this book, the moon is called a *satellite*. I ask the class if they understand the word.

> *Daniel*: I don't get it . . .
> *Teacher*: What? The word *satellite*? It says the moon is a satellite that revolves around the earth.
> *Daniel*: What I don't get is, how does a satellite revolve, usually satellites take pictures.

Yong Sun and other children start searching in their science books. Daniel looks in his book on the moon for a picture to illustrate his idea of what a satellite is, then he shows us a picture of Skylab. Yong Sun finds what he wants in the book, and reads it, "We will soon send a satellite into space and it will help us look at stars and identify things that have moved, so that's one kind of satellite, one that takes pictures like Daniel said but the moon is a different kind of satellite, and the earth is a satellite too."

> *Daniel*: Why would the moon be a satellite if it didn't do much . . .
> *Teacher*: Yong Sun, how can all three of those be satellites, what is a satellite?
> *Yong Sun*: Well it's just like one word can mean different things.
> *Daniel*: What special work does the moon do?
> *Yong Sun*: Well it sort of does the same thing, it kind of goes around a planet.
> *Daniel*: Yeah but how can—

> *Teacher*: Wait can I just ask something? Are you saying that it's a satellite because it goes around a planet?
>
> *Yong Sun*: Yeah like the earth goes around the sun. . . . I'm not really sure why they call the things with cameras a satellite.
>
> *Daniel*: How could, um, if the moon is similar to the, um, to a regular satellite, how could it take pictures?
>
> *Yong Sun*: It doesn't take pictures.
>
> *Daniel*: Then why did you say it's similar to the um—
>
> *Yong Sun*: I didn't say that *everything* is the same!
>
> *Teacher*: What do you think, if you used Yong Sun's definition that it goes around something else, why would the thing that takes pictures be a satellite?
>
> *Daniel*: That's what I don't get, why would that be a special kind of word, 'cause the earth and the moon do the something . . .
>
> *Teacher*: Go around something.
>
> *Daniel*: And usually a special word is where you do things differently.

I ask what is special about the one type of satellite from the other type. Joey says that he thinks the earth is different from the other planets because it is the only satellite that can support life. Jin disagrees with this. He says that he heard on the news that while there may not be life on other planets *now*, there might be in the future. Everyone finds this argument very interesting. After some discussion, I ask, if Joey's comments helped Daniel think how the moon, Skylab, and the earth could all be satellites and still be different. When Joey repeats his statement, slightly doctored to pacify Jin, Dembe starts in:

> *Dembe*: In the newspaper, it said that some aliens they were buried under the Empire State Building.
>
> *Teacher*: What does that have to do with this?
>
> *Dembe*: Well I think that there are some things living on other planets right now.

I included this last interchange between Dembe and myself because I think it is an especially vivid illustration of how this whole unit was a play off of the knowledge children brought in from elsewhere. And like with the first grader's dinosaur stories (see chapter 5), their information is mixed in quality. Science fiction plays off being scientifically plausible. It is also an example of another side comment such as the one I wrote of earlier concerning Ricardo's statement about what would happen to sharks if there were no gravity. In this instance the whole class ooos and ahs and we just leave it. I finish my part in teaching this unit, however, after one more week, and a student teacher continues it. I suggest to him that he take this topic and work with the children to construct science fiction stories—experimenting with teaching science in this manner. So this is an example where a side comment is left for the moment but returns as a more central topic. Another example of this process is the initial comment about birds flying by Amina, which then become central a few days later.

I summarize the discussion between Yong Sun and Daniel and Joey, and then throw in a little demonstration of my own. At the end of my summary, I have Jin run around Joey to demonstrate a satellite. Joey is by far the smallest child in the class, while Jin is large and quite heavy.

> *Hamal*: Jin's a satellite.
> *Timmy*: That's wrong, that's wrong, that's wrong! Jin's bigger than Joey!
> *Teacher*: What difference does that make?
> *Timmy*: It means that if he's bigger, it can't go around, it means that Joey's got to go around him . . .

Jin, Ricardo, and Dembe all think it doesn't matter. Actually, of course two bodies orbit around a fulcrum point (barycenter). Fortunately, I didn't think to try to get them to connect this to levers, or we would still be at this. Timmy repeats, "It's just like the sun, the earth goes around the sun, the moon goes around the earth . . . " I ask why that is; why does the smaller go around the larger? Timmy answers, "because it's bigger." Sook Chin adds the sun has more gravity and that's because it's bigger. Timmy says that this "is like a pattern." I think he's saying that something large can go around something small if it has an orbit.

Ricardo "kind of agrees and kind of disagrees" with Timmy. Timmy repeats his argument but says he "just doesn't know" what he thinks of Sook Chin's explanation. Next Dembe, who agrees with Timmy now, adds her logic.

Dembe: I think it's big and if it's big it really weighs too much and it can't really go around.

Teacher: That seems to be a lot like what Sook Chin said, but anyway I'm sorry, go ahead. . . .

Dembe: And then I disagree with Ricardo but I agree with Timothy, I think that small things have to go around big things because big things can't go around small things, for one thing the sun, I think it weighs too much.

Timmy: If the sun went around the earth, it probably could burn us.

Dembe: Yeah because it would get too close and stuff.

Then there is a short animated discussion of the ways we would all die if this were to be true. Then we go back to making sense of Timmy's assertion. . . .

Teacher: I don't understand that, that doesn't make any sense to me, I mean if the sun goes around the earth or the earth goes around the sun, it still seems to me that they'd still be far enough apart so that we wouldn't burn up.

Timmy: No, because if the sun, the sun went around the . . . see the earth goes around the sun and it can go in its orbit, and it goes around but if the sun went around the earth then the gravity from the earth . . . I just don't think it would work, if it went the other way the sun would get, I don't know how to say it, I know it would be just burning up but I don't know how to explain it.

Alice: I disagree that it might burn you because when the earth goes around the sun then that's just like the sun going around the earth because that's just like the earth moving around the sun, that's turning like the earth usually does so it wouldn't burn us and if the sun goes around the earth it would be like the same thing.

Timmy: There's just got to be something wrong or it wouldn't matter.

Teacher: So Alice, why do you think the earth goes around the sun?

Alice: Um I'm not sure I just know that it doesn't matter which way it goes, if the sun goes around the earth or the earth goes around the sun.

Yong Sun: I disagree with Timothy that we'd all burn up . . . 'cause the earth has an orbit and if the sun went around the earth, the sun would have an orbit too.

Timmy: Yeah but the sun doesn't have an orbit that's why, and also they've gotten something wrong otherwise it wouldn't matter which way it would go so I revise what I said and say now that something's got to be wrong or else the sun would go around the moon or something, something's got to be wrong or I don't know. . . .

I remind him of Sook Chin's explanation, and that seems to pacify him for a moment. But then a whole new argument starts. Joey returns us to the topic of orbits of planets within other orbits. Because of this, larger planets *do* go around smaller planets. "I disagree with Timmy that the moon can't go around the sun because in our science book Mars and Mercury are smaller than Saturn and it still goes around them, it's in a different orbit. . . . " Jin gets very excited about this. He disagrees, "No, if this was Mars and it had a different orbit and Saturn was going around it then Saturn would be like this" [*draws a picture*] (Fig.4.11).

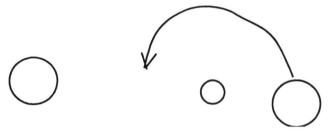

Figure 4.11

Joey says again, "It's in a different orbit, here's Saturn and here's Mars right there [*points*]." Jin still disagrees and keeps interrupting Joey as he tries to explain. So I draw a picture, which is like the one in the book of the planet's orbits around the sun. I ask Joey if this is what he means: "So here's Mercury, it's going around the sun, but in order to go around the sun, Venus has to go around Mercury and the sun, is that what you're saying?" Jin, though, continues to argue for his interpretation of Joey's words: "Yeah but he's saying this is Mars and then it has its orbit and then here's Saturn's orbit and then here's Saturn. I think that's what he's saying."

> *Joey*: Here's Saturn and in order to go around the sun it has to go
> around both of them just to go around the sun.

Teacher: Well I think that is true if this is what you're saying in my
          picture not in that picture?
Joey: Yeah that's what I'm saying.
Teacher: So it's going around the sun as well as going around
          something smaller than it.
Joey: Um-hum . . .
Jin: Well if it's going around it then it has an orbit by it, you know.

Jin gets more insistent in his disagreement, and Joey gets more
vehement in his explanation of *his* argument. "*No*, if I'm, ah, a planet
and then someone else is I'll still be going around it and the other
person's just in a different orbit, or a different place!"

Jin: If it goes round the planet it has to go like this [*he gestures with
       his arms that the planet would circle around the other planet as
       well as around the sun*].
Joey: No it doesn't, I can walk around you but far away.
Jin: I know but you're still going around me.
Joey: I know so it's still going around those other planets.
Jin: But the other planet has to go around it like that . . . closer to it.
Joey: No it doesn't, I'm far, very far away and you're the different
        planet, I go around you and it's not, it's not, and you say you're
        not going around me, I'll still be going around just from farther
        away.
Jin: No 'cause if I were moving that way and you were moving this
       way you'd be going like that . . . [*he indicates that they would
       crash together.*]
Joey: No because if you were the planet and I was Jupiter no not that
        one, Mercury and then you'd be moving too the same way but I
        could still be going around you.
Jin: I know but but you're saying that going around like this going
       around the planet.
Joey: No I'm saying it can still go around a bigger thing just in a
        different orbit.
Jin: I know but like this is still a different orbit, you're saying it goes
       around the sun and the planet so it would go like this like that
       (Fig. 4.12).

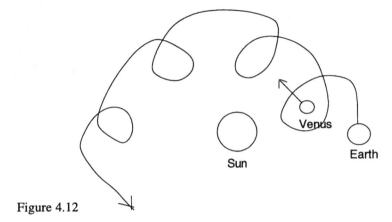

Figure 4.12

Joey: No 'cause if it's going around Venus or Mercury it would go
 around both of them or Venus wouldn't even go around the sun.
Jin: But you said um, that it goes around the planet and the sun so it has
 to go like this? Or like that or something like that. . . . (Fig. 4.13)

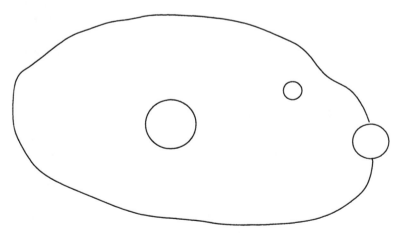

Figure 4.13

Now this one is true, but exaggerated; Jin has now modified his theory to accommodate Joey's in his new drawing, but they continue to argue until I have Joey, Ricardo, and Jin demonstrate Joey's model. I summarize and everyone agrees with Joey. But then it starts up again when Dembe draws this picture to explain why a large thing can't go around a small thing (Fig. 4.14).

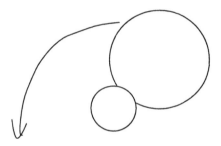

Figure 4.14

Jin says again that if something large were to go directly around the earth it would crush the earth. Joey is adamant, so I stop the argument and ask them all to write in their notebooks what they think of what Joey, Jin, and Timmy are arguing about, then I take a poll and almost everyone says that little would go around big. Alice said she's still thinking about it, Sook Chin has come around to share this opinion, and Dembe isn't sure.

CONCLUSION: THE ROLE OF THE COMMUNITY

In these classes with the third grade, as in those in the first and second grade combination, the shape of conversations and the qualities of the community are intertwined with each other and with the science. The difference is in *my* purposes, *my* role in the two contexts. In the latter class my role is primarily reactive on a superficial level—around the science. My role is primarily proactive—I try to instantiate values that I hold around how children should treat each other. The children and I negotiate the science that is talked about because I hold these values about the way people should interact—there is a dependency between the discourse which springs from these values and the science we are doing. This is also true in the third grade, except my proactive role extends to the science content. I am quite active, trying to shape and center the science. The discourse in some senses follows this. Because I wish to stay with particular ideas and get to particular places in our thinking about those ideas, the discourse patterns have changed. I encourage and stimulate conflict. This feels at odds with my ideals and values about how I think people should respect and value each other. Because I will not give up these ideals, I reshape the science to allow them.

The community in these two classes is, I think, characterized by children entering imaginatively, intellectually, and empathetically into one another's conceptions of the world. This is done in order to understand each other. This thinking becomes critical, and is common to both classes. The entry point to this is different. In the first and second grade, the progression of the community is as simple as described above—listening and hearing each other, then thinking critically. In the third grade, from the start the critical and connected modes of thinking interlayer. This is a reflection of what I am doing, the choices I make. I work in these classes to keep ideas problematic, to generate conflict. I do a balancing act between this and my more fundamental values about how people should treat each other. The ways the children express themselves and interact reflect this. A critical quality of this is how I use conflict in the class to increase the children's need for each other. The children express different ideas and logic in their ways of thinking. Rather than divide the class into factions, differences strengthen the need each child feels for another. By hearing an opinion that is different from your own but is respected, it can cause you to question yourself and modify your thinking. This process is valuable when it is around something engaging, important. Again, this cycles back around to the tension I feel in taking a proactive role shaping the science. To ensure that conflict remains a strengthening quality of the community, I must keep the focus of the conflict of the children's own choice. There is no resolution in this; it is a tension.

This is about knowing certain things—a knowing that enables acting. Not knowing because the things known can be articulated—stated, but rather because those things develop an articulation as they are given substance through what is done in class. The values and beliefs that I think are being articulated concern how people should interact with each other within the context of science. The science is shaped by this as much as the interactions are. In order to enable each child to participate in the inquiry, this unit is about inquiry itself— asking questions (which is by articulating what you know as well as what you don't know) and working on answers (which is through feeling and judging as well as thinking). The subject of the inquiry is the solar system: that's the vehicle for our exploartions. This is not a unit about learning facts about a particular area of science, although it does contain some of that. It's about *thinking* in science, which is something created by people and therefore has people in it. And science, which is a living, growing thing (to me, anyway), has people interacting. This interaction, between people and between people and things, is how it grows. I am not saying that the way the science is portrayed or the way I want the children to interact reflects either science or scientists as I have experienced them. I hold the value that *all* should participate first and I rethink and reshape the science to make this possible. I do this by looking for ways and places that other ways of thinking and knowing—emotional, religious, aesthetic—intersect with the science.

The particular conversations that I have picked to talk about are places where the children and I illustrate various ways of knowing, thinking, and interacting, all of which are both intellectual and otherwise, scientific and otherwise. The conversation between me and Timmy and Jin about gravity and gravity boots is about the relationships between theorizing, questioning, and the phenomena. It's about how different explanations work depending on your purpose. It's also about the relationship between knowing, thinking, and taking chances. The conversation between Ricardo and Yong Sun about whether or not the moon and sun will crash into each other is about the same thing, and also about people trying to understand each other, rather than just asserting their own ideas. The conversation between Daniel and Yong Sun about the word *satellite* is about meaning and understanding of words in context and in isolation: Can fundamental meanings be defined?[4] The conversation about the orbits of the planets about the sun between Jin and Joey is about portraying what you know, knowing with certainty, but still having this knowing questioned and changed. They both portray their knowing as "certain" because they are attempting to communicate their ideas to one another. But because they are attempting to communicate, which also means to hear and under-stand what each is saying, each child's certainty is infused with inherent yet unstated uncertainty. Because they are talking to one another, a statement of knowing becomes a declaration of not-knowing (Habermas, 1991; Heidegger, 1962; Wittgenstein, 1969).

I am actively shaping this class to reflect values and beliefs I already have about science, about children, and about how I think people should interact. I also shape these classes as those values and beliefs take on substance through the concrete realities of what is actually happening, the questions and observations we have about the science, the ideas and qualities the children articulate, and the emotional as well as intellectual ways in which they interact with each other and with me.

NOTES

1. I am awakened to this self-knowledge (Habermas, 1991).

2. See Appendix 1 for a description of the school and classroom setting in which this unit occurs. See Appendix 2 for a discussion of children's pseudonyms.

3. It also makes paramount my role in anticipating who might be able to make those sorts of contributions as well as in knowing when to invite those contributions. The way that I do this I would describe as a process of "nibbling" as well as developing a depth of knowledge about each child. The two are linked, however.

4. Can meaning be divorced from use and context (Wittgenstein, 1968)?

CHAPTER 5

Teaching: Knowing and Learning

In this chapter I argue that a teacher's practice reflects both articulated and unarticulated knowledge. Praxis proceeds from the personal epistemological standpoints of the teacher. This knowledge is constructed from the teacher's prior experiences, and therefore is only partially applicable to particular situations in the classroom. The immediate circumstances in which teaching occurs present different and unique qualities from those in which knowledge and values were created. The classroom environment is also an interactive one. The teacher is, therefore, continuously confronted with the inadequacy of her knowledge. The circumstances and children's activities tell her that she needs to do things differently. In this situation, the act of teaching as an assertion of knowing becomes a recognition of not-knowing. Teaching becomes an occasion for learning about subject matter, children, and self. I offer two examples of teaching in a first grade classroom to give this argument substance.[1] One focuses on an example from my teaching in which parallels between scientific theorizing and storytelling are drawn and capitalized upon. The second example is about Kathy Valentine, the teacher I collaborated with in first and second grade, and her teaching of a social studies unit in which the words fact and opinion are examined while reading biographies of the life of Martin Luther King Jr. This became especially problematic because this instruction occurred during the recent Gulf War, when issues of tolerance and prejudice took on more than philosophical meanings.

As with Jin and Joey in the last chapter, when acting, talking, and teaching in my classes, I expose the things that I think I know. Again like Jin and Joey, I am exposing this knowledge in a changing context;

one that is in flux. Through this process I am recasting those known things as unknown, as questions. The acts of teaching are acts of making assertions; but these assertions quickly become conjectures subject to revision and change—they become opportunities for learning. When teaching, I am often surprised when I realize the things that I am teaching, am learning, that I *know*. And I have noticed that other teachers are, too. When we teach, we act on assumptions founded in knowledge: knowledge about children, curriculum, and teaching. This knowledge is an assumption—unarticulated, unacknowledged— because it has become translated into a value, something we have decided is *of* value and no longer think we have to defend. This knowledge has passed from the intellect and has become beliefs and emotions which are unquestioned, felt to be true. But when we are teaching, things happen to make us aware of those assumptions; to make us think about and question them and the values on which they are based. This questioning and subsequent learning occurs because of the social, interactive qualities of the classroom.

In this chapter I argue that the knowledge base of teachers is both the foundation upon which they are able to teach and a vehicle through which they are able to learn, because through teaching they come to question that knowledge. Teachers know many things and they base their teaching upon this knowledge. Translating knowledge into teaching involves making choices that are based upon the teacher's values and beliefs. Teaching is inherently interactive and social. Because students don't share either the knowledge, the experiences upon which this knowledge is formed, or the teacher's values when she translates what she knows into curriculum, the teacher is continuously reassessing, reforming her knowledge and values. The specifics of the context in which she is using her knowledge challenge that knowledge.

There is an increasing body of work in which researchers and practitioners write about the ways in which teachers' personal and professional selves evolve.[2] In other writings, teachers tell us how the domains of knowledge they bring to teaching are broadened through their teaching.[3] Much can be said about the sources of these "ways of knowing." In general, both personal and professional values and belief systems derive from a variety of sources, but especially from lived experience.[4] These personal experiences and the memberships in sociocultural groups which create them define a person's epistemologic standpoints from which their beliefs, values, and actions are derived.

These epistemologies are created and maintained emotionally as well as intellectually.[5]

I am arguing in this chapter that through teaching we are forced to articulate and act upon our values and beliefs in a context different from the ones in which they were formed. In doing this, our values and beliefs are altered because of this new context—which includes interaction with students—and through the act of articulation and the self-awareness this entails.

The teacher, as well as the children, are members of a community. A community contains people who share some goals, purposes, values, ways of acting and communicating, but not others. The basis of a community is similarity on one or more dimensions—without similarity a community would not exist, could not function. The driving force, however, the life force behind a community, is difference—we need each other because we are different from each other. When we act in a community, we act on an assumption of similarity, but those actions often expose our differences. This exposure motivates change, in ourselves as we learn from this; and in the community, as its members evolve. This process is fundamental to my classroom.

I write about two elementary school teachers: me and a woman whom I work with, Kathy Valentine, both who know a lot about certain things. I know a lot about science and about how to teach science—I have had my Ph.D. in geology for ten years and have been teaching science to children and young adults since 1978. Kathy knows a lot about teaching small children—she has been an elementary school teacher for thirteen years—and about literacy and social studies instruction. I will argue, in this chapter, that as we teach these things that we know so well to children, we both purposely and inadvertently expose ourselves to things that we don't know. This is a function of both *how* we are teaching—with social constructivist means and ideals— and *what* we are teaching. Both process and content become problematic through teaching. When we expose these areas where we don't know the right things in the right ways, that exposure occurs simultaneous with learning. This makes it hard to articulate what is "learned," because it doesn't really occur isolated from previous knowledge or from the context in which learning occurs.[6] But what does happen is that new *meanings* of our choices and values become apparent to us.[7]

I will present two stories of teaching, one by Kathy Valentine and one by me to illustrate my argument. The first story focuses on my teaching a unit about scientific theorymaking—fact and opinion in science—by having children research and write stories about dinosaurs. This raised questions for me about process and about literacy instruction. In the second, Kathy is teaching a unit on Martin Luther King Jr. combined with a part of the social studies curriculum in which the meanings of statements are assessed as either facts or opinions. This teaching occurred during the recent war in Iraq. This context and the context provided by the children in the classroom infused the substance of the unit with intensely felt meanings, which became quite problematic as ideas were shared. In all cases, the teacher's knowledge of "how to teach" enabled us to learn about the children, more about the subject matter, and our own purposes in making certain curricular and pedagogical choices.

FIRST STORY

Dinosaur Stories—Substance Or Process, Choosing Instructional Goals
I decided to teach about dinosaurs and prehistoric life in this first grade classroom because the district science objectives required it. This requirement was rather simplistic: it asked that at this grade level children be introduced to ideas of geologic time scale and the fossil record and be exposed to dinosaur names. I was interested in enabling the children to think critically and creatively in science and about science. This was really the subtext, or maybe the "real" curriculum, for this unit: thinking about where scientific knowledge comes from, how it is constructed, how clues and partial knowledge can be put together to create something with the sometimes misleading appearance of coherence and completeness. Using dinosaurs for this is particularly powerful, I think, because a lot of material about dinosaurs available for children is of varying quality and scientific accuracy.[8]

I decided to teach this unit on dinosaurs using the parallels between story-writing and scientific theorizing, story-reading and interpretation, and the reading and interpretation of the material on dinosaurs found in trade books. If children were to engage in constructing stories about the lives of dinosaurs using the partial evidence—reconstructed morphology, environment, associations—of scientists, they would be participating in realistic scientific activities. The children, in sharing their stories with each other, would subject their thinking to the critical inquiry of me and their peers. I envisioned the vehicle for this unit to be similar to units Kathy had done on story parts and the interpretive reading of stories and descriptions I had read of writing workshops.[9] I had hoped to be able to use these structures to frame our critical assessments of the children's scientific thinking.

I started the dinosaur unit with talk about the things that the children knew or thought they knew about dinosaurs and the sources of that knowledge. I wanted to see the range in the sophistication of their knowledge. Then we talked about whether or not that knowledge was fact or theory or fiction and how those start to blend together when talking about something like dinosaurs. I particularly used the words fact, theory, and fiction with the children because of their importance to my goals in this unit and to connect this unit to other teaching that Kathy had been doing all year in language arts and social studies.[10] I wished to know what the children understood about how ideas about dinosaurs—how they lived, what they did, how they looked—were constructed. I also wanted to open up the discussion to include fictionalized, fantasy dinosaur stories because, to me, this is on a continuum with the scientific theorizing. And I wanted the children to start thinking about the criteria they should be using to judge dinosaur material. This became a discussion of the movie *The Land Before Time*.[11]

I asked the class what kinds of things they had found out about dinosaurs in *The Land Before Time*. Maria Theresa said that she learned that some dinosaurs were egg eaters. Bulli told us that there are big dinosaurs that eat little dinosaurs. Claire added, "It was a tyrannosaurus rex!" I responded that *The Land Before Time* was a story that someone had written, just like *Charlie and the Chocolate Factory*[12] (the children were reading this in class during story time). I said that both are stories and both have authors. Kyong Min, though, disagreed: "It's not real. . . . " So I asked her how she knew that *Charlie and the Chocolate Factory* wasn't real. She responded by listing things in the story that are components of the fantasy. The children debated whether things that were considered plausible had to be real also. Then they talked about why they thought some things were plausible and some things weren't. Other children wanted to continue talking about this, and I also thought it was important in this context. Part of Roald Dahl's power is, I think, that his fantasy is stretched truth, caricatured reality: things that people and especially children really do contemplate. That is also, I think, the power of children's dinosaur stories and these sorts of conversations about what we believe and why, and was what I wanted this unit to be about.

I returned the conversation to *The Land Before Time* and what was real, or stretched truths, or fantasy in that. The children said things like, "dinosaurs are real . . . they did lay eggs . . . eat meat . . . take care of their babies." Each time they said these things, I challenged their statements: "How do you know that, though?" and the children responded with statements about their beliefs, magic, the evidence presented in the story, or constructed by the children from other experiences.

I summarized the children's discussion about what was real or not, what might be real, and why the children thought that. Then I set up the construction of our own stories by reviewing the unit they had done in language arts on story parts—setting, characters, problem, resolution—using these both to construct a story and interpret stories. We went from this to the preliminary construction of a story about the dinosaurs depicted in the mural, *The Age of Reptiles*.[13] This involved more critical thinking and brought more of their ideas about dinosaurs to the surface. I asked the children to start talking about what they thought they saw going on in the picture and gradually helped them to weave a story out of that. I would also periodically interject "why" questions into this. For example, when they said a particular dinosaur was doing something, I would ask them why they thought that and, then, why they thought that the artist felt able to depict the animal in that way—reconstructing their logic and then the artist's logic.

The next thing we did in class was from a handout from a *Ranger Rick* publication on dinosaurs[14] that depicts nine pictures of different dinosaurs and settings such as a volcano and a mesa, that the children could cut out and rearrange into different orders to make stories. After the children constructed their stories, I asked each child to present their story to the rest of the class. This was done by children arranging larger versions of the pictures on the board at the front of the room and then telling their stories using the pictures as props. Then they took questions from the floor. The questioners usually asked the child to clarify some point or give more details or defend the sequence in such a way that the result was an enlargement of the story and the story's logic. This was in essence a rewrite. On a subsequent day, I read back a number of the stories, and each time the child revised it again and again, interactively with the class.

Farzoneh started us off. First she arranged her sequence of pictures on the board, then she began to present her story. I wish to give a full text of her story presentation because it shows how, as an interactive social event, the presentation becomes a constructed act of story-writing. The questions and additions contributed by the class in this piece of dialogue are extremely important components in the science and in the process of writing. But my focus was the science.

> *Farzoneh*: First tyrannosaurus comes and then they see it, but they have to run away, then he sees it. This guy sees it and then the thunderstorm comes and then the mother comes and she sees the babies are hatching. The babies look at the sky because of the thunderstorm. They have to run away but they can't so they try another way but they can't swim and then the volcano erupts.
>
> *Teacher*: And that's the end, the volcano erupts? Okay, let me see if I can say it. The tyrannosaurus rex (*I point*) and the herd of hadrosaurs see tyrannosaurus rex and they try to run away and then the pteranodon sees tyrannosaurus rex, then there is a thunderstorm and the mother triceratops is in the thunderstorm and she sees that her babies are hatching and she wants to get them away from the thunderstorm but they can't go by the rocky cliffs, the rocky cliff is in the way and they can't swim so they can't get across the water hole and there's a volcano too. . . . Very nice story, I liked that story (*we clap*). Everybody, Farzoneh is still up there and she will answer your questions. I personally would like to ask, first of all, who are the characters in the story?

I ask some questions using the story parts that Kathy has introduced to the children, as tools to help develop critical reading skills. I wish to model a form of critical questioning which would lead to elaborating and rethinking the stories. I am interested in developing the children's thinking around the content of their writing rather than the mechanics of writing. My interest is not so much in the literary value of their stories, but rather in the scientific value. Then other children start asking questions. These questions, however, were usually about why Farzoneh had made the narrative choices that she had made intertwined with discussions of alternative choices and the variations in reasoning that might lie behind those choices.

For example, Tatyana asked Farzoneh why she had put the picture of the tyrannosaurus where she had, which led to a discussion between the two girls, and Chen, Cory, and Claire about the predatory habits of tyrannosaurus, and whether or not the mother triceratops would be with her young and if so, whether or not she would be helping them and how. I push this along by asking, "Would the mother triceratops take care of her babies, or do the eggs just hatch and the babies are all by themselves? How do you know that the mother triceratops is going to take care of her babies?" Farzoneh replies, "'Cause she doesn't want them to die. . . ."

> *Teacher*: She doesn't want them to die? But some animals lay their eggs for their babies and then the babies are born and they're not there, the mothers and fathers aren't there. Birds have their eggs and the babies hatch and the mothers take care of the babies, but snakes don't. Snakes lay their eggs and their mothers and fathers go away and when the babies hatch the babies are all by themselves. . . .
>
> *Chen*: Alligators do.
>
> *Teacher*: Alligators . . . do they leave their babies all alone or do they take care of them?
>
> *Chen*: They don't take care of them.
>
> *Teacher*: They don't take care of them? You're saying that the mother triceratops was there when her babies hatched. Do you know if that's true? [*Farzoneh makes a face.*] You think that might be true? Is that a guess, a theory? [*Yeses.*]
>
> *Kyong Min*: How do you know the mother dinosaurs take care of their babies? How did the dinosaur know that the babies would be born?

Kyong Min and Farzoneh talk for a short while about why Farzoneh thought the mother was taking care of the babies, but Tatyana wants to know more about the manner of the interactions between the mother and young: "How come you need to put the mother's swim with the babies. How come she swims, why did you put it right there? Why did you put the babies over there and not over there?"

Farzoneh: Because I thought when she was, she saw the thunder-storm she was running and she saw her babies hatch.

Teacher: Oh, I see, so she was running and then she saw the babies hatch. She didn't run over to see if the babies hatched? Oh.

Farzoneh, in essence, reconstructs her story as she talks about her choices, her reasoning, and the science with the rest of the class. This continues in the next class, which I open by reading a transcribed version of Farzoneh's story. But Farzoneh has decided that she wishes to tell it herself a different way.

Teacher: This is Farzoneh's story. There was a tyrannosaurus coming. And a herd of hadrosaurs saw it and ran away. A pteranodon saw it and flew away. Then a lightning storm came and scared the tyrannosaurus away. A mother triceratops was scared by the lightening. As she tried to run away, she saw her eggs were hatching. She and her babies tried to run away but they couldn't climb over the rocky cliffs and they couldn't swim across the water hole, so first the babies died in the volcanic eruption and then the mother died. And that's the end. Farzoneh has revised some of her story and she wants to tell you her new version of the story. She's kept the pictures the same but she's rewritten the story. She's revised it.

Farzoneh: First he comes to eat those but they look at him because he's coming to eat the babies.

Teacher: Oh, the pteranodon is coming to eat the babies?

Farzoneh: So the stor [?] comes and then he has to run away but he ate the babies so she can't find them, she went, she wouldn't go and find her babies but she didn't care so she went here, but she couldn't go over the rocky cliffs so she went here, but she couldn't swim and then she, the volcano came and then . . . but they still didn't die, only the babies did because he ate them.

Teacher: 'Cause the pteranodon ate them?

Farzoneh: And this because she went close . . .

Teacher: So now the story is the tyrannosaurus. . . . There was a tyrannosaurus and the hadrosaurus saw him and ran away, and pteranodon came and the pteranodon tried to eat the baby triceratops and the mother, is that the mother or the father triceratops now? *[Farzoneh answers: "Mother."]* The mother triceratops came looking for the baby triceratops and couldn't find them and she looked and she looked and she looked in the rocky cliffs but she couldn't really get over them because they were rocky cliffs and she couldn't find them and she looked by the water hole but she couldn't go any further looking because the water hole was in the way and then the volcano came and what happened with the volcano?

Farzoneh: The babies died because of him [*the pteranodon*] and the mother died because, um, she was close to the volcano.

Teacher: Ah, so the babies are dead because the pteranodon ate them and the mother triceratops died in the volcano. Do you want to answer some questions? [*Many children murmur "sad ending."*] Those are comments—do you want to take comments too, Farzoneh, or just questions?

Farzoneh: Comments and questions.

Cory: That's a sad ending, that's my comment.

The children again start questioning Farzoneh's narrative and debating the reasoning behind it. Bulli asks, "Um, why did the, wait a second, I think the pteranodon, um, oh why did he eat the babies?" And I ask, "Is the question, Bulli, is the question why did the pteranodon eat the babies or why did Farzoneh think that pteranodons would eat babies?" Bulli wants to know the second, but Ok Ran the first. "I think it really was hungry!" Farzoneh explains. Once again, I return the conversation to the debate about whether or not the children know or can theorize that mother dinosaurs look after their young: "How would you know that that might be true? I think the last time that I asked that question and Chen remembered about alligators, the mothers have their babies hatch out of eggs and the mothers aren't there to take care of their babies. Why wouldn't a triceratops be just like a mother alligator?"

Kyong Min: They were different.

Maria Theresa: They're not alligators.

Ok Ran: The mother alligator stays with the babies, when the babies hatch. I saw it on a book, that the mother stays, the mother stays with the eggs, the eggs hatch, and then the mother is there!

Teacher: Claire, can you think of any reason to think that mother triceratops take care of their babies?

> *Claire*: I'm not so sure because a bunch of people said yeah and there aren't any people who have seen dinosaurs so we will never know and I wouldn't be so sure about that.

I ask the children what sort of things we could do to be able to say what mother dinosaurs do with their young. Paula suggests that we look in books; Bulli and Chen suggest a dictionary. Ok Ran suggests asking their moms or dads. Claire thinks we could go to a museum. I settle on looking in books, "Well you know we have all these books over here and maybe you guys could be looking to see if there is any evidence for that. That's all that we could do in this room, I think."

My role in the storytelling is to question foundational assumptions in the science; the children picked up on this and started doing it for each other, also. I did this, for example, by asking them how they *knew* the mommy dinosaurs looked after their young, how they *knew* that certain dinosaurs ate certain things or behaved in certain ways or lived in certain places. This was to generate discussion on the content of their storytelling rather than to critique the stories by literary criteria. That's not to say that the two—the content and the form—weren't linked or the development of the two weren't linked, because I think that they were. For example, Farzoneh wrote her story so that it opens with a problem, which is based upon a number of embedded assumptions about the nature of dinosaurs—where they live, what they do—and her resolutions are also based upon assumptions. The way that she moves the story by adding problem after problem continues this and plays upon this.

At the end of this phase of storytelling, I listed questions on a poster and said that maybe we needed to try to find out about them. Then we looked at books on dinosaurs and modern analogues. This was within cooperative learning groups at this point, with one question per group but one book per child. Each child would use a book and then share what they had learned with others in their group, after this, we had a large group discussion.

The question about how dinosaurs care for their young or even whether or not they do seemed from the start to be the most compelling to the children. It is also the one about which I could present a number of different current theories and also pull in modern analogues to dinosaurs such as birds and alligators; so that's the one I concentrated on. We had a very interesting discussion about the logic behind the various theories about whether or not dinosaurs and different dinosaurs in different ways took care of their babies. As counter examples to their theorizing, I used modern animals. We started doing more research on that topic and then I asked a colleague who had documented a family of hawks to come in to the class and give a slide presentation about how hawks bring up their babies. The result was that some members of the class continued doing research on dinosaurs and others started to research birds, and all continued to write and share their stories. But this final process was conceived of and used by me to motivate research and thinking, which resulted in new writings—not explicit rewriting and perfecting of one piece of work. In other words, we focused *out* from our writings rather than *in* on the writings themselves.

This was not really what I had expected that we would be doing. I purposely modelled the initial framing of the curriculum of this unit after descriptions I had read of writing workshops. I found that because I had certain goals in mind about the substance of the children's writing, that I had to lay aside the workshop's writing-sharing-editing-rewriting cycle. I stopped pursuing the literacy aspect because I perceived the goals of the two, literacy and science instruction, to be in some senses antithetical—for example, envisioning stories as "complete thoughts," which I understood to be one of the writing workshop goals rather than as vehicles for articulating questions. This was a disquieting choice for me to make; I felt that in doing this I was forfeiting the literacy instruction I had planned.

Although I had planned purposely that the instructional goals of the unit were to be the creative and critical qualities of scientific thinking, I had never really critically examined those values in myself. Through this teaching I came to do this and to see those values as potentially problematic. The child Farzoneh, whose story is the springboard for much of this unit, is from a traditional, conservative culture in which knowledge is widely regarded as received, not created, and in which a woman's place is to live within that knowledge, rather than to challenge it. Many of the other children in the class come from similar cultures. All of these children would be returning to these cultures. In many ways I have a planned political purpose in teaching children to be critical and creative thinkers, but I have done most of this thinking in the abstract, divorced from particular interactions with particular children. How defensible are these choices, really? How would I feel, as a parent, if my daughter's teachers based their instruction at a fundamental level on values radically different from my own?

When I teach science to children, a major belief that I bring to the curriculum is that science is a place where children are involved in *active* learning. There is no place for passivity in science, no place for uncritical knowledge. This is an important issue for me as a scientist, for a person who knows what it means to act as a scientist, but also as a woman, as a person interested in teaching science to girls and minorities. But is my urging little girls who appear to be passive in school to be active learners in a social context really effective? Is it okay for me to be urging this on children, whose success might be more dependent on knowing certain things in certain ways rather than being critical, creative thinkers?

SECOND STORY

Martin Luther King Jr.—
The Personal And The Political In The Social Constructivist Classroom
This is a story about how a teacher's pedagogical actions are infused with moral and ethical choices, and about how a teacher can become aware of those *as choices* through her teaching. To introduce this, I will tell some short anecdotes about my own and other's experiences of schooling as political.

I went to junior high and high school during the second half of the 1960s and early part of the 1970s. I lived in a conservative corner of northwestern Connecticut, in a farming town peopled primarily by second-generation Swedes, and a minority of English and Scottish colonial descendents. My social studies and history teachers came from New York or Boston. Many were politically active outside the community and frustrated by the political inactivity of the community.

The common joke among my peers, when we talk about American history classes in high school, is that classes never get beyond the Civil War. My personal experience was that we never did anything *but* the Civil War. We would start with Jacksonian Democracy and end with Reconstruction. In five out of six years, we read *Civil Disobedience* in classes. Why was this? I would argue that this choice of curriculum relates to the political purposes of my teachers: purposes that maybe they didn't wish to state or even defend to the community, but purposes that were nonetheless rooted in values and moral judgements that they were willing to act on in this covert sort of way.

My mother did all of her schooling in the 1930s in Brooklyn, New York. The majority of her teachers were first- and second-generation German-Jewish immigrants. Many of these teachers were politically active, in the community, their union, nationally, internationally, and around economic and social issues—they were union activists; they housed refugees. These teachers brought these concerns to their teaching but rarely overtly, explicitly. Usually the political, moral content of their teaching was submerged within other parts of the curriculum—what children read in Reading or Civics and how it was discussed, what children wrote about in composition or worked problems on in math—not explicit, but *there*.

I have a friend who was schooled in economics and left-wing politics who taught business education to coloured children in South Africa in the early eighties. The formal curriculum concerned simple mathematics, balancing checkbooks, and keeping a ledger. What he really taught was in *how* he taught these things, and in particular, in the conversations that went on in class about this curriculum. The curriculum was in the pedagogy as much as in the content of the subject matter.

In these three examples, teachers were acting as political moral agents. They were moved to do so by the intensity of feelings they had about particular issues focused and activated by circumstances of the times in which they were teaching. These same times also made these moral, political choices around how curriculum was depicted more apparent and potentially more problematic. My teachers and my mother's were often called upon to defend their teaching by parents who did not agree with the teacher's beliefs. My friend, teaching in South Africa, counted on his students and their parents to keep the things going on in his class secret.

During the week in January 1991, when Martin Luther King Jr. Day was celebrated, Kathy read biographies of Dr. King to the children. Then the children together composed a pattern book about King's life in which each sentence began with the phrase, "My dream for a better world is . . ." This unit was combined with a unit from the social studies curriculum in which the meanings of the words fact and opinion were examined both in the contexts of the books being read and the book written by the children.

Kathy's understandings of literacy teaching and teaching students whose primary language isn't English has led her to emphasize the structure of sentences and stories as a means to enable both interpretation and communication. Her pedagogy invites interaction with the children, both as a group and as individuals. Kathy continued this while reading about Martin Luther King Jr. combined with working on the meanings of the words fact and opinion. This combination allowed Kathy to attempt something very political in this class—to portray her own moral beliefs about racism, softened by intertwining that portrayal with the social studies curriculum. Her beliefs and those of the authors of the books were portrayed as personal opinion. Kathy's relativistic portrayal of her moral views concerning racism was maintained through her choice of process, in which she expressed her beliefs about the development of voice in the children. The children have ideas that differ from Kathy's, and the publicness of this sharing and debate was heightened by circumstances: the Gulf War. This created dilemmas—the substance of this unit was problematic to some parents of children in the class, particularly within the context of the Gulf War. There are children in her classroom and in the school from Iran, Palestine, Israel, Saudi Arabia, and Kuwait. These children brought their own and their families' beliefs about racism as experienced in their cultures to the class. The perceptions of many of these families were that the Gulf War, Sadam Hussein's attacks on Israel, and the Israeli treatment of Palestinians were all racist. Their desires concerning the resolution of this racism may or may not be the same as that sought by Martin Luther King Jr. in the United States in the 1960s or by Kathy in this class. Other parents agreed with Kathy's values and political purpose and wished to make these ideas more explicit. They objected to allowing the children to voice different views. Still other parents thought discussion of these ideas shouldn't be part of public schooling at all. In this teaching, neither process nor substance are the "private property of the teacher."[15] Rather, the curriculum is "a medium evoking the critical reflection" of the teacher. This happens because the act of teaching is a public and social one.

The examination of the structural components of language—the use of the words fact and opinion—in a moral context deviates from the purely syntactical way this unit is normally taught. For example, the handouts which come with the text for this social studies unit involve classification of a series of statements on eighteenth-century British pirates. These sentences can be classified as either fact or opinion through a syntactic analysis, without any factual knowledge of pirates. By combining this unit with a controversial subject matter in a classroom in which discussion of meanings is invited ("What does the word segregation mean, anyway?"), the child is asked to examine the contextual meaning of ideas in the books and as felt in their own lives and experiences. The meaning of the words *segregation* and *prejudice* is different and multiple for a Palestinian child, a girl from Bangladesh, a child from Iran with relatives in Kuwait, a white middle-class American boy, a girl from inner-city Detroit—all of whom were in this classroom. It is different yet again from the lived experiences of the teacher. These personal contexts for meaning are also different from the context induced through a sympathetic (empathetic) consideration of the life of Martin Luther King Jr. All of these personal contexts and derived beliefs are invited by the process of this teaching. Because this teaching was done through people sharing different ideas and beliefs, these ideas and beliefs went from the tacit, felt, emotional state to the intellectual and articulated.[16]

This is different from what individual parents want—to avoid moral issues entirely or to preach particular viewpoints. This is *the* American dilemma of the role of school in moral education—should moral values be explicitly taught in schools, or is this education the private prerogative of individual families? The teacher is caught in the middle because her teaching directly reflects her own moral choices and ethical code. In this instance, Kathy's beliefs about racism and her beliefs about the rights of children to say the things that they believe are both exposed. Because this is done publicly during the Gulf War when sensitivities were particularly acute about many issues, Kathy had to articulate her foundational values. This act of articulation of previously assumed, tacit values requires that they be rerationalized, the logic behind them reconstructed within the concrete particulars of that moment. It means the development of a critical consciousness about those values.

DISCUSSION: PLACES OF CONFLICT
AS PLACES OF CHANGE

A teacher's foundational knowledge, the knowledge upon which she makes assumptions in order to be able to teach, can be thought of as a standpoint—the "place" in which her professional being is grounded. This place reflects her experiences and identities: it is from these experiences and identities that her standpoints are constructed.

Sandra Harding, in the book *Who's Science? Who's Knowledge?* writes about feminist standpoint theory as an epistemology which arises from an articulation of an individual's membership within historically and socially constructed communities. For example, a person who would call herself an African American, working-class woman, would also recognize that particular naming is a manifestation of certain systems of values, beliefs, and ways of thinking and believing derived from memberships in these groups. These memberships are multiple, and the values, goals, and means that each entail are often in conflict. Values derived from being working class can be at odds with those derived from being a woman. The values are formed, however, from the "lived" experience of the person through her membership in these groups and the interrelationships among her experiences of these groups. This situates the experience of the individual—experience has meaning and significance because it is socially constructed with and by a subset of certain kinds of people. Harding goes on to argue that because this ontology is personally and experientially derived, epistemology is as well—ways of knowing are derived from ways of being. This becomes translated into doing particular things in particular ways. It becomes manifested through methods of acting.[17]

Harding, and Dorothy Smith in *The Everyday World as Problematic*, discuss how articulating a personal lens can become a foundation for asking questions that drive research. I am suggesting in this chapter that an articulation of this lens acts, for the individual, as a vehicle in developing a critical consciousness of personal beliefs and values; the pursuit of questions developed in this process feeds back to a reexamination of the lenses and the values derived from them. This is a background/foreground argument, like the ones I have pointed out in previous chapters to talk about how conversation on one scientific topic can shift to be about a different topic; it explains how the focus of a community is dynamic and changing. In the community of the classroom, we as teachers act upon beliefs and knowledge; but this acting can cause us to articulate these in a new community, one which is different from the communities in which the beliefs and knowledge were formed. This causes us to rethink both the values, the knowledge, and their source. This process is a vehicle for learning about ourselves and about those people or things causing us to do this thinking.

Harding doesn't explicitly write about a standpoint position as evolving and changing because, I think, she writes primarily of a standpoint as a "possession" of an individual rather than as a dynamic construction created through the continuing interplay of the individual with the group. Smith hints at this because she is discussing the interactions of sociologist(s) and the individual(s) they study arising from different standpoint positions. This is not unlike my descriptions of the interactions of teachers and students. I would argue that any articulation of a standpoint acts to alter that stand, particularly if a person occupies multiple and potentially conflicting standpoints. Both the act of articulation—the way in which something comes to be articulated is implicitly critical—and reflection on that articulation because of the new context in which it occurs act to alter a stand.

Both of these are illustrated in my "stories." I think this is because the articulations that I am writing about are occurring during and through praxis, and not divorced from praxis. They are what Dewey or Schon[18] call "reflection-in-action": they are articulations constructed within a context framed by the individuals involved, but also by a purpose. Teaching is purposeful action. This articulation—what is done in a class, the curriculum—derives meaning from a retrospective understanding of historical context and a forward-looking recognition of the purpose, the needs it addresses. This purpose, the goals of teaching, directly reflect the teacher's initial standpoint and are both maintained and altered because of interactions between people and between people and subject matter in the class. The needs of the future rewrite the past.[19] For example, a teacher draws on her knowledge within the domains of the discipline, the learner, and the milieu in order to act; but enabling action is not the goal in itself. Rather, the goal is in the results of that action. A teacher may know certain things about a child and she may know that she has particular goals for that child (e.g., to learn to read). She may draw on her knowledge of subject matter, teaching, and the child to formulate actions which enable this goal. That goal, through this procedure, takes on concrete yet changing particulars from the evolving knowledge the teacher is using to formulate it within the context created by the child. These new concrete meanings act, in turn, to rewrite the past, or at least the interpretation that the teacher puts upon the past.

Habermas argues that communication fulfils three purposes: to make statements about actions, to make statements about the quality of those actions, and to make statements about how we feel about those actions. These statements are in fact claims made by the person speaking; claims about what is true, about the speaker's beliefs, and about a person's feelings. A hearer evaluates these claims and judges them. This hearer can also be the person making the claims. Habermas, in his later writings, argues that the articulation of beliefs in a new context causes them to be altered. This alteration can be congruent with the original beliefs—they can be merely enlarged or constricted in application—or they can be challenged and more fundamentally altered.

A teacher, in portraying a subject matter in a particular way or in choosing to teach in a particular manner, is also making claims, either implicit or explicit, about the subject matter and about what is "proper" behavior.[20] All of this is done within a context constructed by the interactions of people, ideas, and things. This is not a passive context. Some of the things a teacher does work, others don't; most work in part. It is also true that for these claims there is an audience of children that judges these claims and will express their judgements, given the opportunity, again either explicitly or implicitly.

When thought of in this way, the "pedagogical knowledge"[21] of a teacher becomes another example of a standpoint. A teacher's knowledge of students, learning, milieu, subject matter, and how to teach that subject matter are constructed from abstract moral and ethical values and more concrete experiences of teaching and subject matter both as it is encountered in school and in the world outside of school. A teacher's ways of knowing, as Schon points out, are "knowledge in action."[22] Therefore, they are most constructively thought of as dynamic ways of knowing; ways of knowing that are both specifiable—a teacher knows certain things in certain ways—and continuously altered and evolving, or unspecifiable. It is teacher knowledge that is created in the act of teaching, when the different things that a teacher knows are integrated in the choices that define an action. Those things that the teacher knows are transformed through that integration—the sum is not a pure addition of parts, the things interact with each other and interact within the context of the act; and that knowledge is transformed through implementation. An act doesn't stand in isolation; rather, it follows other acts, and actions succeed it.[23]

The actions of a teacher are also interactions with students. This interaction becomes a vehicle for teachers to define their own knowledge, and recognize what they know and don't know. A teacher's acts of teaching can be thought of as claims to knowledge. By asserting these claims in public, they are opened up to judgement and critical evaluation. By making a claim of certainty of knowledge, of what to do, a teacher makes a complementary claim of not knowing, of uncertainty.[24] This becomes a vehicle for learning and a vehicle for recognizing and examining the moral underpinnings of particular choices, representations, and beliefs.[25]

Shulman (1986) describes pedagogical content knowledge as knowledge of how to teach which entails an intersection of subject matter knowledge, knowledge of children, and milieu. Teachers can say what they know about a particular student at any one time, but this knowledge is continuously altered as the teacher and student interact and the student interacts with others in the teacher's presence. That knowledge of that student is also contingent upon the teacher's knowledge of the other domains —this knowledge specifies the form that the teacher-student interaction will take. The teacher's knowledge of the student does not exist out of the context constructed to contain the other domains of teacher knowledge or out of the interdependent evolution of that knowledge. Shulman emphasizes that pedagogical content knowledge draws upon a teacher's knowledge of multiple domains which intersect in enabling the act of teaching, but this intersection is one of mutually dependent variables. The different domains of teacher knowledge are located within a web a intersupporting beliefs, facts, theories, and ethical choices. An articulation of this knowledge takes on particular meaning and substance in the context of the act of teaching. This context is different from the ones in which the knowledge was originally constructed. This articulation can also make obvious the things a teacher doesn't know and give the teacher pathways to learn.

In teaching the unit on dinosaurs, I *knew* what I wanted to teach, how I wanted to teach it, and why. Because of the particulars of the children and the context of this teaching, I found myself questioning this knowledge. I was making a claim about knowledge and ways of doing things which I became increasingly uncertain of through those actions. The past contexts in which my knowledge of the subject matter and how to teach that subject matter were formed—that of being a woman scientist in a male-dominated field—were different from those in which I tried to apply that knowledge. In this particular instance, I abandoned one set of values and goals—about using a writing workshop model to teach scientific theorizing—and I am still questioning others—about the morality of teaching science in the way that I do. Kathy, in teaching the way that she does, learned new facets and interpretations of subject matter. She learned things about her students and their beliefs which broadened and extended her own ideas or caused her to rerationalize and rethink those ideas in this new context. In both cases, Kathy's teaching and my own, we came to learn about subject matter, teaching, our student's, and ourselves through our teaching. Our teaching was predicated upon an articulation of things we knew, and this articulation became a vehicle for questioning this knowledge and learning.

NOTES

1. The teaching described in this chapter occurred in a first grade class in the year previous to that described in the rest of this book. For a full description of the school, classroom, and children please see Appendices 1 and 2.
2. For example, Connelly & Clandinin (1990), Stories of experience and narrative inquiry; Johnson (1989), Embodied knowledge; Paley (1979),*White teacher*; Heath (1983), *Ways with words: Language, life, and work in communities and classrooms.*
3. Examples are: Ball (1990), *Halves pieces and twoths: Constructing representational contexts in teaching fractions*; Lensmire (1992), *Intention, risk, and writing in a third grade writing workshop.*
4. Harding (1991), *Whose science? Whose knowledge? Thinking from women's lives*; Belenky, Clinchy, Goldberger, Tarule (1986), *Women's ways of knowing: The development of self, voice, and mind*; Dewey (1902/56), *The child and the curriculum.*
5. Two references which I have found particularly helpful to me in formulating these ideas are Jurgen Habermas (1991), *Moral consciousness and communicative action*; and Hannah Arendt (1978), *The life of the mind* .
6. Schon (1990), *The theory of inquiry: Dewey's legacy to education.*
7. Schwab (1976), Education and the state: Learning community.
8. I believe that people in general make sense of the world and their lives through the use of stories and of storytelling. An example of a teacher making similar use of story telling in the classroom to make sense of children is Vivian

Paley (1990), *The boy who w ould be a helicopter.* I am also extending this idea to help my understanding of how children think about subject matter and I am using storytelling as a tool to challenge these understandings--I also teach the subject matter through storytelling.

9. Graves (1983), *Writing: Teachers and children at work*; Calkins (1986), *The art of teaching writing*; Applebee (1986), Problems in process approaches: Toward a reconceptualization of process instruction; Willensky (1990), *The new literacy: Redefining reading and writing in schools.*

10. An example of Kathy's teaching in which these words are used is the next story in this chapter, concerning Kathy's teaching of the life of Martin Luther King Jr.

11. Spielberg, Lucas, Kennedy, & Marshall (1988), *The land before time.*

12. Dahl (1964), *Charlie and the chocolate factory.*

13. Zallinger, *The age of reptiles.*

14. Brans, ed. (1989), *Ranger Rick's NatureScope: Digging into dinosaurs.*

15. Belenky, Clinchy, Goldberger, & Tarule, *Women's ways of knowing: The development of self, voice, and mind,* page 219.

16. Habermas (1991), *Moral consciousness and communicative action.*

17. Smith (1991), *The everyday world as problematic.*

18. Dewey (1933), *How we think: A restatement of the relation of reflective thinking to the educative process*; Donald Schon (1983) *The reflective practitioner: How professionals think in action.*

19. For example, Marx (1983), Theses on Feuerbach; Buck-Morss (1990), *The dialectics of seeing: Walter Benjamin and the arcades project.*

20. Apple (1979), *Ideology and curriculum*; Linda MacNeil (1988), *Contradictions of control: School structure and school knowledge.*

21. Shulman (1986), Those who understand: Knowledge growth in teaching.

22. Schon (1983), *The reflective practitioner: How professionals think in action.*

23. Kerr (1981), The structure of quality in teaching.

24. Wittgenstein (1969), *On certainty.*

25. Habermas (1991), *Moral consciousness and communicative action*; Kathleen Weiler (1988), *Women teaching for change: Gender, class and power*; Schwab (1976), Education and the state: Learning community.

CHAPTER 6

Conclusion

In this work I have tried to show how relationships are constructed and developed. Teaching, learning, and science are all fundamentally about relationships between people and between people and things. These relationships are developed, they change and evolve over time, as an interplay between those involved (both animate and inanimate), as each side of the relationship is affected by the other. Relationships begin with statements (implicit or explicit) of assumptions and of purposes. As the relationships alter, assumptions are challenged and changed, and purposes grow and shift direction.

I began this work claiming that it was to be about method, how and why we do the things that we do. I have built up an argument that the things that we do, in science, in the classroom, and as we interact with each other, are done for a purpose. A purpose guides and shapes our actions and also develops and evolves as we act. As this purpose shapes our actions, the actions become method. A difference between traditional, scientific definitions and uses of the word *method* and the one that I have constructed is that I have tried to show that method develops (it isn't preexistent, it isn't a standard of behavior) as relationships between people and phenomena, people and people, evolve. People develop norms for these ways of acting because of the demands of both the relationship and of the purpose itself. Methods and their norms underlie scientific ideas, discoveries, procedures and the construction and need for community. Because it reflects an evolving relationship and changing purposes, method itself changes through time—it is a tool, rather than an end point. Another word for this "might" be "knowledge." Knowledge of facts and ideas and of ways to do things is an end point of what we are doing in class, but it also exists before we do things and guides our actions. This first knowledge changes and grows. Knowledge is a vehicle for learning because it is acted upon and shared with others. In this work, this knowledge is of science, of each other, and of teaching—and all evolve.

Relationships are also tools, not end points. For this reason, the traditional "scientific" idea of the dichotomization of subject from object is a fiction. In realty this relationship shifts and changes also, whether or not this is acknowledged. The relationships described in this work are between the children and the phenomenon we are examining, between me and the phenomena, between children and children, and between me and the children. Each relationship results in two things; the construction of science and the construction of a community. Science and communities aren't things that exist separate from person and phenomena; they exist in the conceptual space between the phenomena and the actor. Science *is* a relationship and communities *are* relationships. Each relationship is shaped through a dialogue between partners and also between those partners and ideals and needs formulated outside the relationship. These ideals and needs are not just the manifestation of an individual's thinking, but are also constructed and shaped through the interactions among people in the class. Ideals (values, beliefs, goals, dreams) and needs are formed through conversation, within a community. It is these ideals and needs and their means of formation that keep the relationships dynamic, prevent them from reaching a climax, fulfilling themselves. That lack of closure, of coming to an end, drives the community within the class, and causes people to need and appreciate each other.

In this work, I have written of the words *design*, *pattern*, *method*, and *community*. I have suggested, but not defended, the idea that these are legitimate goals as well as means of teaching in general and science teaching in particular. In each chapter I have worked to develop the meanings of the words, in science, in teaching, in relationships between people. I have worked to develop the interrelationships between these words—these words and their applicability in my stories is through an organic interdependence. It is because of this interdependence that they are legitimate, and, I would argue, unavoidable goals, of teaching and of science teaching. In this final chapter, I would like to underline this interdependence. I will do this by recapitulating the meanings I have given to each word.

The first word that I talked about at length is the word *design*. The word *design* has two meanings as I use it in this book. Design is both a noun and a verb—the end result of designing is a design, a pattern. A design is constructed through framing—given meaning differentially, comparatively; meaning is dependent on context. The act of framing creates a background and a foreground from the whole of the phenomenon. By doing this we, in turn, create lenses, develop selective vision. The net result of this process can be that the background, the ignored parts of the phenomenon, become forgotten, are lost. Rather, in this work, I argue that this process of differentiation and use can remain an interplay of the background and the foreground. This can lead to the development of a critical consciousness, an awareness or questioning of context and the process of differentiation.

Design, as a verb is an interactive process between person, materials, purpose, and context, reflecting assumptions about all of these. In the act or process of designing, these assumptions also compose the background. When the design is completed, reflecting upon that design or putting the design to some use can cause us to think back on those assumptions and reconsider. The act of design is purposeful: it expresses a need, is directed toward a need. It is this need that underlies our assumptions, and conversely, our assumptions underlie our perceptions of need. Recognizing this in combination with an understanding of the interplay of background/foreground which makes up the design can also generate a critical consciousness concerning that need.

Design as a verb serves cyclical conceptions of time, as patterned (repetitive) action. As a noun, it serves progressive conceptions of time because it addresses needs: for example, what the children are doing with soap bubbles, what I am doing in teaching, what we are constructing as science—all of these embody patterned action, but they also address needs. What we are doing and the needs we are addressing also shift and change through the foreground/background interplay which I generate and encourage. The design—of science, of interaction, of teaching—is a tool as we (myself, the teacher, and the children) construct a community in the classroom. Because of our designs, we become people with a shared purpose, language, and methods of acting. These are vital—they can grow and change. Curriculum is a design and is formulated through the design process as are science and community.

The concept of design that I outline is critical for understanding science—how science explains and acts as a vehicle to create new objects, materials, understandings, and knowledge—the role of people in science, how science changes and evolves. The concept is also critical for understanding the idea of community. The scientific community is a subset of the larger community. The scientific community has its own ways of communicating and acting; its own special questions. All of these, though, are derived from those of the larger community, constructed and maintained in a relation to the larger community. The word design captures the qualities of human agency fundamental to an understanding of both science and community.

The second and third words that I talk about are *pattern* and *method*. Designs are the cumulative effect of patterns: they contain patterns. Patterns are characterized by variables situated in a relationship. Defining these variables defines the foreground. Pattern as design (the noun) is composed of a background and a foreground, and exists as an interplay between the two. Therefore, pattern has the same potential to foster critical thinking as does design. The ability to construct a pattern, to design a pattern is dependent upon our ability to create a foreground selectively—move some elements of a phenomenon to the fore and others to the back. The decisions that we go through to make this differentiation are often buried by the things that we are able to do in and with the foreground. If we can remember to critically confront ourselves with things we *can't* do with the foreground, we can remind ourselves of those decisions, remind ourselves of the things we have excluded, and reconstruct the foreground/ background relationship and the assumptions buried within the relationship.

Patterns are created through repetition and relationships. Patterns in science and in class both reflect relationships and construct relationships. There are patterns in relationships between people and between people and things; both result from a purpose. Such patterned relationships define method. Patterns in relationships between people define community. Because patterns reflect relationships, they can alter as relationships alter. The ideas of pattern and method follow from design. They are components of design, make up design, both the noun and verb. As such, they are components of both science and community. They are the means of interpreting (through description, making sense of, doing things with) phenomena. Patterns don't always appear to be created by people (although they are, if only passively, by selective vision); sometimes they appear to be "found." This is why the concept of design in science is so important. Through the idea of design, human agency is recognized.

The fourth important word is *community*. Communities are constructed through a medium: in this book and these classrooms, this medium is the pursuit of the science. A community is composed of people who are simultaneously different and the same. Similarities are constructed (not necessarily present beforehand) by developing a common language and ways of doing things framed by the medium, the science. This process is driven by a shared purpose. Differences between people drive the need for community—a shared need for each other. The essence of community is people interacting with each other because each can contribute something different and unique toward a purpose, toward fulfilling a mutual need. Unlike a discourse community, in the community in my classroom, hierarchical power relationships don't develop because of my actions to keep the need, the questions, which drive the community unfulfilled. The idea of community focuses the word *relationship*. When I say that science, teaching, and learning are fundamentally about relationships, relationships that can not be adequately described by the subject-object dichotomy, I am arguing that the relationships are reciprocal—all sides contribute, and the contributions of all sides are formative and *important*. That is an expression of the foundational ideals of community.

This leads to the teacher's role, my role, in enacting the above four words. As the teacher, I act as a designer of experiences and activities. By choice, my actions are proactive around instantiating values about how children should interact, but reactive about the science—the science follows from the conversation that results from the interactions of the children. The teacher's choices reflect standpoints which, in turn, reflect personal history and ways of knowing. Acting on this knowing introduces opportunities to learn, because whenever I act it basically doesn't work out in some dimension(s). Assertions of knowing (the basis of praxis) are also statements of not-knowing, of uncertainty. They are also questions.

As I teach, I act on my values, I impose those values on others. Oftentimes these values, formed from different experiences, reflecting different parts of my history, are actually in conflict with each other or come into conflict with each other when enacted in a social situation with others who come from different backgrounds and histories. Since vital communities contain people who are both fundamentally different and the same, conflict is an integral, essential part of community.

For example, the most obvious place of conflict in my values (and this is illustrated throughout this work) is between my desire to impose ways of acting and interacting on the children yet take a reactive role in the science. The two value choices are linked—much of my discussion about community hinges on the idea that social interactions and the interactions which compose "science" are coconstructed, interlinked. In separating them from each other as I plan my classes, as well as when I am actively teaching, I am setting myself up to be continually at the focus of this conflict.

A second and equally fundamental conflict is between me and the children. My value choices arise from my history but the children are not blank slates, lacking values or scientific knowledge and understanding. There is a conflict between how I think people should act and how the children assume they should act. This is conditioned by the fact that we are both in the setting of school. We inherit roles and relationship expectations that we didn't create, a conflict not of our making. This is heightened, I would argue, because I am rarely explicit about how I think the children should act. Therefore, they never state their assumptions about how they should act, and so the conflict rarely becomes articulated, talked about. It remains a struggle beneath the surface. This is how learning and change occur on both sides (mine and the children's). If the struggle were explicit, on the surface, sooner or later a resolution would be reached and the problem would appear to disappear. The point is that if the community is to remain alive, vital, this struggle can't and shouldn't disappear.

There is an obvious conflict in roles here—as I have outlined the conflicts between values and portrayed them as opportunities to learn and change, I am portraying myself as a learner as well as the children. When the children explain a phenomenon or state a theory in class conversations, when they create a design for the bubble solution, when I set up a class, we are all saying "I know" in one way or another. This statement is fundamentally in opposition to the actuality of it, which is to say, "I really don't know and actually I know I don't know." There is a conflict between the role of the knower and the role of the learner.

To be a learner requires more than just a statement of not-knowing; it also requires an internal recognition of not-knowing. It is hard to combine within yourself this recognition with the social and other demands of a situation which ask you to claim that you do know. I would argue that this tension between knowing and learning is fundamental to science and to teaching (and, because both are social, is why community is also fundamental to both). It is the driving force behind the curiosity that is central to both. The difference between science and teaching is, I believe, that in science having ever to articulate this fundamental form of not-knowing can be avoided, while this articulation (recognition) is central to teaching. It can be buried in science because of science's progressive nature: the present buries the past, future desires and goals bury the past and the present. There can be an accumulation of knowledge without an accumulation of wisdom.

In teaching, knowing more means knowing less (as in science) and also recognizing this (which isn't necessarily true in science). For example, I know a lot about science, but as I teach and use this knowledge, I am again and again confronted by things I don't know, by new subtleties of understanding, by new questions that generate new connections. As I teach I come to know a lot about the children I am working with—about each individual's qualities, history, beliefs, and desires. As I consider this knowledge and act on this knowledge in my interactions with the child I find that this knowledge is partial. The more I know, the more I realize I don't know. This is the basis of my claim that I take a reactive role in my teaching, that I set up potential experiences for the children in science and with each other and then I react to shape those experiences based upon what the children show me. I can only do this because I recognize that I know a lot and also know almost nothing.

So much has been written on what teachers need to know, but I am aware of little that addresses this "knowing that isn't knowing" which I am arguing is central to both teaching and the discipline of science. In the introduction to this book I claim that I will address three conversations:

- The learning science conversation, particularly the theories of the role misconceptions play in inhibiting learning. A subconversation here is the knowledge that children bring with them and what teachers ought to do with that knowledge.
- The teacher knowledge/learning conversation and the idea of pedagogical content knowledge. This has implications for

teacher education—what prospective teachers should be taught in their preservice programs.

The sociocultural learning conversation, particularly the idea that, for cognitive and emotional reasons, learners' cultures must be incorporated, somehow, in both the curriculum and the teachers' pedagogy.

Central to all of these are claims about teacher's knowledge—the knowledge that they should have and how they should use that knowledge. In this book I am not making an argument for a particular kind of knowledge that teacher's should have. Rather, I am arguing for an attitude *toward* knowledge, that knowledge is not an end point: it is a starting point for learning. Acting upon this knowledge doesn't reify that knowledge. Rather, the assertions of knowing and the knowledge itself become increasingly questionable. As a teacher, the more I know, the more aware I am that to explicitly state this knowing would act to fix it in one place, solidify something that should never be made solid. Knowing for me doesn't lead to direct action; it leads to the creation of possibilities.

Embedded in this are value assumptions about the purposes of education that have nothing to do with imposing a canon of knowledge and societal beliefs on a child. Rather, I am suggesting as an end point to education the same attitude toward knowledge I am claiming to manifest in my teaching—that knowledge has little value except as a starting place for asking questions. The societal beliefs, the standards for acting that I am imposing on the children are both vehicles in imparting this attitude toward knowledge and goals in themselves. It would be dishonest for me to claim otherwise. The knowledge and attitude toward the discipline, the ways the children interact with each other and with me, and the development of a community are linked. None is possible without the others.

The question is, how defensible are any of these as educational goals? Looked at in isolation, each ideal entails questionable outcomes. For example, respecting children, their ideas, values, and history necessitates redefining what science is. Valuing the community and its evolution sometimes means not staying with topics long enough to reach a closure satisfactory to me as a trained scientist. When I don't act as an authority in the one domain, science, does it make questionable my right to act as an authority over the children's actions?

These seem to be inherent paradoxes. Embedded in this education is a reverence for knowledge as well as a questioning of that knowledge. There is a similar paradox in the values that underlie the class. I would argue that it is this paradox which feeds the need for community. A vital community embodies both a love of things as they stand and a love of change. A vital community must both know and learn. If that is so, that these paradoxes form the foundations for the community (the community of science, of the class), then the paradoxes must be acknowledged and maintained as vital life forces. The goals of this education become defensible through the cyclicity of this argument. To question the goals would necessitate stepping outside the argument—something that a person within the community, involved in the teaching, is not able to do.

School and Classroom Descriptions

The times that I taught first grade and the first and second grade combination, I worked with Kathy Valentine, the classroom teacher, for all other academic subjects. The classroom teacher in the third grade class was Sylvia Rundquist. In the body of the text I refer to these teachers by their correct (real) names by their choice. During the time that I was working in third grade I was also collaborating with the art teacher of the school, Phyllis Victoria. This collaboration does not feature in this work, but it did frame the projects that I was doing in this room. I have not explicitly discussed this in the chapter that revolves around the third grade class.

My involvement at this school was through an internship with the Michigan Partnership for a New Education. The projects that I was involved in were collaborative with the classroom teachers and, in the case of the third grade, with the school's art teacher. In each case, the teaching collaboration was around integrating science and literacy teaching and, in third grade, science, literacy, and art.

I collected the data used in this book from transcripts of audiotapes—I audiotaped each class and transcribed the tapes myself. I also kept copies of the majority of the children's written work. The children were always aware of the audiotaping going on and quite interested in what I was doing. The children periodically requested to listen to the tapes, and would then comment on them. The children also knew that I was writing about my teaching in the classes and using the classroom discussions in these writings. I asked the children to help me pick their pseudonyms, listed in Appendix 2.

In transforming transcripts to stories I have reduced and edited what was said by both the children and me as well as descriptions of what we did. In doing this and in choosing to focus on science content (rather than, say, control issues) I have, deleted much of the everyday activity of the class. I would like to describe some of that here.

I tried, in my teaching in these classrooms that were not solely my own, to conform to and respect the classroom teacher's rules and methods of procedure for classroom control. The methods of classroom control that I found myself using were first to clap my hands in a rhythmic pattern to get the children to stop whatever they were doing and listen to me. In doing this, I would clap first and then they were expected to clap the same pattern back. I also used a timer to constrain activities. The timer had a bell and when the bell went off children were expected to follow some prearranged pattern of activity. I turned the lights off to get the children to stop their activities immediately— they were expected to freeze when the lights were off and wait for instructions.

Classroom discussions were usually teacher-centered—I determined who would talk and usually what they would talk about. To do this I required the children to raise their hands and be recognized by me before they could speak. Often a child gave a semiformal presentation of an idea or of some item and then the procedure was that they controlled the conversation, again semiformally—children who wanted to ask questions or make comments raised their hands and were recognized by the speaker. Classroom discussions in the first and first-second grade combination usually occurred in a "learning circle"—the children and I would sit in a circle at the front of the room. Discussions in third grade occurred with the children at their desks, while I tended to walk about the room. As I say, these discussions were controlled by me in a semiformal manner. Yet they almost always became conversations in which the children directly addressed each other rather than waiting for my recognition to talk. These free conversations were punctuated by me taking the control back and choosing who would talk. So discussions would usually start with me posing a question or asking for a description, calling on a number of children until this pattern broke down into a freer discussion. I would allow this discussion to go on for a few minutes and then I would stop conversation and return to my initial pattern of calling on people.

In all classes the children were seated in groups of desks, usually three or four facing each other rather than in a particular orientation in the room. In the first and first and second grade combination I did the seating arrangements by agreement with Kathy Valentine. In third grade the children's seating was primarily done by Sylvia Rundquist, with some suggestions by me and Deborah Ball, the mathematics teacher. In all classes these seating arrangements played an important role in the social and academic qualities of the classes. In particular in my teaching, experiments and informal discussions were carried on within groups.

Children's Country of Origin and Pseudonyms

FIRST GRADE

Country of Origin	Pseudonym
Bangladesh	Bulli (f)
Ghana-Malawi	Kojo (m)
Iran	Farzoneh (f)
Korea	Kyong Min (f) Chun So (f) Ho Sook* (f) Ok Ran (f)
Malaysia	Titon (m) Yasin (m) Mira (f)
Pakistan	Ahmed (m) Amina (f)

(continued next page)

FIRST GRADE *(continued)*

Country of Origin	*Pseudonym*
Palestine	Hanan (f)
People's Republic of China	Yu* (m)
Russia-Bangaladesh	Tatyana (f)
Sri Lanka	Vijay* (m)
Taiwan	Chen (m)
United States	Claire (f)
	Cory (m)
	Mike (m)
	Sondra (f)
	Paula (f)
Venezuela	Maria Theresa (f)

* English as Second Language student. These children did not speak English and were in a pull-out program for approximately thirty minutes per day during which they received English language instruction. The form of this instruction was what I would call "immersion"—the children were involved in reading and writing books in English in which the meanings of words became apparent through context and use. The children also participated in activities such as cooking, gardening, and field trips, in which they learned English by speaking it. Typically, a child spent one to two years in these classes.

FIRST AND SECOND GRADE COMBINATION

Country of Origin	*Pseudonym*
Egypt	Ahmed (m)
India	Sakti (f)
Korea	Kwanhyo (f) Ho Sook (f)
Malaysia	Tity (f) Teton (m)
Nepal-India	Suni (m)
Nigeria	Abeni (f)
Pakistan	Shumshad (m)
People's Republic of China	Meiying* (f) Sueh-yen (m) Danping (f)
United States	An'gele (f) Emily (f) Paula (f) Andy (m) Ricky (m) Thomas (m) Cory (m) Benjamin (m) Dan (m)
Yugoslavia	Alyosha (m)

* English as Second Language students

THIRD GRADE

Country of Origin	Pseudonym
Birundi	Dembe (f)
Brazil	Estevao* (m)
Costa Rico	Ricardo (m)
Egypt	Amina (f) Hamal* (m)
Ethiopia	Selamawit* (f)
Japan	Sen* (f)
Japanese American	Evelyn* (f)
Kenya	Mwajuma (f)
Korea	Yong Sun (m) Sook Chin* (m)
Korean American	John (m)
Malaysia	Jihad (m)
People's Republic of China	Jin (m)
Russia	Antoninya* (f)
United States	Alice (f) Daniel (m) Joey (m) Karen (f) Kristin (f) Timothy (m)

* English as Second Language Students

References

Apple, M. (1979). *Ideology and curriculum.* London: Routledge and Kegan Paul, 1979.

Applebee, A.N. (1986). Problems in process approaches: Toward a reconceptualization of process instruction. In A. Petrosky & D. Bartholomae (Eds.), *The Teaching of Writing,* (pp. 95-113). Chicago: University of Chicago Press.

Arendt, H. (1964/77). *Eichmann in Jeruselem: A report on the banality of evil.* New York: Penguin Books.

Arendt, H. (1978). *The life of the mind.* New York: Harcourt Brace Jovanovich.

Azimov, I. (1966). *The universe: From flat earth to quasar.* New York: Avon.

Ball, D.L. (1990). *Halves pieces and twoths: Constructing representational contexts in teaching fractions.* National Center for Research on Teacher Education, Craft Paper 90-2. East Lansing, MI: Michigan State University.

Ball, D.L. (1993). Moral and intellectual, personal and professional: Restitching practice. In M. Buchmann & R.E. Floden, (Eds.), *Detachment and Concern: Topics in the Philosophy of Teaching and Teacher Education,* (pp.193-204). New York: Teachers College Press.

Barnes, H. (1963). Introduction. In J.P. Sartre, trans. H. Barnes, *In Search of a Method,* New York: Vintage Books.

Belenky, M. F., Clinchy, B. M., Goldberger, N. R., & Tarule, J. M. (1986). *Women's ways of knowing: The development of self, voice, and mind.* New York: Basic Books.

Brans, J. (Ed.) (1989). *Ranger Rick's NatureScope: Digging into dinosaurs.* Washington DC: The National Wildlife Federation.

Buchmann, M. (1986a). *Teaching knowledge: The lights teachers lives by.* Institute for Research on Teaching, Occasional Paper 106. East Lansing, MI: Michigan State University.

Buchmann, M. (1986b). Role over person: Morality and authenticity in teaching. *Teachers College Record*, 87, 529-544.

Buchmann, M. (1989). *The careful vision: How practical is contemplation in teaching?* National Center for Research on Teacher Education, Issue Paper 89-1. East Lansing, MI: Michigan State University.

Buck-Morss, S. (1990). *The dialectics of seeing: Walter Benjamin and the arcades project.* Cambridge MA: The MIT Press.

Calkins, L.M. (1986). *The art of teaching writing.* Portsmouth, NH: Heinemann.

Chandrasekhar, S. (1987). *Truth and beauty: Aesthetics and motivations in science.* Chicago: The University of Chicago Press.

Connelly, M., & Clandinin, J. (1990). Stories of experience and narrative inquiry. *Educational Researcher, 19*(5), 2-14.

Dahl, R. (1964). *Charlie and the chocolate factory.* New York: Knopf.

Delpit, L. D. (1992). Acquisition of literate discourse: Bowing before the master? *Theory into Practice. 31.* 296-302.

Delpit, L.D. (1986). The silenced dialogue. *Harvard Educational Review. 58*(3), 280-298.

Derrida J. (1976). *Of grammatology.* Baltimore: Johns Hopkins University Press.

Derrida, J. (1987). *The truth about painting.* Chicago: University of Chicago Press.

Dewey J. (1902/56). *The child and the curriculum.* Chicago: University of Chicago Press.

Dewey, J. (1933). *How we think: A restatement of the relation of reflective thinking to the educative process.* Boston: D.C. Heath and Company.

Dewey, J. & Bentley, A.F. (1949). *Knowing and the known.* Boston: The Beacon Press.

Dreyfus, H.L. (1991). *Being-in-the-world: A commentary on Heidegger's being and time, division I.* Cambridge, MA: M.I.T. Press.

Driver, R, Geusne, E., & Tiberghienn, A. (1985). *Children's ideas in science.* New York: Open University Press.

Evans, C.L., Stubbs, M.L., Frechette, P., Neely, C., & Warner, J. (1989). *Educational practitioners: Absent voices in the building of educational theory.* Wellesley College Center for Research on Women, Working Paper 170. Wellesley, MA: Wellesley College.

Fish, S. (1980). *Is there a text in this class: The authority of interpretive communities.* Cambridge, MA: Harvard University Press.

Foucault, M. (1979). *Discipline and punish.* New York: Vintage.

Foucault, M. (1980). *Power/knowledge: Selected interviews and other writings. 1972-1977.* New York: Pantheon Books.

Gadamer, H.-G. (1976). *Philosophical hermeneutics.* Los Angeles: University of California Press.

Gamow, G. (1961/70). *The creation of the universe.* New York: Bantam Books.

Graves, D.H. (1983). *Writing: Teachers and children at work.* Portsmouth, NH: Heinemann.

Habermas, J. (1991). *Moral consciousness and communicative action.* Cambridge MA: The M.I.T Press.

Harding, S.M. (1991). *Whose science? Whose knowledge? Thinking from women's lives.* Ithaca NY: Cornell University Press.

Hawkins, D. (1974a). I, thou and it. In *The informed vision: Essays on learning and human nature.* (pp. 48-62). New York: Agathon Press.

Hawkins D. (1974b). Messing around with science. In *The informed vision: Essays on learning and human nature.* (pp. 63-75). New York: Agathon Press.

Heath, S.B. (1983). *Ways with words: Language, life, and work in communities and classrooms.* New York: Cambridge University Press.

Heidegger, M. (1962). *Being and time.* New York: Harper.

hooks, b. (1990). *Yearning: Race, gender, and cultural politics.* Boston: South End Press.

Irigaray, L. (1985). *The speculum of the other woman.* Ithaca, NY: Cornell University Press.

Johnson, M. (1989). Embodied knowledge. *Curriculum Inquiry, 19,* 361-377.

Johnson, M. (1987). *The body in the mind: The bodily basis of meaning, imagination, and reason.* Chicago: University of Chicago Press.

Keller, E. F. (1985). *Reflections on gender and science.* New Haven: Yale University Press.

Kerr D.H. (1981). The structure of quality in teaching. In J. Soltis, (Ed.), *Philosophy and education: Eightieth yearbook of the national society for the study of education.* (pp. 61-93). Chicago: University of Chicago Press.

Kristeva, J. (1973/1986). The system and the speaking subject. In T. Moi, (Ed.), *The Kristeva reader.* New York: Columbia University Press.

Kristeva, J. (1986). Women's time. In T. Moi, (Ed.), *The Kristeva reader.* New York: Columbia University Press.

Kuhn, T. (1970). *The structure of scientific revolutions.* Chicago: University of Chicago Press.

Lakoff G. (1987). *Women, fire and dangerous things: What categories reveal about the mind.* Chicago: University of Chicago Press.

Lakoff G. & Johnson M. (1980). *Metaphors we live by.* Chicago: University of Chicago Press.

Lampert, M. (1985). How do teachers manage to teach? Perspectives on problems in practice. *Harvard Educational Review, 55,* 178-194.

Lensmire, T. J. (1992). *Intention, risk, and writing in a third grade writing workshop.* Unpublished Ph.D. dissertation, Michigan State University.

Levi-Strauss, C. (1963/76). *Structural anthropology.* New York: Basic Books.

Levi-Strauss, C. (1966). *The savage mind.* Chicago: University of Chicago Press.

MacNeil, L. (1988). *Contradictions of control: School structure and school knowledge.* New York: Routledge.

Maher. F.A. (1987a). Inquiry teaching and feminist pedagogy. *Social Education, 51*(3), 186-192.

Maher. F.A. (1987b). Toward a richer theory of feminist pedagogy: A comparison of "liberation" and "gender" models for teaching and learning. *Journal of Education, 169*(3), 91-101.

Maher F.A., & Tetraeult, M.K.T. (1993). Doing feminist ethnography: Lessons from feminist classrooms. *Qualitative Studies in Education, 6*(1), 19-32.

Marx, K. (1983). Theses on Feuerbach. In E. Kamenka, (Ed.), *The portable Karl Marx.* New York: Penguin.

McDiarmid, G.W. (1989). *What do teachers need to know about cultural diversity: Restoring subject matter to the picture.* East Lansing, Michigan: National Center for Research on Teacher Education, Michigan State University.

Moi T. (1986). Marginality and subversion: Julia Kristeva. In T. Moi, (Ed.), *Sexual/Textual politics: Feminist literary theory.* New York: Routledge.

Moi, T. (1986). *Sexual/Textual politics.* New York: Routledge.

Moi. T. (1985). Helene Cixous: An imaginary utopia. In T. Moi, (Ed.), *Sexual/Textual politics: Feminist literary theory.* New York: Routledge.

Moi, T. (1986). Introduction. In T. Moi, (Ed.), *The Kristeva reader.* New York: Columbia University Press.

Noddings, N. (1984). *Caring, a feminine approach to ethics and moral education.* Berkeley: University of Califormia Press.

Norris, C. (1982). *Deconstruction: Theory and practice.* London: Methuen.

Paley, V.G. (1979). *White teacher.* Cambridge MA: Harvard University Press.

Paley, V.G. (1981). *Wally's stories.* Cambridge MA: Harvard University Press.

Paley, V.G. (1986). On listening to what children say. *Harvard Educational Review, 56*(2), 122-131.

Paley, V.G. (1990). *The boy who would be a helicopter: The uses of story telling in the classroom*. Cambridge, MA: Harvard University Press.

Paley, V.G. (1992). *You can't say you can't play*. Cambridge, MA: Harvard University Press.

Piaget, J. (1964/72). Development and learning. In C.S. Lavatelli & F. Stendler, (Eds.) *Readings in child behavior and development*. New York: Harcourt Brace Jovanovitch.

Polanyi, M. (1966). *The tacit dimension*. New York: Doubleday and Company.

Popper, K. (1958). *Conjectures and refutations: The growth of scientific knowledge*. 1-65. New York: Harper and Row.

Resnick, L.B. (1983). Mathematics and science learning: A new conception. *Science 220*, 477-478.

Rommetveit, R. (1980). On 'meanings' of acts and what is meant and made known by what is said in a pluralistic world. In M. Brenner, (Ed.), *The structure of action*. New York: St. Martin's Press.

Rorty, R. (1991). *Objectivity, relativism, and truth: Philosophical papers*. Cambridge: Cambridge University Press.

Roth, K. J. (1987). *Learning to be comfortable in the neighborhood of science: An analysis of three approaches to science education*. East Lansing Michigan: National Center for Elementary School Teaching, Michigan State University.

Sartre, J.-P. (1963). *In search of a method*. New York: Vintage Books.

Sartre, J.P. (1956/65). *Being and nothingness*. New York: Citadel Press.

Scholes, R. (1985). *Textual power: Literacy theory and the teaching of English*. New Haven, CT: Yale University Press.

Schon, D. (1983). *The reflective practitioner: How professionals think in action*. New York: Basic Books.

Schon, D.A. (1984). Generative metaphor: A perspective on problem-setting in social policy. In A. Ortony, (Ed.), *Metaphor and thought*. Cambridge: Cambridge University Press.

Schon, D.A. (1990). *The theory of inquiry: Dewey's legacy to education*. Presented as The John Dewey Lecture, at the meeting of the American Educational Reasearch Association. Boston, MA.

Schwab, J.J. (1976). Education and the state: Learning community. In *Great Ideas Today 1976*, (pp. 234-271). Chicago: Encyclopedia Britannica.

Schwab, J.J. (1978). The practical: Translation into curriculum. In I Westbury & N. Wilkof, (Eds.), *Science, curriculum and liberal education:* Selected essays. Chicago: University of Chicago Press.

Shulman, L.S. (1986). Those who understand: Knowledge growth in teaching. *Educational Researcher, 15*(2), 4-14.

Smith, D. E. (1991). *The everyday world as problematic*. Chicago: Northeastern University Press.

Spielberg, S., Lucas, G., Kennedy, K., & Marshall, F. (1988). *The land before time* [Film]. Los Angeles: Universal Pictures.

Spielberg, S., Lucas, G., Kennedy, K., & Marshall, F. (1977). *Star wars* [Film]. Los Angeles: 20th Century Fox Films.

Stevens, S. (1974). *Patterns in nature*. Boston: Little, Brown.

Thompson, D'A. (1961). *On growth and form*. Cambridge: Cambridge University Press.

Vygotsky, L. (1978). *Mind in society: The development of higher psychological processes*. Cambridge MA: Harvard University Press.

Walkerdine, V. (1990). *Schoolgirl fiction*. New York: Verso.

Walton, R.K. & Whanson, R. (1989). *Birding by ear: A guide to bird song identification*. Boston: Peterson Field Guide Series, Houghton Mifflin.

Weiler, K. (1988). *Women teaching for change: Gender, class and power*. South Hadley, MA: Bergen and Garvey.

Weiler, K. (1991). Freire and a feminist pedagogy of difference. *Harvard Educational Review, 61*, 449-474.

Whitford, M. (Ed.) (1991). *The Irigaray reader*. Cambridge, MA: Basil Blackwell.

Willensky, J. (1990). *The new literacy: Redefining reading and writing in schools*. New York: Routledge.

Wilson S.M., Shulman, L., & Richert, A. (1987). 150 different ways of knowing: Representations of knowledge in teaching. In J. Calderhead, (Ed.), *Exploring teacher thinking*. Eastbourne, England: Cassell.

Winograd. T & Flores, F. (1986). *Understanding computers and cognition: A new foundation for design*. Norwood, New Jersey: Ablex Pub. Corp.

Wittgenstein, L. (1968). *Philosophical investigations*. Oxford: Basil Blackwell.

Wittgenstein, L. (1969). *On certainty*. New York: Harper and Row.

Zallinger, R.F. *The age of reptiles* [Mural]. New Haven, CT: Peabody Museum of Natural History.

Index

application. *See* use
argumentation. *See* community
Arendt, H., 6, 7, 104, 163
    presentation of self, 8

beliefs, 203

causality. See relationships
certainty, 192-193, 202-03, 224
community, 58, 92, 109-10,
    228-31
    a process, 48
    argumentation in, 195-200
    conflict, role of, 142, 201,
    231-33
    connected thinking and, 172
    construction of, 43, 45
    defined, 11, 45
    designed, 56
    differences and similarities
    in, 207
    discourse, Foucauldian, 158,
    192-93
    discourse, role in, 141-42,
    175-176, 201
    evolving, 58, 104-05, 141-
    42, 201, 207
    method and, 137, 138
    needs, 228
    patterned, 56
    processes, 152-53
    purposeful, 58, 137, 138
    qualities of, 200
    relationships in, 228
    scientific, 175-76
    teachers as members of, 207
    values, 228

conflict. *See* community
connected thinking, 60, 172,
    192-93, 201
context
    role of, 61
conversation. *See* discussion
critical consciousness, 220
critical thinking, 18, 60, 192,
    201

Derrida, J., 4, 7, 9
design, 9, 57, 228-31
    ability to see, 52-54
    agency and, 127
    as creative act, 18
    as dialectic with materials,
    37, 41
    as "made" 126-27
    as metaphor, 57
    as pattern, 138
    as purposeful activity, 25,
    53
    bubble structures, 36
    in community, 49
    in teaching, 26, 36, 53-54
    method, and, 11, 54
    modification of, 40-41
    problems of realization,   36,
    45
    purpose of, 36, 127-28
    relation to background/
    foreground, 19, 48-49, 63-65
    relation to known and
    unknown, 54-55
    relation to patterns, 10, 25,
    57, 61
    relationships and, 57-58

repetition in, 25, 57-58
    Schon, D., 25
Dewey, J., 136
    reflection in action, 222
Dewey, J., and Bentley, A.,136
differences. *See* similarities and
    differences
discussion
    argument, role of, 35
    conventions and, 138
    evolving qualities, 38
    explanation and, 104
    function of, 18-20, 60, 80-81
    goals and, 157
    patterns in, 20
    procedures in, 180
    qualities of, 138, 200

experience
    teacher knowledge and, 205-
    07
experiment(s)
    active role of experimenter in
        shaping, 34, 46
    children's, 72, 88-92
    defined, 55
    designed, 55
    explanation and, 104
    locating variables, 55
    observation, relation to, 22
    patterns in, 92
    role of, 60
    systematic, 86, 92-94, 95-
        102, 104
    surprise in, 38
    teachers role in, 34
    technique, 20
explanations
    construction of, 27-29, 79
    relationship to observation,
        29-30

Foucault, M. 7, 104, 114, 176,
    192

Gadamer, H.-G., 5

Habermas, J., 6, 104, 163, 203,
    223
Harding, S., 221-22
Hawkins, D., 58
Heidegger, M., 9, 52-53, 61,
    143, 192-93, 203
hooks, b.
    yearning, 7

identity
    background/foreground, 4
    context: role of, 4
    defining, 4
    framing, 4-5
    history, 4, 5
    naming, 4-5
    reducing into parts, 4
inquiry, 202

judgment(s), 104
    criteria for, 122

knowing, 104-05, 192, 201-2
    articulating, 120, 143
    cyclicity in, 164
    expressed as assertion, 142,
        205-06
    expressed as question, 142,
        206
    felt, 192-95, 206
    "opinion" and, 120
    qualities of, 143-44
    tacit, 136, 192, 205-06, 220
    ways of, 136
knowledge
    as method, 227-28
    assumed, 157
    claims, 163, 223, 224
    function of, 208
    learning, and, 206
    pedagogical, 223
    teacher, 224
    testing, 165-66
known. *See* relationships,
        known to unknown

Kristeva, J.
  explanations, construction
    of, 48
  female subjectivity, 10
  meaning, constructing, 4
  method, 8
Kuhn, T., 165-66, 176

language
  role in community, 176
learning
  as relationship, 227-28
Levi-Strauss, C., 136
  ritual: role of, 8

meaning(s), 4, 108-09, 181
  context and, 104, 106, 109,
    114, 202
  conventions, role in
    constructing, 114
  defining, 137
  differentiating meanings,
    114, 121, 192
  evolving, 109, 222
  felt, 208
  intrinsic qualities of object
    and, 106
  new, 207
  relationships and the
    construction of, 109
  testing, 134
metaphor, 41-42, 71, 77
  generative, 42-43, 45, 75-76
  role in explanation, 39
method, 228-31
  as hegamonic, 137
  as patterned action, 137, 138
  as relationship, 227
  defining, 8, 10-11
  developing norms, 227
  evolving, 227
  in communicating, 94
  in construction of a
    community, 94-95
  in science, 227
  limitations, 11
  patterns, and, 10, 92

purpose of, 10
purposeful action and, 127,
  227
relationships, role in, 11-12
representing to known and
  unknown, 54
role of, 7, 8
systematic, 58
  See also Sartre, J-P.
moral education, 220

not-knowing, 205, 232

object
  differentiation of, 4
observation, 25
  constructing patterns, 74
  relationship to
    experimentation, 34, 68
  relationship to explanation,
    34

pattern(s), 10, 87, 109, 228-31
  assumptions within, 66
  as blinding, 137
  as hegamonic, 137
  as reductive, 65-66, 134-35,
    137
  as tools, 35, 136
  causality and, 103
  components in, seeing, 63
  construction of expectations
    and, 60
  construction of theories and,
    74
  context and, 137
  correlation between, 68, 73-
    74, 77
  defined, 59, 107, 117-18,
    122-23
  describing, 64, 125
  design and, 123-24, 138
  experiments and, 92
  explanatory, 66, 135
  extending, 67
  irregularities and, 119, 135-36
  "made," 67

metaphoric construct, 59, 136
method, and, 59, 87, 92, 123-24, 138
perspective and, 59, 118
relation to background/foreground, 19, 48-49, 63-65, 104
relation to experimenting, 78
repeating, 25, 107, 129-30
repetition and, 57-58
relationships and, 57-58, 59
seeing, 102
systematic, 58, 60
uses of, 136
pedagogical knowledge. *See* knowledge
Polanyi, M., 34, 136
purposes
of education, 234-35
reflecting needs, 58

reflection
purposes of, 5-6
reflection in action, 222
relationships
as tools, 228
causality, 21, 103, 163
components of, 11
constructed, 227
evolving, 227-28
hierarchical, 104
in a community, 228
known to unknown
tension between, 8, 53
subject-object, 3-4, 6-7, 10, 228, 231
See also subject-object, community
Rommetveit, R., 4
Rorty, R., 138

Sartre, J.-P.
method, defining a, 7
need, 7, 58
Schon, D., 25, 54, 137, 223
design as a dialectic, 36

metaphor, 42
reflection in action, 222
Schwab, J., 58, 143
science
as relationship, 227-28
aspects of, 5
assumptions in, 215
feminist issues in, 156, 158, 169, 216-17, 225
history of, 184
metaphor, and, 136-37
nature of, 5, 8, 61, 202, 233
patterns and, 65, 134, 135-36
process, 5
reductive, 134
story telling in, 208
teleological arguments and, 169
theories of, 208
religion and, 169
Shulman, L.,
pedagogical content knowledge, 224
similarities and differences
examination in the construction of identity, 5
reflections on context: causing, 5
Smith, D., 221-22
social constructivism, 207
standpoint theory, 205-07, 221-22

teaching
as purposeful, 26, 200, 222
as relationship, 227-28
decisions in, 33
designed, 56
evolving, 13, 54, 225
goals, 5
interactive, 206
nature of, 8, 233
patterned activity, 56
problematic, 207
reflection upon, 5
social, 206
standpoint theory in, 222

teacher
  as learner, 232
  beliefs, 143, 201-02
  choices, 141, 143, 206, 216
  learning, 205-06, 208
  practice
  role, 141, 180, 200, 215, 231
  values, 143, 201-02, 205-06,
  216, 231
    as choices, 217, 220
teacher knowledge, 13, 205, 234
  assertions of, 205-06
  evolving, 18, 220-25
  experiences and, 231
theories in science
  children's, 77
  evolving, 175
  explanatory, 45
  role of, 26
  testing, 175-76

thinking
  convergent, 157
  divergent, 157
tools
  nature of, 34
  teaching as, 34

uncertainty, 192, 202, 206, 224
understanding
  construction of, 4
unknown. *See* relationships:
  known to unknown
use (application), 4

values, 104, 203

ways of knowing, 202
  dynamic, 223
Wittgenstein, L., 53, 181, 203
writing workshop, 216

www.ingramcontent.com/pod-product-compliance
Ingram Content Group UK Ltd.
Pitfield, Milton Keynes, MK11 3LW, UK
UKHW02085628025
455677UK00006B/56